ONE ROAD, MANY DREAMS

ONE ROAD, MANY DREAMS

CHINA'S BOLD PLAN TO REMAKE THE GLOBAL ECONOMY

DANIEL DRACHE, A.T. KINGSMITH & DUAN QI

BLOOMSBURY CHINA

LONDON • OXFORD • NEW YORK • NEW DELHI • SYDNEY

BLOOMSBURY CHINA
Bloomsbury Publishing Plc
50 Bedford Square, London, WC1B 3DP, UK

BLOOMSBURY, BLOOMSBURY CHINA and the Diana logo are trademarks of
Bloomsbury Publishing Plc

First published in Great Britain 2019

A catalogue record for this book is available from the British Library

Library of Congress Cataloguing-in-Publication data has been applied for

ISBN: TPB: 978-1-9123-9204-9; eBook: 978-1-9123-9206-3

2 4 6 8 10 9 7 5 3 1

Typeset in Minion Pro by Deanta Global Publishing Services, Chennai, India
Printed and bound in Great Britain by CPI Group (UK) Ltd. Croydon, CRO 4YY

MIX
Paper from
responsible sources
FSC® C020471

To find out more about our authors and books visit www.bloomsbury.com
and sign up for our newsletters

CONTENTS

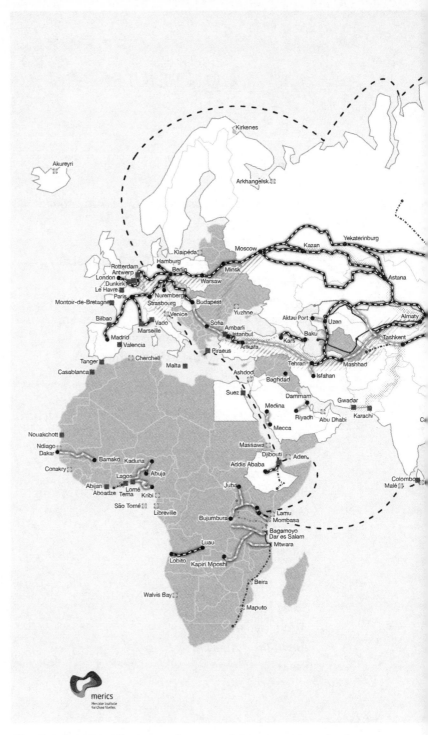

China's Belt and Road Initiative has created a transcontinental infrastructure consisting of a network of railroads, ports and pipelines running across 88 countries. *Source*: Merics 2018.

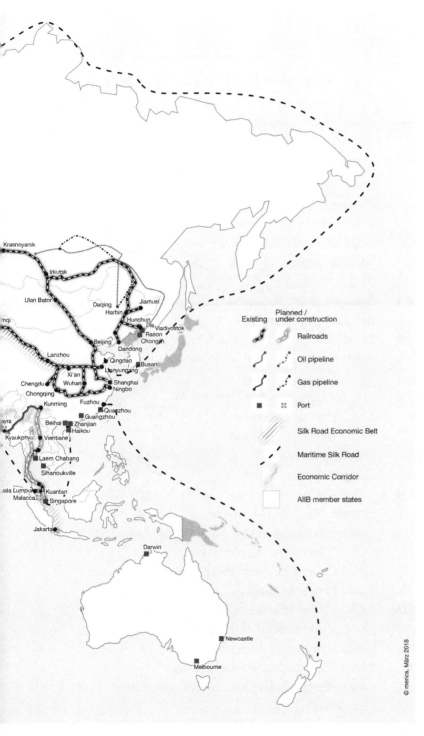

	Existing	Planned / under construction	
			Railroads
			Oil pipeline
			Gas pipeline
	■	▨	Port
			Silk Road Economic Belt
			Maritime Silk Road
			Economic Corridor
			AIIB member states

Krasnoyarsk
Irkutsk
Ulan Bator
Daqing
Jiamusi
Harbin
Hunchun
Vladivostok
Rason
Chongjin
Beijing
Dandong
Lanzhou
Qingdao
Busan
Xi'an
Lianyungang
Chengdu
Wuhan
Chongqing
Shanghai
Ningbo
Kunming
Fuzhou
Quanzhou
Guangzhou
Beihai
Zhanjian
Haikou
Kyaukphyu
Vientiane
Laem Chabang
Sihanoukville
Kuala Lumpur
Kuantan
Malacca
Singapore
Jakarta
Darwin
Newcastle
Melbourne

© merics, März 2018

vii

LIST OF ABBREVIATIONS

ADB	Asian Development Bank
ADBC	Agricultural Development Bank of China
AfDB	African Development Bank
AIIB	Asian Infrastructure Investment Bank
ASEAN	Association of Southeast Asian Countries
BIT	bilateral investment treaty
BOC	Bank of China
BoCOM	Bank of Communications
BRI	Belt Road Initiative
BRICS	Brazil, Russia, India, China, South Africa
CBRC	China Banking Regulatory Commission
CCB	China Construction Bank
CCP	Chinese Communist Party
CCTV	China Central Television
CDB	China Development Bank
CEA	French Alternative Energies and Atomic Energy Commission
CETA	Comprehensive Economic and Trade Agreement between the EU and Canada
CFLD	China Fortune Land Development Co., Ltd, a leading industry city operator in China
CGN	China General Nuclear Power Group
CMB	China Merchants Bank
CHEXIM	Export-Import Bank of China
CIS	The Commonwealth of Independent States
COVEC	China Overseas Engineering Group
CNNR	China National Nuclear Corporation
CPECC	China Petroleum Engineering & Construction Corporation

CSRC	China Securities Regulatory Commission
DBAR	Digital Belt and Road
EEA	European Environment Agency
EFSI	European Fund for Strategic Investment
ERDF	European Regional Development Fund
G7	Group of Seven: Canada, France, Germany, Italy, Japan, the United Kingdom and the United States; the European Union is also represented
G20	Group of Twenty: Argentina, Australia, Brazil, Canada, China, France, Germany, India, Indonesia, Italy, Japan, South Korea, Mexico, Russia, Saudi Arabia, South Africa, Turkey, the United Kingdom and the United States; the European Union is also represented
GLOF	glacial lake outburst floods
H-1B	A visa allowing US employers to employ foreign workers in specialised occupations
HSBC	Hong Kong and Shanghai Banking Corporation
ICBC	Industrial and Commercial Bank of China
IADB	Inter-American Development Bank
ICC	International Criminal Court
IMF	International Monetary Fund
IRENA	International Renewable Energy Agency
LNG	liquefied natural gas
MPI	Multidimensional Poverty Index
MSCI	Includes Morgan Stanley Capital International and MSCI Barra
NDRC	National Development and Reform Commission of the People's Republic of China
NSR	New Silk Road
OBOR	One Belt, One Road
OECD	Organisation for Economic Co-operation and Development
PBOC	People's Bank of China
PRC	People's Republic of China
RCEP	Regional Comprehensive Economic Partnership

ROI	return on investment
RTA	regional trade agreement
S&P	Standard & Poor's
SASAC	State-owned Assets Supervision and Administration Committee
SCO	Shanghai Cooperation Organisation
SICC	Singapore International Commercial Court
SOE	state-owned enterprise
SPC	Supreme People's Court
TAZARA	Tanzania-Zambia Railway Authority
TBNA	Tianjin Binhai New Area
TBEA	Tebian Electric Apparatus Stock Co. Ltd.
TIR	*Transports Internationaux Routier* (International Road Transports)
TPP	Trans-Pacific Partnership
UNFCCC	Paris Global Warming Convention
WTO	World Trade Organization
ZTE	Chinese Multinational Telecommunications Equipment and Systems Company

LIST OF FIGURES

PREFACE

'One Belt, One Road': China's Investment Blitz

Daniel Drache, A. T. Kingsmith and Duan Qi

IMPATIENTLY BIDING ITS TIME

Five years ago China announced the creation of a new initiative called 'The New Silk Road' – also called One Belt, One Road (OBOR) or the Belt and Road Initiative (BRI) – to link China more closely with its neighbours and to the wider global community. The focus is on building infrastructure all around the globe: railroads, ports, roads, factories – the nervous system of the modern economy.[1] These projects are designed to promote economic development and to gain unprecedented political influence. So far its investment club of nations has 80-plus partners and five Chinese provinces with more ready to join in 2019. China has committed what appear to be staggering sums of money (more than a trillion dollars) in long-term soft loans to its partners in this enterprise.[2] The scale is unmatched in history – only the American Marshall Plan that rebuilt western Europe after the Second World War is somewhat comparable, but One Belt, One Road far surpasses it in scale and imagination.

BRI is an extraordinary enterprise that is transforming our world. It extends China's influence, provides it with new allies and

---

[1]For the most up-to-date head count of member states, see Frank Umbach, 'China's Belt and Road Initiative and Its Energy-Security Dimensions', RSIS Working Paper No. 320, 3 January, 2019 http://www.rsis.edu.sg/rsis-publication/rsis/chinas-belt-and-road-initiative-and-its-energy-security-dimensions/

[2]No one knows for sure because the data is incomplete and estimates by economists range between two and eight trillion dollars. All references to currency are in USD.

strengthens its economic power. Presently, contrary to China's former leader Deng Xiaoping's astute policy advice, China is neither 'biding its time nor hiding its strengths'. The initiative poses a major challenge to the existing economic and political order – especially the current global structure. It can be perceived as both a challenge and a threat by the Americans, the world hegemon. What is unique about BRI is that it can seemingly accomplish its expansionist goals without resorting to force or conquest. As we shall see in this volume, designed to introduce BRI to a broader audience, what China is smartly doing is using soft power to maximise its global position. Some may say this is a form of neocolonialism, but others have argued it is a creative initiative that avoids the direct dependency that existed in past imperialist practice.

In it, we introduce BRI to the non-China specialist by providing concrete examples of the many projects marking the growth of this initiative. We use a wide range of sources, official and academic, including Chinese materials. We draw on our political economy perspective to provide a comparative framework, and the insights of our own experience: Duan Qi is a Chinese economist based in Beijing; Adam Kingsmith is a specialist in soft power at York University; and the principal author of this volume, Daniel Drache, has in recent years lectured and given TED talks in China, receiving important feedback from senior Chinese officials and many China experts, both critical and insightful.

Aside from time spent in China and other countries witnessing BRI in action, Drache recently travelled to Ethiopia, a least developed country with a very low per capita income and a population of 110 million people, and one of the many African countries that are part of this initiative. He was struck by the way in which China is using BRI to further its influence in Africa. In Addis Ababa, China built the permanent administrative home of the 54-member African Union, a gleaming 20-storey architectural showpiece named after Nelson Mandela. China also built the Addis Ababa–Djibouti railway (759 km/472 miles long), giving landlocked Ethiopia a port on the Horn of Africa. Today, the city is booming as billions of dollars of Chinese investment in construction, mass transportation and urban development have poured into the city.

Its burgeoning presence in Africa is just one facet of China's global enterprise. Readers will also learn more about what China is doing in the EU, Kazakhstan, India, Pakistan, Indonesia, Sri Lanka, the Philippines and a host of other places, as it builds infrastructure and closer links – not just establishing new economic and political beachheads, but also replacing old ones linked to the current world order. Our purpose is to capture the scale of this enterprise and to evaluate the likelihood of its success.

We approach the initiative with badly needed scepticism to shed light on China's role in the global economy. The critical questions that decisively matter are: can China sustain the huge costs involved? Are the new partnerships with these other countries sustainable? What about corruption? What will happen if recipient countries cannot meet their debt obligations? Is China's government capable of long-term management of such an ambitious project? What could go wrong and how could that affect the global economy?

Five years is a fleeting moment in world history and it may be premature to make judgements about the long-term viability of what China is doing. It is possible that future political and economic factors may limit outcomes, causing China's soft-power strategy to fail. History also tells us that dominant powers do not willingly leave the stage of history to make way for brash new challengers. BRI may not transform the world, and it may not elevate China to superpower status, but it is innovative, has captured our attention and we need to know more about its geopolitical, economic and cultural aspects as well as about the Chinese model of state capitalism. It is our aim to provide this badly needed information: is it within China's reach to remake the global economy organised around its core interests? Or will China inevitably stall in mid-flight trying to do something seemingly implausible?

IF THERE WAS A WAY TO SUM EVERYTHING UP . . .

If it was possible to sum up why so much is at stake for both the world's richest countries and the poorest on the planet, we would say this: it is a costly mistake to underestimate the economic and political significance of the BRI for China, balanced precariously between the ascendant Asian century and the American Stars & Stripes, losing its pre-eminence. Whatever its design flaws, it will continue to serve Beijing's global interests. It is doubtful that threats and bullying will knock China's elites off their chosen path. It has not worked at any time in the last eight decades and is not likely to when China is economically and militarily an ascendant world power. If we are honest about it, Washington Republicans and the Trump administration want to see China's global initiative fail and its geopolitical ambitions stopped in their tracks.

They have launched a tsunami-sized crippling trade war against China's political elites. The nationalist Far Right in Europe and elsewhere are exploiting anxieties and longings for a past multilateral order that is no longer sustainable.[3] They are angered by the shift in power moving irreversibly towards Asia. Up until now China has not slowed down, and it intends to seize this moment of flux with its gigantic Belt and Road Initiative. Its plans will include the major investments in public goods, education, regional integration and infrastructural projects that draw on its own experience and diplomatic skills to build a world order. China intends to advance its own interests as well as those of the Global South, which is struggling with the legacy effects of poverty and underdevelopment. The truth is that to succeed China needs to develop a long-term commitment towards countries impacted by the many negative changes in the global trade order.

In the first five years China has built nearly 200 hydroelectric dams worldwide, 41 gas and oil pipelines, and 203 railway lines, roads and bridges in Africa and South and Central Asia. China has also invested

---

[3]Helmut K. Anheier, 'The Decline of the West, Again', *Project Syndicate*, https://www.project-syndicate.org/onpoint/the-decline-of-the-west-again-by-helmut-k--anheier-2018-10

in green energy, public health, new information technologies, a digital city, and an assemblage of ocean-going ports often called its 'string of maritime pearls'.[4] In a global era, every investment it makes is designed to respond to both internal and external forces; high on its list are poverty eradication, community development, commercial opportunity, regional economic integration, and, of course, China's strategic security interests. There is a lot going on in all of its projects at numerous levels, including high levels of debt for many of its recipients competing with the promise of badly needed investment to accelerate local growth. The European Council on Foreign Relations find parallels between China's disastrous Great Leap Forward and the Belt and Road's sprawling, open-ended ambition. It criticises China's investment spending spree harshly, as 'China's great leap outward'.[5]

Hard-wired into its architecture is room for hundreds of projects of all kinds. A majority would be considered by some experts to be in the category of conventional infrastructural investments of the bricks and mortar variety, such as roads and bridges. But from a developmental perspective, they are nonetheless essential for high-risk, high-poverty countries. Some of the more eclectic or ground-breaking include the Longyangxia gravity dam on the Yellow River in Qinghai Province, China; the Quaid-e-Azam solar park in Pakistan; the Dawood Wind Power project, the world's largest wind farm; The Digital Belt and Road International Centre of Excellence Bangkok (DBAR ICoE-Bangkok); the China-Pakistan Economic Corridor, a $46 billion project ending at the Arabian Sea port of Gwadar; the China-Laos Railway Project; the new Yalu Bridge in North Korea; Turkey's third nuclear power plant; and Kiev's fourth metro line.

[4]Derek Watkins, K.K. Rebecca Lai and Keith Bradsher, 'The World Built by China', New York Times, 18 November, 2018 https://www.nytimes.com/interactive/2018/11/18/world/asia/world-built-by-china.html; Keith Bradsher and Li Yuan, 'China's Economy Became No. 2 by Defying No. 1', New York Times, 25 November, 2018 https://www.nytimes.com/interactive/2018/11/25/world/asia/china-economy-strategy.html
[5]The European Council on Foreign Relations, '"One Belt, One Road": China's Great Leap Outward', 10 June, 2015 http://www.ecfr.eu/page/-/China_analysis_belt_road.pdf [Accessed October 2018]

The expectation is that each major investment will have significant impacts for communities and people. Many will be transformative economically and others will surely disappoint. But all this – a final reckoning – is in the future.

If our analysis had to be reduced to a single element, we would underline this fact: China's global infrastructural initiative is a case study of an ascendant world power learning painfully through trial and error, the difficult but invaluable lessons of timing and sequencing its complex construction projects. They face many obstacles across continents without the guarantee of immediate success. Inevitably, out of thousands of projects the results will be mixed or worse. Indeed, history tells us that this kind of accomplishment can never be guaranteed in advance, but mastering the top-down timing and sequencing of these massive infrastructural projects is indisputably a key factor. For many reasons its investment coalition could still go off the rails as a casualty of great power politics, bureaucratic interference and excessive centralised planning. About 15 to 20 ventures remain troubled, mired in corruption by local politicians or facing rising anger from social movements against China's intrusive presence in domestic affairs. If this is the downside, China is also a quick study of its diplomatic savoir faire to meet people's rising expectations in some of the poorest countries in the world.

CHINA'S COMPARATIVE ADVANTAGE

It is also important to emphasise that China has a policy advantage because its global strategy has its immediate origins in the 2008 global financial crisis and its response to the banking crisis. China took a bold approach to ramping up public spending on infrastructure. In his new book, *Crash: How a Decade of Financial Crisis Changed the World*, Adam Tooze guides us through these momentous events in which the Chinese government agreed to an increase in spending amounting to 12.5 per cent of GDP, more than double the US fiscal stimulus at 5 per cent of GDP passed in 2009.[6] Ten years later, China

---

[6] Adam Tooze, *Crashed: How a Decade of Financial Crisis Changed The World* (Allen Lane, 2018).

can still see the benefits of its massive stimulus infrastructural-focused package in responding to the global financial crisis.

From a theoretical standpoint, one of its priorities is its ability to conceive, plan, execute and after-service its thousands of investments, which is in no small part explained by its tightly controlled planning and sequencing mechanism. This is why the Middle Kingdom is perceived as a risk taker and disruptor of Western-dominated global finance industries. For Chinese state-owned enterprises (SOEs), it creates new market access to sell a range of heavy industry and consumer goods, from clothing and sewing machines to electrical equipment, trucks of every description, bullet trains, the ubiquitous urban passenger bus, hydroelectric transformers and even whole factories. Their aim is to flood the market with Chinese big-ticket items such as cars, trains, buses and earth-moving equipment to capture significant market share for Chinese enterprises and global actors. They may even raise their prices once they have a dominant share. One thing is clear: as Chinese domestic growth slows, Beijing needs this 'spatial fix'. Its Communist leadership is intent on challenging the market for Western goods and services in African and Asian countries and competing with the West for over 2 billion potential consumers on these continents.

Another of China's goals is to emphasise international cooperation as a primary goal of exercising soft power. For the current Chinese leadership, the Information Age's concept of connectivity linking hundreds of millions of users through social media and the Internet offers a powerful sense of historicity, with its strong overlays of both national pride and economic openness, depending on one's viewpoint. Not surprisingly, this observation is based on the extensive, earlier mixed experience of China's political elites investing in Third World partnerships.

In the 1960s and 1970s, China, under the sway of revolutionary fervour, backed dozens of anticolonial and anti-imperial liberation struggles in Africa and Asia. Beijing's commitment to Third World solidarity has long been a foundation stone of its diplomacy. The 1955 Bandung Conference, attended by 29 newly independent African and Asian countries with over half of the world's population, marked the trailblazing beginning of the postcolonial era. Nasser, Nehru, Sukarno, Nkrumah, Tito and Zhou Enlai, its often controversial, iconic leaders, attended and actively participated in what later became the beginning of the Non-aligned Movement.[7] Despite all their differences, they agreed on a common Declaration of Principles for international development for the poorest countries in the world. The long-term consequences of Bandung are visibly present in the Belt and Road Initiative; 22 of the original Bandung countries are part of the China club today![8] Currently, many of those countries are core 'common interest' members of the Belt and Road Initiative, including Zimbabwe, Kenya, Tanzania, Egypt, Mozambique and, more recently, Sudan. Vietnam, Laos, Burma and Cambodia are important allies and recipients of China's infrastructural investments.

Energy security is also one of China's top strategic goals. One of its priorities has been to target oil from Saudi Arabia, oil from the Persian Gulf countries, and fossil fuel and energy resources from the republics of central Asia as well as Mozambique. By protecting its delivery routes, China expects to leverage its extensive investments in oil and gas pipelines, as well as new-found coal deposits, to acquire 'policy connectivity'. It is looking to consolidate its need for energy security with diverse partners such as the Eurasian Economic Union, the Bright Road Initiative of Kazakhstan, the Kenya Investment Authority, DeWe Security, the UK–China Fund, and the French Alternative Energies and Atomic Energy Commission (CEA).

China's elites intend for Beijing, at some point in the future, to find itself astride a parallel world-trading order, with its BRI

---

[7]Jürgen Dinkel, *The Non-Aligned Movement: Genesis, Organization and Politics (1927–1992)*, (Brill, 2018).
[8]They are as follows (with the names used at the Bandung Conference 1955 in brackets if different from their current names): Afghanistan (the Kingdom of Afghanistan), Cambodia (the Kingdom of Cambodia), China, Egypt (the Republic of Egypt), Ethiopia (the Ethiopian Empire), India, Iran, Iraq (the Kingdom of Iraq), Jordan, Laos (the Kingdom of Laos), Lebanon, Libya (the Kingdom of Libya), Nepal (the Kingdom of Nepal), Pakistan (the Dominion of Pakistan), the Philippines, Saudi Arabia, Sri Lanka (the Dominion of Ceylon), Syria (the Syrian Republic), Thailand, Turkey, Vietnam (the State of Vietnam and the Democratic Republic of Vietnam) and Yemen (the Mutawakkilite Kingdom of Yemen).

strategy as the deep anchor for transcontinental, land and maritime corridors of economic activity and security. The institutional pillars for a China-friendly international order are now becoming visible. With the establishment of the Asian Infrastructural Investment Bank (AIIB) and the slow-paced, 16-nation Regional Comprehensive Economic Partnership (RCEP) comprised of Asian nations and Asia-Pacific states, Beijing's political elites have entered a period of global institution building. But whether this plan to remake the global economy succeeds is another matter. The difficulty of re-engineering global international relations should not be underestimated. All these demanding and challenging plans depend on whether Beijing preserves leadership unity and maintains a stable domestic political system. The Chinese authorities' recent decision to remove the constitutional restriction on the maximum number of terms a president can serve has been widely criticised in the Western press. It gives the President enormous power over the government, Party and military with few checks and balances. It clears the way for Xi Jinping, the chief architect and champion of the BRI, to stay in power indefinitely and ensure China's growth and expansion for a decade or longer.[9] In any event BRI is supposed to end in 2049, which, if it does, would be a world record!

THE GLOBAL RACE FOR INFLUENCE-BUILDING

Globally based private finance and multinational construction firms are struggling to match China dollar for dollar, but so far are barely in the race for sustainable economic growth. Is this about to change in the next decade? Beijing's strategy relies on narrow ledge bilateral concession bargaining, which uses the law of contracts as a powerful lever to set the terms and conditions it negotiates. China has depended on this legal device to establish close working relationships with governments of every political stripe throughout Africa, Asia and Latin America. As we will come to learn, concession

---

[9]Chris Buckley and Keith Bradsher, 'China Moves to Let Xi Stay in Power by Abolishing Term Limit', *New York Times*, 25 February, 2018.

bargaining serves to build friendly 'relationships' (*guanxi*) for political, solidarity-enhancing purposes by offering large-scale financing of infrastructural deals at discount rates and legal guarantees of non-interference in domestic affairs in the awarding of contracts. At the same time, narrow ledge contractualism shifts attention away from green proactive environment principles, human rights protection and stronger work and employment standards. In the worst cases, it is an example of myopic, eyes-shut-tight policymaking.

The deeper and potentially explosive issues are that Chinese investments concentrated in a city or maritime area creates anger and feeds anti-China sentiment from the locals and social movement actors against the 'foreigner' in their midst. Economically, China's investment blitz can come at a spiralling cost; what mainstream economists are quick to call 'debt distress'. This occurs in high-risk economies where there is the possibility of default on the loans used to build expensive, capital-intensive mega-projects – an outcome that would be disastrous for poor countries with high levels of unemployment and shaky economies.

There are a lot of countries that find themselves on the extreme or high-risk list for previously having borrowed from international lenders as well as China. Many Belt and Roaders' debts are carried over from the past. Nonetheless, they are welcome members of China's investment blitz, including Bangladesh, Egypt, Iraq, Myanmar, Pakistan, Malaysia, Indonesia, Vietnam, Sri Lanka, Laos, Sudan, Democratic Republic of the Congo, South Africa, Ghana and Kazakhstan, to mention some of the more familiar troubled economies. So far no 'Roader' has quit China's investment club because of debt distress. Many of the liberal economists' predictions that the host countries' enormous debts cannot be repaid are exaggerated. Nor have any of Beijing's many partners defaulted, though some might in the future.

Instead China has had to renegotiate terms and conditions with about a dozen countries, cancelling some of the debt and increasing the pay-back period. China has made a calculated risk investing in the-bottom-of-the-economic-ladder countries shunned in recent times by Western financial institutions. It seems to have found a complicated way both to invest in infrastructure development and spur local and regional growth, potentially in new and innovative ways. Even here a word of caution is in order. We will find out that the economics of infrastructural projects are not in sync with the practices and priorities of local elites. Certainly, China is giving these countries some badly needed breathing room by assigning the local state a primary role in steering the economy, an approach that worries free market economists.

MANY POTENTIAL DEVELOPMENT FAILURES?

For countries in Africa and Asia, Western aid has far too often been a terrible and tragic failure, and the development gap has actually widened since the 2008 global financial meltdown. Despite the billions of dollars in aid money, the development gap, measured by per capita income, remains large, seemingly unbridgeable and highly visible. With China investing billions of public money cheaper than any global bank or hedge fund can offer, which African or Asian partner doesn't want so-called free money, even with strings attached? The answer appears to be very few indeed. Africa south of the Sahara is home to more than 1 billion people with a per capita income of $2660. Even if for some countries of sub-Saharan Africa (SSA) 'incomes have more than doubled over three decades, levels remain very low'.[10] Southeast Asian countries, home to 650 million people, have a per capita income of $6500, measured in 2005 values.

The emergence of a 'natural constituency of the poor and forgotten' is another way to describe China's club of nations, but belonging to it should not be confused with a more formalised community with a carefully negotiated consensus on fundamental issues. This is possible only if China's diverse partners have a lot in common. Many of Beijing's partners, like India and Pakistan, are 'frenemies'

---

[10]Alice Sindzingre,'The Detrimental Consequences of Dependence and Externalisation: Sub-Saharan Africa's Mixed Prospects' (seminar, 'Narrowing the Development Gap', Ismeri-Europa, Poggio Mirteto, 18–20 June, 2018).

locked in tense decades-long conflict. As a generalisation, Beijing's partners are a heterogeneous lot divided by geography, language, religion and political loyalty. China's natural constituency is based on something more powerful, visceral and immediate: the need for investability, particularly for high-risk countries gripped by poverty.[11] Nonetheless, the notion of the 'forgotten constituency of the poor' is a powerful concept that requires a different logic to make sense of China's core interests and why the China club keeps growing and growing.

With so much at stake, one consequence is that many countries once part of Washington's friendship circle are taking a second look at Chinese-led institutions, coalitions and bilateral negotiations.[12] Where American elites promote raw nationalistic 'American Firstism', Chinese authorities offer a complex Faustian bargain to their investment club of nations – the compelling promise of international cooperation and poverty alleviation, all the while expanding its core interests and looking towards the future.[13] The Asian Development Bank's recent report does not exaggerate when it states that China has overtaken all Western development banks in infrastructural investment. Sceptics need to confront the fact that it is walking the walk and talking the talk. Western investment in global infrastructure since 2016 runs a distant second.[14] If further proof is needed, China's ascendancy can be measured and tracked through the global ranking of its banks, now among the world's largest financial institutions.

---

[11]Dambisa Moyo, *Dead Aid: Why Aid is Not Working and How There is a Better Way for Africa* (Penguin, 2009).

[12]Mireya Solís, 'Trump withdrawing from the Trans-Pacific Partnership', blog, Brookings Institution, 24 March, 2017 https://www.brookings.edu/blog/unpacked/2017/03/24/trump-withdrawing-from-the-trans-pacific-partnership/ [Accessed October 2018]

[13]Tan Weiping, 'Chinese Approach to the Eradication of Poverty: Taking Targeted Measures to Lift People out of Poverty', (speech, Expert Panel on the Implementation of the Third UN Decade for the Eradication of Poverty [2018–2027], Addis Ababa, 18 April, 2018) https://www.un.org/development/desa/dspd/wp-content/uploads/sites/22/2018/05/15.pdf [Accessed October 2018]

[14]*Meeting Asia's Infrastructure Needs* (Asian Development Bank Institute, February 2017) https://www.adb.org/sites/default/files/publication/227496/special-report-infrastructure.pdf [Accessed October 2018]

THE LONG REACH OF SOFT POWER DIPLOMACY: TRAP OR OPPORTUNITY?

It appears that the BRI is a striking example of China's growing influence at a time when states have come to rely on the 'soft power' of leadership, values and ideas to defend and expand their core interests. With 800 million of its people lifted out of poverty since the 1990s on a scale never before achieved in human history, China's leaders have a highly credible alternative narrative to liberal internationalism. The magnitude and scale of its investment is one of the biggest tests since opening to the global economy. Soft power may be less flammable than military might, but it is not without its risks of explosive confrontation and regional conflict. China has faced Washington's diplomatic ire to its plan to build a multi-nation, transnational coalition, adding to escalating China-US tensions. Trump's America First policies shocked many, especially with the American withdrawal from the multi-lateral Trans-Pacific Partnership (TPP). Much has happened since, as Washington has unilaterally begun a trade war with China, Canada, Mexico and the EU. In 2018, Washington imposed $60 billion in punitive tariffs against Chinese imports and has threatened to impose $250 billion in additional punitive tariffs.

The Chinese are certainly not the first rising world power to embrace this high-priced ambition to build vast regional networks and commercial beachheads in order to reconfigure the grooves of global commerce. It is useful to recall the fact that, in the 19th century, many Western governments initiated earth-shaking, audacious policies that transformed the institutions of global commerce at times of great change and momentum. Sceptics expected such projects to fail because they seemed too technically complicated, reckless for their time, and, thus, irresponsibly costly. Inevitably, expectations of a profitable return on investment in the medium term were low to nil at best. In the long term, sceptics were proven wrong.

The massive undertaking in building the Suez and Panama Canals, the railway-building frenzy in North America in the 19th century, and, of course, the spectacular engineering feat of China's

Three Gorges Dam offer but a few of the most obvious examples of such projects considered doubtful, and disasters waiting to happen. It is fair to say that history has never seen an initiative similar to OBOR. The closest rival was perhaps the Marshall Plan, the US initiative launched in 1947 to rebuild the ravaged infrastructures of Western Europe after the Second World War. In today's dollars, it cost a modest $130 billion, but OBOR dwarfs Marshall in size, scope and ambition.

The learning curve behind successful infrastructural projects has always been steep. Often by trial and error, states and investors have leveraged technological advancements, financial risk-taking, global financial markets and public indebtedness for state-inspired ends.[15] In her controversial book *Dead Aid* Dambisa Moyo documents decades of wasted money spent on investment projects in Egypt, South Africa, Nigeria, Ethiopia and Malaysia funded by the World Bank and other institutions despite their transparency and accountability norms.[16]

Crony capitalism is a global problem today, not unique to China's bilateral partnerships. The lesson that the Panama Papers and a steady stream of exposés in the global press teaches is that without strong regulation, the state-market interface gives powerful business interests licence to rig the awarding of public contracts, overcharge for services and pay off state officials. Since the global crisis, the business press has carried a torrent of stories about recidivist corporate criminality.[17] Malaysia's massive Malaysia Development Berhad (MDB) fund scandal is only the latest tawdry example implicating Goldman Sachs in the bank's 'disgusting' role in the bribery and embezzlement scheme, according to angry comments from Anwar Ibrahim, the likely future prime minister of Malaysia. The government is demanding $600 million in reparations from

[15]John Haltiwanger, 'Globalization and Economic Volatility', in Marc Bacchetta and Marion Jansen (eds), *Making Globalization Socially Sustainable* (International Labor Organization and World Trade Organization Publications, 2011) https://www.wto.org/english/res_e/booksp_e/glob_soc_sus_e.pdf [Accessed October 2018]

[16]Dambisa Moyo, *Dead Aid: Why Aid is Not Working and How There is a Better Way for Africa* (Penguin, 2009).

[17]Adam Tooze, op.cit.; Harry Glasbeek, *Capitalism: A Crime Story* (Between the Lines, 2017).

Goldman, which the bank charged in fees from the state investment fund.[18] The lesson here is plain. China's funding of BRI projects will have its predictable share of fiascos and failures, like any investor. All the signs point to the fact that Beijing's elites face a perennial threat from debt distress and corruption.

So, the question of finding ways to engage China's principal strategy and its highly specific model of state capitalism is a top priority. The logical place to start is to follow the investments, map the power networks arising from China's global infrastructural investments, and analyse the ways in which it is organised both institutionally and bilaterally, seemingly without a rigid template. A one hundred per cent success rate is not an option. Yet despite appearances, we will discover that Chinese authorities do have a highly functional, complex model of investment-led growth and development driving the BRI forward. We focus on the great diversity of projects and their very important regional dimensions. The theoretical component of *One Road, Many Dreams* has incorporated some of the best thinking of David Harvey's 'spatial fix' for an ascendant economy facing structural constraints, as well as the robust appeal of Edward Said's 'imagined geographies' for Chinese political elites. We also rely on Paul Krugman's 'geography of trade' to explain the economics of its investment strategy, E.P. Thompson's 'narrow ledge of contractual law' for negotiating hundreds of deals, and the complex way Joseph Nye's concept of 'soft power' impacts China's ideas and interests.

WHAT THE READER CAN EXPECT
It would surprise no one to discover that the debates surrounding China's large-scale infrastructural investments are highly polarised between 'Sinomaniacs' and 'Sinophobiacs', to use the language of Jonathan Fenby.[19] While many see China's 'opening to the world' in a

---

[18]Stefania Palma, 'Malaysia's Anwar demands more than $600m in reparations from Goldman', *Financial Times*, 26 November, 2018 https://www.ft.com/content/b14a4d2e-f05d-11e8-ae55-df4bf40f9d0d

[19]Jonathan Fenby, *Tiger Head, Snake Tails: China Today, How it got There and Why it has to Change* (Simon & Schuster UK, 2012).

positive light, others have a dim view of the attendant dangers. Such considerations about the turnkey role of the state in the economy, international power politics, the effectiveness of China's investment strategy, pollution control, and China's poor record on human rights, freedom of speech and lack of freedom of the press cannot begin to explain Beijing's rationale and motivation in the OBOR initiative. These binaries operate as a distorting lens obscuring the larger dynamics and uncertainties in motion. Instead, China relations, particularly after Trump's election, have to be understood in terms of multiple contested realities about China's core interests and soaring project costs.

Therefore, we have divided the book into two parts to make the narrative easier to follow. Part I, 'China's Deep-pocket Pragmatism', focuses on bilateral dealmaking along the OBOR. Part II, 'Beijing's Vaulting Global Ambition', traces China's vested self-interest and its impact on global politics. In the process, we have pinpointed some of the most creative and sustainability-focused projects, as well as those we call 'sparklers', investments with catalytic potential.

The question of how China is going to reach into its deep pockets to pay for this massive investment initiative is examined in detail. China's model of infrastructural development is analysed in relation to its important consequences for domestic steel and construction industries, which are suffering from overcapacities and shrinking markets. There is also an empirical focus, which scrutinises the strategic importance of the economic corridors and maritime beachheads that China is establishing from a regional perspective. Finally, our investigation examines data from 20 of the most influential projects in order to more clearly identify the way China is addressing the global infrastructural deficit in its many partner countries.

MANY CONFLICTING CROSS-CURRENTS

We also ask: why is the Silk Road, this ancient commercial highway of economic and cultural goods, travelled by warriors, itinerant merchants, holy men and explorers, such an iconic, powerful metaphor for modern China today? Can Chinese policymakers appropriate the ancient Silk Road's complex iconographic policy for commercial and geopolitical purposes?

As the reader will discover, the ancient Silk Road has a limited role in the official narrative. It is more accurate to stress that its greatest value is as part of Beijing's global branding exercise. We have also included a chapter on governance troubles; what we describe as the entanglements of transparency, responsibility and accountability in managing a multitude of projects across more than 80 partner states. It examines the ways China is attempting to walk a fine line between top-down control from Beijing and a more inclusive and locally driven model of bilateral cooperation. The final chapter explores two provocative but relevant questions: What has China accomplished? What is its long game?

What is not crystal clear to Western publics is whether China's new initiative is designed to challenge American hegemony outright; to find new ways to coexist or redesign the global economy with different rules and institutions that place China within a multi-stakeholder epicentre and make the US, EU and Japan its global rivals and tense collaborators. Sometimes we describe this great power capitalist rivalry as a high-wire act in which American fear about the future collides with China's newly self-confident ascendancy. It is easy to see why either Great Power could lose their balance in a typical misstep in a winner-take-all shoving match, the classic trigger for an international relations systemic meltdown. Such meltdowns occurred in 1914 and again in 1939, igniting complex chains of events that plunged the world into chaos and global warfare. Today it is impossible to predict which leader, Xi or Trump, will be the first to blink or how the Asian Age will be accommodated by Western interests in the medium term.

THE STORY UP UNTIL NOW
It should be clear that with the multilateral international order in continual crisis, there is a pressing need for the general public to have access to a larger policy analysis and long-term view of the many aspects of China's premier foreign policy initiative. Are we on the

cusp of another epic-making journey, where China will have changed the world with its massive public works programme and leadership ambitions? How is it going to do this? Will the planet be better off, more solidaristic and greener? And how will it likely end – for better or for worse?

Part I

China's Deep-pocket Pragmatism

1

Money and Power: China's Bespoke Global Infrastructural Deal

In September and October 2013, during a state visit to the Central Asian countries, the President of China, Xi Jinping, proposed the New Silk Road and Belt, the largest socio-political development model in modern Chinese history since China joined the world economy.[1] In his speech, he wanted to draw a parallel between his proposal to extend China's influence on land and sea and the golden era in Chinese history that marked China's expansion to the west and to the south, and the establishment of trade routes joining China's old capital Xi'an with ancient Rome. It covered a vast area, measuring 10,000 km (6210 miles) from east to west and 3000 km (1860 miles) from north to south. It joined present-day Xi'an in China to central Asia, and opened up trade links throughout the vast region of Asia,

---

[1]Xi Jinping, 'Opening Plenary' (speech, World Economic Forum Annual Meeting 2017, Davos-Klosters, Switzerland, 17–20 January, 2017) https://www.weforum.org/agenda/2017/01/full-text-of-xi-jinping-keynote-at-the-world-economic-forum [Accessed October 2018] Beginning in 2013, China's premier foreign policy strategy has been called by different names, including the New Silk Road (NSR) and, most recently, the Belt Road Initiative (BRI). In official documents it is often called, prosaically in English, the One Belt, One Road initiative (OBOR), which hardly does justice to its ambition and magnitude. On nomenclature, for the sake of simplicity, we interchangeably use the unofficial title, the New Silk Road, with its official designation the Belt and Road Initiative, issued by the National Development and Reform Commission, Ministry of Foreign Affairs and Ministry of Commerce of the People's Republic of China, with State Council authorisation, on 28 March, 2013, available at http://english.gov.cn/beltAndRoad [Accessed October 2018] Daniel Drache (TEDx talk, Factory798, UCCA, 16 September, 1017), http://v.youku.com/v_show/id_XMzEwOTgzMDg4NA==.html [Accessed October 2018]

North Africa and the countries lining the Mediterranean coast.[2] Giving it the name 'Belt and Road' in the English version hardly does justice to the scope and magnitude of China's ambition.

By the Ming era (1368–1644), China was the largest economy in the world and its traders led international commerce. Today, China is often called the 'workshop of the world', dominating global commerce and having overtaken the US' pole position some years ago, a fact that no longer shocks many.[3] The simple and most easily understandable explanation is that as European and Japanese economies have stagnated, those of India and China have surged. The G7 economies continue to be richer on a per capita income basis, but China's 17-year-old Shanghai Cooperation Organisation (SCO), with Russia, India and Pakistan among its members, includes countries with larger economies and populations. A sister organisation of the One Belt, One Road, the SCO may be part of Beijing's grand plan for a new international order that is an alternative to American-dominated groupings. For the time being, it is a work in progress without a clear timeline other than the group's annual meeting.

Since the original 2013 announcement of the New Silk Road and Belt, China has made immense amounts of development money available to any 'Roader' that wants to join its audacious global infrastructure investment network, popularly renamed One Belt, One Road (OBOR), and more recently rebranded as the Belt and Road Initiative (BRI). Critics are divided on what the real cost will be in the end, as estimates vary considerably. According to data assembled by the RWR advisory group since 2013, contracts worth about $1.1 trillion in 87 BRI countries. Approximately 17 new countries joined China's investment club in the last three years alone. If anything, these numbers are expected to increase as other states want to be part of the BRI. Not even the end date is certain, but Chinese scholars are of the view that Beijing's

---

[2]*Miles upon Miles: World Heritage along the Silk Road,* brochure (Hong Kong Museum of History, February 2018).
[3]Martin Wolf, 'How the West should judge a rising China', *Financial Times,* 15 May, 2018.

premier global initiative will run to 2049.[4] If so, it will, arguably, be the largest and costliest infrastructural development venture in history, with an estimated price tag of more than $4 trillion, easily surpassing the $130 billion Marshall Plan in today's dollars. The final cost may even surpass the total stimulus spending shelled out by the G7 between 2007 and 2008 to rescue global capitalism from the financial crisis.

We don't know how many projects are associated with China's global initiative, but a recent estimate puts the number of contracts at more than 15,000, a number that continues to grow.[5] When completed, China will have spent an estimated $5 trillion on its globe-spanning land and maritime initiative, linking Asia and Europe in ways never before thought possible. At this point, no one can say for certain what it will cost and how many thousands of infrastructural projects will be undertaken. Each year, Chinese authorities are signing more deals and adding new countries from Africa, Asia, the Caribbean and, eventually, quite possibly, the European Union as a single signatory.

So far, 11 European Union members and another five non-EU Central and Eastern European countries have signed agreements with China and the commercial group 16+1, another Chinese initiative to deepen cooperation with 11 EU member states and 5 Balkan countries.[6] Each of these countries has negotiated major infrastructural deals, giving China a major presence in the EU. This Chinese involvement in the EU is a large and important step towards realising its geopolitical goal of building a vast corridor of economic exchange between Europe and Asia with connecting corridors to Africa and the Middle East.

---

[4]Lei Zou, *The Political Economy of China's Belt And Road Initiative* (World Scientific Publishing, 2018).

[5]Nadège Rolland, 'China's Belt and Road Initiative' (National Bureau of Asian Research, Asia Insight podcast series, 20 March, 2018) https://itunes.apple.com/us/podcast/asia-insight/id1363281533?mt=2 [Accessed October 2018]

[6]The 16+1 format is an initiative by the People's Republic of China aimed at intensifying and expanding cooperation with 11 EU member states and five Balkan countries (Albania, Bosnia and Herzegovina, Bulgaria, Croatia, the Czech Republic, Estonia, Hungary, Latvia, Lithuania, Macedonia, Montenegro, Poland, Romania, Serbia, Slovakia and Slovenia).

The priority areas for cooperation are in the fields of investments, transport, finance, science, education and culture.

The One Belt, One Road was also enshrined in the Party Constitution in 2017, recognition of just how important it is regarded to be by China's ruling elite.[7] OBOR is a foundation stone of public policy that cuts across different ministries and strategic objectives. The geographical maritime dimension has now become a central tenet of Chinese planning, and was adopted as a priority government policy in 2016. Significantly called Vision for Maritime Cooperation, it is also a wide-ranging policy statement, including a very important, but overlooked, subsection on security issues.[8] China has defined three potential target areas for economic cooperation: infrastructure, high technologies and green technologies. Some would add a fourth, namely development and international cooperation. Each of these priorities is seen through the Chinese lens of self-interest. Still, it is very difficult to map, let alone understand, all of its aspects since there are more than 15,000 contracts with 80 countries – if Latin American partners are included.

In 2017, China added yet another Silk Road corridor: China intends to traverse the Northwest Passage in the Arctic in the summer months. Specially designed and ordered by Beijing from Korean builders, the ships China is using have icebreaking capacities of up to 2 m (6½ ft) and are able to transport liquefied gas on the Polar Silk Road between China, Russia and Finland, a transoceanic passage navigable at the top of the world due to global warming.[9] All these examples illustrate a simple constant: many top-level Western policymakers have underestimated the depth of China's global vision and China's ability to implement its grand design. What precisely is missing from their perception?

---

[7]Thomas S. Eder, 'Mapping the Belt and Road Initiative: This is Where We Stand', Mercator Institute for Chinese Studies, 7 June, 2018 https://www.merics.org/index.php/en/bri-tracker/mapping-the-belt-and-road-initiative [Accessed October 2018]
[8]Thomas S. Eder, ibid.
[9]Sebastian Murdoch-Gibson, 'Arctic Corridor', 7 March, 2014 (youTube video, 3:47) https://www.youtube.com/watch?v=jovIfvlE4fI [Accessed Ocotber 2018]

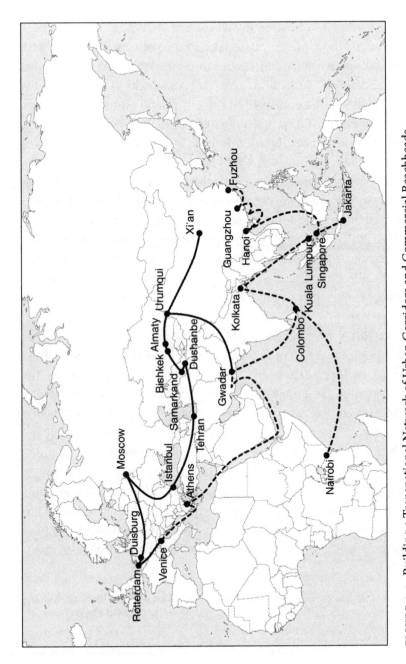

FIGURE 1.1 Building a Transnational Network of Urban Corridors and Commercial Beachheads

Source: Bloomberg News, 10 May, 2017 https://www.bloomberg.com/graphics/2017-china-belt-and-road-initiative.

ITS MANY MOVING PARTS AND GRAND DESIGN

Beijing wants to build a network of urban-linked rail, road and sea corridors connecting the principal densely populated cities in Asia to their large and bustling European counterparts. Xi'an, Moscow, Tehran, Istanbul, Rotterdam, Kolkata, Hanoi, Athens and Venice are all major links in a transnational chain of land and sea connectors (see Figure 1.1). You could imagine an ocean freighter departing from Fuzhou, a transportation hub in southeastern China's Fujian province, and making stops in Hanoi, Colombo and Gwadar in Pakistan before making port in Athens, then unloading cargo in Venice, with Rotterdam the final port of disembarkation. The Suez Canal facilitates the long voyage, particularly for oil, and China's strategically located ports – called the 'string of pearls' – provide a safe harbour for China's global shipping lanes.[10] Make no mistake; the OBOR is designed as a commercial superhighway moving goods and people over vast distances from China into the heart of Europe and the West.

For China, it is important to draw attention to the very large and important sea component of its infrastructural initiative. China's policymakers have acquired parallel maritime routes for shipping gas and other strategic commodities around the world, which will secure China's strategic energy needs. Seven new strategic ports have already been constructed, essential for the building of a network of secure oceanic trade routes in order to assist China in securing its strategic vision in the region. It has Kyaukse in Myanmar, Port Klang in Malaysia, Colombo and Hambantota in Sri Lanka, Bagomoyo in Tanzania, Djibouti City in Djibouti and Gwadar in Pakistan. The Chinese have also signed a 99-year lease to build the new port of Darwin in Australia.[11]

[10]Gurpreet Khurana, 'China's "String of Pearls" in the Indian Ocean and its Security Implications', *Strategic Analysis* 32(1) (2008), pp. 1–39. http://www.academia.edu/7727023/Chinas_String_of_Pearls_in_the_Indian_Ocean_and_its_Security_Implications [Accessed October 2018]
[11]Helen Davidson, 'Chinese company secures 99-year lease of Darwin port in $506m deal', *The Guardian*, 13 October, 2015. https://www.theguardian.com/australia-news/2015/oct/13/chinese-company-secures-99-year-lease-of-darwin-port-in-506m-deal [Accessed October 2016]

A Chinese state-owned enterprise bought Zeebrugge, Belgium's second-largest port, in 2018. By no means is Beijing's buying spree likely to be over anytime soon.

A network of economic agreements stretching from Beijing to London underpins this BRI superhighway as an expanding amount of finance is made available to foreign governments. According to Kevin P. Gallagher, Associate Professor of Global Economic and Development Policy at Boston University, this is possible because Beijing is willing to take on more risk.[12] A recent G-24 report showed that the Western-backed multilateral development banks (MDBs) have become highly concerned about their credit ratings and have become less willing to lend to certain groups of countries, whereas China's banks can rely on deep Chinese capital markets.[13]

Where '1' is low risk and '10' is high, the average OECD risk rating for the World Bank's Top 20 recipients of energy finance is 5.5, excluding the United Kingdom. The Chinese banks' risk average is just a bit higher at 5.63, but 10 countries on China's list that do not appear on the World Bank's have an average risk rating of 6. In terms of Chinese energy financing recipients (2005–2017), Russia leads the pack with $42,700 million, Brazil follows with $39,256 million, while Pakistan ($24,613 million), Angola ($8900 million) and India ($7705 million) round out the top five.[14] Importantly, this is not only an economic but a political trend, as Chinese financial banks seem willing to take on more risk due to the fact that China's foreign policy is not to discriminate on the basis of the borrowing governments' domestic policies and behaviour. By contrast, the MDBs, such as

---

[12]Kevin P. Gallagher, 'Risk and reward in China's overseas development plan', *Financial Times*, 7 May, 2018.

[13]Chris Humphrey, *Infrastructure Finance in the Developing World: Challenges and Opportunities for Multilateral Development Banks in 21st Century Infrastructure Finance* (Seoul, Intergovernmental Group of Twenty Four on Monetary Affairs and Development, 2015) https://www.g24.org/wp-content/uploads/2016/05/MARGGK-WP08.pdf [Accessed October 2018]

[14]Kevin P. Gallagher, Rohini Kamal, Junda Jin, Yanning Chen and Xinyue Ma, 'Energizing Development Finance? The Benefits and Risks of China's Development Finance in the Global Energy Sector', *Energy Policy* 122 (2018), pp. 313–321.

the World Bank, often have a set of tough austerity domestic policy conditions that make it less willing to finance certain governments.[15]

The big picture idea is that the financial and infrastructural supply lines connecting dozens of countries with Western Europe, Russia, Central Asia and China will operate like a giant artery, expanding commerce and deepening trade. Bloomberg captured the zeitgeist of China's sweeping campaign to remake the global economy and boost economic growth in these words:

> From Bangladesh to Belarus, railways, refineries, bridges, industrial parks and much else is being built. In Colombo, a new city larger than Monaco is taking shape near Sri Lanka's main port. With an estimated total investment of $13 billion spanning about 25 years, the new city is shaping up as the poster child for China's grand plan.[16]

It is apparent that Chinese authorities have learned the basic lesson history teaches about the complex ways in which free trade and infrastructure are inextricably linked. Mind-boggling projects such as the Trans-Siberian railway (9289 km/5772 miles long) and the railways built during the golden age of railway construction in 19th-century North America changed the dynamics of space and time in their historical era and had vast economic impacts, irreversibly altering the lives of people, communities, markets and entire regions. These hinge-turning events were also burdened with debt and were high-risk, low-return investments. Many failed spectacularly. Others transformed the economic grooves of global geography. For instance, the completion of the Suez Canal in 1869 'brought India nearly 6,000 miles closer to western Europe, vitally altering the pattern of trade relations which had previously existed to the great benefit of the United Kingdom'.[17] It is China's ambition

---

[15]Gallagher et al., op. cit.
[16]'Chinese Spending Lures Countries to its Belt and Road Initiative', *Bloomberg News*, 10 May, 2017 https://www.bloomberg.com/graphics/2017-china-belt-and-road-initiative/ [Accessed October 2018]
[17]Jules Hugot and Camilo Umana Dajud, 'Trade Costs and the Suez and Panama Canals', CPEII Working Paper No. 2016–29, 5 December, 2016.

to bring modern China and Europe thousands of kilometres closer by building land and sea routes to shrink the once bounded forces of space and time. China's grand design involves investing in time-saving superhighways of commerce for the trans-shipment of goods and the movement of peoples, creating closer links between Africa, the Middle East, Central Asia and Western Europe.

Focus on the dynamic importance of infrastructure has always been on the agenda of states around the world, particularly those in the Global South and the many industrial metropolises in the Global North. Economic geographer Paul Krugman provided the key insight in his highly acclaimed book, *Geography and Trade*. He observed that once regional economies are established and become sufficiently strong with robust economies of scale – such as China, which has accomplished this in record time – local demand will keep the majority of manufacturers inside their manufacturing belt. So, the challenge, in Krugman's terms, is to figure out how national and regional markets can use locational theory to map the geographic dynamics, creating new opportunities in sectors with sufficiently low transportation costs to share in what he calls 'footloose' production that is not tied down by natural resources.[18]

This is where China enters the theoretical picture with its deep pockets and investment blitz across the globe. Its strategic policy epitomises the powerful benefits of locational theory and economic geography working in tandem. It relies on altering the relationship between the centre and the periphery by linking regional manufacturing hubs to their local urban centres in new ways to lower transportation costs, generate employment and stimulate demand in local markets.[19] Many experts have identified the absence of infrastructure as a key structural factor holding back the economic development of many countries that do not have adequate, continuous and round-the-clock electricity, fully functioning roads, clean water,

[18]Paul Krugman, *Geography and Trade* (MIT Press, 1993), p. 22.
[19]Michael Piore and Charles F. Sabel, *The Second Industrial Divide: Possibilities for Prosperity* (Basic Books, 1984).

modern airports, and effective and safe railroads, not to mention global-reaching telecommunications systems.[20]

What China cannot know beforehand, and what experts have great difficulty in predicting accurately, is whether the investment push by China's policy banks will be intense enough to be transformative. Will its big vision, structural-transformative projects be more than run-of-the-mill, bricks-and-mortar investment in energy hubs and public works? In the best case scenario, will they trigger a very different kind of growth process, one that is supportive of long-term structural change in the economy, including strengthening regulatory institutions, investing in human capital, and an environmental pro-innovation dynamic?

Infrastructure by itself cannot take the critical place of well-functioning institutions with their embedded rules and practices, but from historical experience, institutions also seem to arise in intense periods of infrastructural-led development. Recall Roosevelt's introduction of the New Deal in the 1930s to rescue American capitalism, which was in the grip of worldwide economic depression, and the radical consequences of Keynesian economics that legitimised the need for the modern welfare state. In theoretical terms, this is a big idea and one that China can run with if it understands and learns how to manage the timing and sequencing of its investment drive. When completed in a decade's time or longer, these corridors, supported by their infrastructural DNA, will integrate and bind together dozens of countries in new ways. That is the expectation and goal. Transportation systems, the mass movement of people and new information technologies will redirect global flows of commerce in response to these powerful incentive structures, which are paid for and managed by China, and built with Chinese technology and capital goods manufactured in China.

To better grasp the many implications of China's global investment plans, we need to focus our minds on the central role

---

[20]Daron Acemoglu and James Robinson, *Why Nations Fail: The Origins of Power, Prosperity and Poverty* (Crown Publishers, 2012); Paul Collier, *The Bottom Billion: Why the Poorest Counties are Failing and What can be Done About It* (Oxford University Press, 2007); Thomas Piketty, *Capital in the Twenty-first Century* (Harvard University Press, 2014).

played by all kinds of infrastructure in promoting social cohesion and supporting transformative economic growth. The catch-all term 'infrastructure' typically characterises technical structures, such as roads, bridges, tunnels, water supply systems, sewers, electrical grids and telecommunications networks, and can be defined as: 'the physical components of interrelated systems providing commodities and services essential to enable, sustain, or enhance societal living conditions.'[21] But it means much more than that.

INFRASTRUCTURE: THE NERVOUS SYSTEM OF THE MODERN ECONOMY

When they use the term *infrastructure*, experts are referring to the structures, institutions, systems and facilities that serve a state, city or region.[22] In other words, infrastructures are the services and facilities necessary for any economy to function for exchange, production, distribution and consumption purposes. Economic growth, or what economists call economic development, is always the highest priority in all economic issues. Gene Grossman and Elhanan Helpman have divided economic development into three types: the first considers the accumulation of 'broad' capital, including human capital, and different types of physical capital of the more traditional sort, invested in roads, motorways, airports and harbours; the second type applies to external economies such as ports, shipping infrastructure, airports and logistics hubs; and the third concentrates on industrial innovation as the engine of growth.[23]

Infrastructure of every description is a cornerstone of a stable and productive society that impacts people's lives by giving them access to clean water, sanitation, transportation and public goods such as education, information and communication, and medical care. The advanced, capitalist-world countries that

[21]Committee on Infrastructure Innovation, National Research Council, *Infrastructure for the 21st Century: Framework for a Research Agenda* (Academy Press, 1987).

[22]François Bourguignon and Boris Pleskovic, *Rethinking Infrastructure for Development* (The International Bank for Development and Reconstruction, 2008).

[23]Gene Grossman and Elhanan Helpman, 'Endogenous Innovation in the Theory of Growth', *Journal of Economic Perspectives* 8 (1994), pp. 23–44.

are high-performance success stories all have some of the best infrastructure in the world, from high-tech ports capable of handling hundreds of millions of tonnes of containers annually, autobahns and superhighways for truckers and the movement of millions of tonnes of freight, to the very best capital intensive systems of logistics and communications.

Some scholars sharpen the term further by distinguishing between 'hard' and 'soft' infrastructure: the former refers to the large physical networks necessary for the functioning of a modern industrial nation such as roads and waterways, sewer systems, electricity and telecommunications. The latter refers to all the institutions that are required to maintain the economic, health, cultural and social standards of society. These include the financial, education, health care, and government and law enforcement systems, as well as emergency services.

To grasp all the elements of China's unique, history-making BRI epic drama, its global infrastructural story needs investigating, documenting and telling in some considerable detail. Who is part of it? Which countries want to join? What is China's long-game vision of infrastructural politics? To put it bluntly, what are the odds it will succeed?

THE ONE BELT, ONE ROAD CHINA CLUB
In real time, China's expertise in infrastructure development has plenty to offer its partners in this sprawling global spending initiative. Half of China's partners are drawn from the ranks of what the World Bank might refer to as low-income, essentially poor countries facing all kinds of developmental traps. They could be landlocked without access to a major ocean. Many are dependent on an abundance of resources for export to foreign markets and little else. Others have little access to technology, are handicapped by weak institutions and authoritarian governments. Many have been devastated by civil war and deep ethnic divisions. So, all these countries are looking for a way forward and to get on their feet; Beijing is the go-to power. It has partners in Eastern Europe (Hungary, Serbia, Belarus and Russia), Western and Central Asia (Iran, Turkey, Kazakhstan, Kyrgyzstan and Uzbekistan), East and

Central Africa (Tanzania, Kenya, Uganda, Rwanda, Burundi and South Sudan, along with Eritrea, Ethiopia and Somalia), and Southern and Southeast Asia (Indonesia, Malaysia, Laos, Vietnam and Cambodia). Saudi Arabia is also a major partner and one of China's largest suppliers of oil and gas. Pakistan, Bangladesh, Sri Lanka and the Maldives are critical partners with major Chinese investments that function as a regional counterweight to India.

It makes geopolitical sense that the OBOR initiative is concentrated in Northeast Asia, Southeast Asia, South Asia, Middle Asia and Middle Eastern countries. China has also secured early and significant support from the BRICS states (Brazil, Russia, India and South Africa). This, too, is hardly astonishing. According to the World Economic Forum's *Positive Infrastructure Report*, the world will face a global infrastructure deficit of $2 trillion per year over the next 20 years.[24] With only $24 trillion coming from the world's leading economies, it leaves a shortfall falling somewhere between $16 and $47 trillion.[25] Business will also need to step up to the plate by increasing infrastructure investments from the current $63 billion to $250 billion by 2020, a target the private sector is unlikely to meet. So OBOR's billions will not be enough to erase the global infrastructural deficit, by any standard, it is an impressive first and second step.

China's own model of development is based upon mastering giant engineering infrastructural projects like the Three Gorges Dam, which took 10 years to construct, cost billions of dollars, spans more than 2 km (1 mile) of turbulent rivers and gorges rising 181 m (594 ft) in height, and supplies the super-metropolis of Shanghai

[24]World Economic Forum, 'Infrastructure and Connectivity', in *The Global Competitiveness Report 2015–2016* http://reports.weforum.org/global-competitiveness-report-2015-2016/infrastructure-and-connectivity/ [Accessed October 2018]; McKinsey Global Institute, *Southeast Asia at the crossroads: Three paths to prosperity* (2014) http://www.mckinsey.com/global-themes/asia-pacific/three-paths-to-sustained-economic-growth-in-southeast-asia [Accessed October 2018]

[25]Norman F. Anderson, 'A new vision for infrastructure will save doomed global economy', *The Hill*, 16 April, 2015 http://thehill.com/blogs/pundits-blog/finance/239007-a-new-vision-for-infrastructure-will-save-doomed-global-economy [Accessed October 2018]. For more on the Global South's infrastructural deficit, see the *Meeting Asia's Infrastructure Needs* report by the Asian Development Bank, available at: https://www.adb.org/publications/asia-infrastructure-needs [Accessed October 2018]

with its electricity. According to Jin Liqun, President of the recently launched Asian Infrastructure Investment Bank (AIIB), the official rationalisation for the OBOR initiative comes from China's own experience: 'It illustrates that infrastructure investment paves the way for broad-based economic social development, and poverty alleviation comes as a natural consequence of that.' Speaking from the perspective of the AIIB, he went on to say that, 'We want to create something new that combines the strong features of private companies with those of multilateral development banks.'[26] While the AIIB has already contributed significantly to infrastructural initiatives, it has increased operations gradually, investing $1.52 billion in infrastructure in 2016, $5 billion in 2017 and a projected $10 billion in 2018.[27]

There are other similarly remarkable Chinese projects that are less well known in popular discourses in the Global North, but which are equally impressive. For example, the diversion of water in the Yangtze, Yellow and Huaibe rivers will fundamentally change the flow and direction of the water while the massive new locks being constructed will lift ocean-going freighters hundreds of metres.

For North Americans, it may come as a shock that China, with its late entry into transcontinental railway development, is unequalled in building high-speed trains and now has 80 per cent of the world's bullet trains.[28] Beijing recently completed the much-admired 1308 km/ 812 mile-long high-speed rail line between Beijing and Shanghai in record time, a transportation route that carries tens of thousands of Chinese people daily at speeds of up to 300 km/h (186 mph). It is hard to wrap your head around so much Chinese development without encountering its record of achievement in the area of infrastructure development.[29]

[26]Jamil Anderlini, 'Lunch with the FT: Jin Liqun', *Financial Times*, 21 April, 2016.
[27]James Kynge, 'How the Silk Road plans will be financed', *Financial Times*, 9 May, 2016.
[28]Economist News Desk, 'The lure of speed: China has built the world's largest bullet-train network', *Economist*, 13 January, 2017.
[29]Simeon Djankov and Sean Miner (eds), *China's Belt and Road Initiative: Motives, Scope, and Challenges* (Peterson Institute for International Economics, 2016).

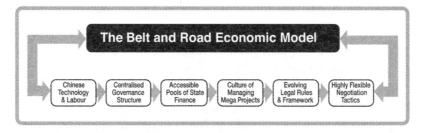

FIGURE 1.2 China's Infrastructural Economic Model
Source: China Pivot Working Group, Robarts Centre for Canadian Studies, York University, 2018.

It will surprise many that Global North countries are on another AAA investment list that, while not formally part of the OBOR global initiative, is nonetheless swept up in China's global repositioning strategy. The UK, the EU and the US are already long-standing commercial partners with China. Commercial investment properties from hotels to shopping centres, mass media, financial services, electrical facilities and industrial groups of every description, as well as nuclear and sustainable energy, are among the many sectors that Beijing has been investing in for over a decade. Recently, China Southern Airlines ordered $6 billion worth of Airbus aircraft, another indication of the deep commercial relationship between China and Europe in this critical leading sector. Since 2015, China Southern Airlines has ordered more than $15 billion worth of new aircraft from Airbus and Boeing, and will continue to place orders as it adds transoceanic routes to many countries.[30]

CHINA'S MODEL OF INFRASTRUCTURAL DEVELOPMENT

What China brings to its model of infrastructure-centric investment and development (see Figure 1.2) is seemingly bottomless pools of state financing at very low interest rates, leading management expertise and proven Chinese technologies of different kinds that it has developed and which it manufactures, installs and maintains once the project is completed. It has proven conceptualisation and execution expertise. This expertise did not just appear out of thin

[30]'China Southern Airlines Orders 20 Airbus Jets Worth $6 Billion', *China Daily News*, 27 April, 2017.

air: in the 1950s, after liberation from Japanese occupation, Stalin sent 80,000 Soviet engineers and military advisers to China to help build Tiananmen Square, roads, bridges, the Beijing subway and the Great Hall of the People. In Wuhan, you can see the massive dual-purpose railway and car bridge, a mastodon of a structure that took eight years for Soviet 'friendship workers' to complete.

Now there are seven bridges and one tunnel connecting the three cities of Wuhan. In this sense, the Chinese have long since abandoned the Soviet monumental style of infrastructure. Today, many are crane-like suspension bridges with intricate systems of enormous wires and support pylons. Others are inspired by successful Chinese experiences and the latest advances in functionalist engineering. Chinese engineering technology is also very influenced by Western advances in building technology and construction methods. Mao expelled the Soviet engineers and advisors as a consequence of the Sino-Soviet split in the early 1960s, a pivotal moment that probably did more to change the course of Chinese engineering and infrastructure building than any other development. It forced Chinese professionals to acquire their own engineering skills, methods and designs to build China's vast infrastructure. When Deng opened China to global markets in the late 1980s, this process began to accelerate rapidly.[31]

Since then, China has developed its own in-depth expertise in complex engineering projects, and large-scale infrastructure management is part of the curriculum in many engineering universities. Strictly speaking, the most recent iteration of China's economic model is not as new as it appears. A large part of the rationale behind it is to breathe new life into China's mass production industries, which are in need of new markets as China's growth slows. These will supply the machinery, parts and equipment used in these unparalleled infrastructure projects across the globe. Steel, construction and coal industries have already been hit by large-scale layoffs because these industries are suffering from a glut of

[31]Personal interview with the Dean of Engineering, Wuhan University of Technology and Engineering, September 2017.

18

overcapacity. For the Chinese economy, the OBOR is, for all intents and purposes, a multiyear stimulus package to boost exports and create new markets for Chinese products in the heavy goods sector. For many observers, China is an export success story and accused of 'dumping' its excess manufacturing capacity in its neighbours' markets. The fact that China can be both of these things at once speaks to the many conflicting roles Beijing plays in the global economy.

For each large-scale project China delivers everything, from a workforce of thousands of Chinese workers if required, to the maintenance of equipment and the supply of new parts and their assembly when needed. It is not unusual for China to send a small army of personnel and labourers for the surveying, construction, training and management of its massive railway-building projects. At the height of the construction of the Tanzania-Zambia railway in the early 1970s, it is estimated that more than 60,000 African and 13,500 Chinese workers were employed to build the railway.[32] In many projects since, China no longer supplies all or part of the labour force, though it is unclear presently how many Chinese 'special contract' workers are part of the BRI. China has localised employment in many African countries according to recent 2015 research by Sautram and Hairong, who have studied Chinese hiring practices across the African continent. As one expects, there are variations in Chinese enterprises and projects. They write: 'on average, locals are more than 4/5 of the employees at 400 Chinese enterprises and projects 40 in African countries'.[33] The proportions are much lower for top managers and significantly lower for engineers and other professionals.

In Ethiopia, for instance, Chinese workers are training the drivers of the newly completed Metro. Along the way, Beijing has acquired a deep management culture skilled in overseeing highly engineered,

---

[32]Jamie Monson, *Africa's Freedom Railway: How a Chinese Development Project Changed Lives and Livelihoods in Tanzania* (Indiana University Press, 2009).

[33]Barry Sautman and Yan Hairong, "Localizing Chinese Enterprises in Africa: from Myths to Policies," HKUST Institute for Emerging Market Studies, Thought Leadership Brief no. 5 (2015), https://iems.ust.hk/assets/publications/thought-leadership-briefs/tlb05/hkust_iems_thought_leadership_brief_tlb05.pdf.

capital-intensive projects. The official view is that, in 1980, when mainland China replaced Taiwan in the Bretton Woods institutions:

> We [Chinese] had nothing but hundreds of millions of Chinese. Then, we started to borrow to build infrastructure, and some were worried about debt creation. But the benefits of infrastructure investment appeared 25 years later, when the economy started to take off. At the same time, other countries were borrowing to sustain consumption.[34]

AN INCIPIENT LEGAL FRAMEWORK FOR COMMERCIAL DISPUTES

For much of the first five years, BRI has had a minimalist governance structure with no formal provision for commercial or state investor-dispute mechanisms. The latter would be foreign to Chinese legal culture, but modern China has an extensive practice of commercial dispute resolution. Initially China's global infrastructural model was, to say the least, incomplete, without a strong legal dimension.

In 2018, Beijing announced partnerships with both the Singapore International Commercial Court (SICC) and the Dubai International Financial Centre (DIFC) Courts for the purposes of mediating disputes along the BRI. The SICC was established by the Supreme People's Court (SPC), China's highest domestic court, and was created specifically to resolve international disputes, even those that have no connection with Singapore and are not governed by Singaporean law. To paraphrase British legal dispute expert William Jones, a key feature of the SICC is that it maintains an international bench of judges and is often addressed directly by foreign counsel. The fact that foreign lawyers are subject to strict controls (for example, they cannot advise on PRC law in China) makes it unlikely that the court would be willing to allow non-Chinese judges or counsel to play such a role.[35]

---

[34]Jonathan Fenby, *Tiger Head, Snake Tails: China Today, How it got There and Why it has to Change* (Simon & Schuster, 2012), p. 12.
[35]Bryan Cave and Paisner Leighton, 'Belt and Road Insights: China announces new courts for resolving Belt and Road disputes', Lexology, 22 March, 2018 https://www.lexology.com/library/detail.aspx?g=9b2a23d2-a461-4e89-96a4-adeb3ecf7e20 [Accessed October 2018]

China's system of commercial arbitration, which hears disputes and makes nonbinding awards, is very different from commercial arbitration in the West because the state intervenes directly through the courts in accordance with Chinese legal provisions, a fundamental difference from Anglo-American practice and the notion of the separation of powers. Such provisions take into consideration the validity of the arbitration award, the making of arbitration procedures and the enforcement of awards in accordance with local laws and regulations.[36]

With the SICC and DIFC Courts moving into place, the critical question remains: How will the BRI's newly appointed courts practically address these existing challenges? After all, increased disputes along the BRI are likely to encounter some of the world's most difficult commercial environments, which have weak investment protections, and slow and cumbersome legal processes.[37]

Beijing's legal fix has, in theory, addressed an important need, but it is unclear how BRI partners will respond to the relatively untested framework. Importantly, the BRI courts underscore how China is slowly working to revise the current rules-based order. According to the Centre for Strategic and International Studies report, the courts will focus, at least initially, on disputes between commercial investors rather than between states or between investors and states.[38] However, given the BRI's record of intensifying expansion from Asia to the Arctic and on to cyber and outer space since its announcement in 2013, the ambitions and reach of its courts might grow as well. As more and more BRI projects are agreed to, China would naturally prefer to play by its own rules.

---

[36]China International Trade Lawyers, 'Arbitration System of China', 17 January, 2012 http://www.cn-linked.com/en/view.php?id=237 [Accessed October 2018]

[37]As a 2018 report from the Center for Strategic & International Studies points out, across all BRI partner countries the average time for resolving a commercial dispute through a local court is 621 days. The report is available at https://www.csis.org/analysis/all-rise-belt-and-road-court-session [Accessed October 2018]

[38]Jonathan E. Hillman and Matthew P. Goodman, 'All Rise? Belt and Road Court is in Session', Center for Strategic & International Studies blog, 26 July, 2018 https://www.csis.org/analysis/all-rise-belt-and-road-court-session [Accessed October 2018]

A SUPPLY-AND-DEMAND ANALYSIS OF THE NEW SILK ROAD – THE ROLE OF PIVOTAL REGIONAL ACTORS

China's global infrastructural project, with its newly minted dispute resolution provision, is a work in progress. Most importantly, the BRI has recently been made part of the Party Constitution, giving it extra-legal clout and authority at the top of the hierarchy. Embedding it in the Constitution gives it a unique status and legitimacy, and is a sign that BRI will outlive Xi's presidency.[39] As a state priority, OBOR is a new form of soft power diplomacy and can be used most effectively across different regional markets in South Asia, Central Asia, Russia, the Middle East, the EU and Africa, supported by China's 'core' industrial sectors.

State-owned enterprises are key actors in the Chinese model of infrastructure development, which some economists estimate exceeds 50 per cent of China's GDP.[40] These state-owned enterprises supply the onsite know-how, offer critically important managerial expertise and are legally responsible for ensuring these complex mega-projects are completed on time. They also sign contracts with their China club bilateral partners. Contracts are awarded without open competition bidding and all equipment is made by Chinese manufacturers. Many of these economic construction and engineering giants are based in China, operate globally and have their origins in the building of China's modern, highly efficient infrastructure.

China's global supply chains give its state-owned enterprises the inside track, supplying all the equipment needed for building hydroelectric power installations, port facilities, the rolling stock and equipment for railways, roads and public facilities of every description. In his book on China's industrialisation, James McGregor calls these supply chains 'anointed national champions to lead China's international ambitions and serve as guarantors of Party supremacy'.[41]

[39]Chris Buckley and Keith Bradsher, 'Xi Jinping's Marathon Speech: Five Takeaways', *New York Times*, 18 October, 2017.
[40]James McGregor, *No Ancient Wisdom, No Followers: The Challenges of Chinese Authoritarian Capitalism* (Prospecta Press, 2012), p. 86.
[41]James McGregor, op. cit., p. 154.

These corporate structures are protected by the 1994 Company Law Reform, which gave them decision-making powers and access to preferential financing. The biggest SOEs compete head-on with the world's biggest firms on the Fortune 500 list. Recently, the government has reduced the number of these economic giants largely through mergers. At a global level, they are the interface between China's infrastructure initiative and its 'core' industries in power generation, oil and gas, telecommunications, steel, construction and equipment manufacturing.

For the next critical period, China and SOEs will be in an active recruitment phase in the hopes of broadening and deepening China's list of partners from the current number. Its highly flexible negotiating tactics with countries at such different stages of development and in so many regions of the world have worked to China's advantage.[42] In extending loans to various developing economies, China has brought them into its sphere of influence and thus made them vulnerable to Chinese pressure. Some economists believe that recipients will be trapped in a vicious cycle of debt and easy credit, which will increase China's leverage over 'One Roaders' such as Cambodia, Laos and Thailand. For instance, when the Sri Lankan government was on the brink of default, it asked for more loans from China.

One would think this would be a counterintuitive move on the part of the Sri Lankan government, but the Chinese authorities seized this as an opportunity to bail out the government. Some experts see a pattern of commercial penetration followed by China's use of hard power as strategic leverage. Other policy experts are looking at the range of projects themselves and putting a brave face on the growing Chinese influence, describing it as China meeting unmet infrastructural needs through easy credit and benevolent investment.[43]

China has multiple goals and interests, depending on the region's resources and geopolitical importance. For instance, in Central and

[42]Mark Blyth, *Austerity: The History of a Dangerous Idea* (Oxford, 2015).
[43]Brahma Chellaney, 'China's Debt–Trap Diplomacy', *Project Syndicate*, 24 January, 2017 https://www.project-syndicate.org/commentary/china-one-belt-one-road-loans-debt-by-brahma-chellaney-2017-01 [Accessed October 2018]

Eastern Europe, including Hungary, Belarus and Serbia, China's investments and commitments have provided local elites with new social and economic development opportunities, as well as an incentive to make new foreign direct investment in important sectors that are of interest to Beijing. Central and Eastern Europe are geopolitically valuable because they connect Europe to Asia for advancing regional market strategies that will enhance China's already very large presence in Europe, negotiating bilateral investment deals both with more countries and in more markets.

The Middle East and Western Asia covers a hugely diverse regional economy of the United Arab Emirates, Saudi Arabia, Iran and Turkey. China's goals are many: to deepen market access, to have an influential role in the social and economic transformation of the region, and to recruit new partners for Beijing's global economic initiative. The prize for China is to achieve secure energy access to the oil and gas reserves as well as for other kinds of primary resources strategically located midway between Europe and East Asia.

Central Asia, including Kazakhstan, Kyrgyzstan and Uzbekistan, is also a critical region in China's growth coalition and occupies a complex space in both China's and Russia's security perimeters. It is important for its natural resources, particularly oil and gas reserves, and links China to foreign energy markets. If China's investment initiatives in the region are successful, it will enable China to achieve enhanced energy security from countries located in its own backyard.

Southern and Southeastern Asia, comprising Indonesia, Malaysia, Laos, Vietnam and Cambodia, are part of China's backyard and central to its security scenarios. These countries are embroiled in complex, contentious and century-long relations, border issues and fundamental questions of national sovereignty. The OBOR initiative is seen regionally as a primary vehicle for social and economic development, with an emphasis on the social as much as the economic. As a result, Southern and Southeastern Asia are seen by Beijing as important regional hubs, waypoints for the export of goods and services as well as other market-centric growth opportunities.

Still, the fit between the 'supply' and 'demand' from both China and the governments of its growth coalition has, to date, been very successful, because the demand for new infrastructural funding is a priority for many low-income countries.

ENDING THE POVERTY TRAP: A GLOBAL PRIORITY

The United Nations has recently reported on the state of the world's infrastructure across many regions and continents. It found that 2.5 billion people are without proper sanitation and indoor toilets.[44] It blames 'bad economics' or poor infrastructure, which allows millions of people every year, most of them children, to die from diseases associated with inadequate water supply, sanitation and hygiene. Chronically inadequate infrastructural development is not just a symptom, but is a causal factor in much of the poverty and immiseration in Asia and Africa according to the Asian Development Bank's most recent 2017 report.[45] Recently, poverty experts have constructed more powerful analytical tools and have developed the widely accepted Global Multidimensional Poverty Index (MPI). They estimate that a total of 1.45 billion people from 103 countries are multidimensionally poor. Multidimensional poverty accounts for the profile of overlapping deprivations experienced by each poor person. This framework produces a more accurate understanding of poverty; a condition that experts agree can no longer be understood simply as a function of per capita income.

What we need to focus on is the intensity of poverty's many dimensions. What makes the index so pertinent is that it aggregates this marginalisation of 'the poor and forgotten' into a number of meaningful indexes that can be used to inform and develop policies 'that tackle the interlinked dimensions of poverty

---

[44]*State of the World's Cities 2006/7: The Millennium Development Goals and Urban Sustainability: 30 Years of Shaping the Habitat Agenda* (UN Habitat, 2006) https://sustainabledevelopment. un.org/content/documents/11292101_alt.pdf [Accessed October 2018]

[45]*Asian Development Outlook 2017: Transcending the Middle-Income Challenge* (Asian Development Bank, 2017) https://www.adb.org/publications/asian-development-outlook-2017-middle-income-challenge [Accessed October 2018]

together'. The critical measures are health (nutrition), education (number of years of schooling) and standard of living (water and sanitation).[46]

The latest report of the Oxford Poverty and Human Development Initiative presented findings demonstrating that 48 per cent of poor people live in South Asia and 36 per cent live in sub-Saharan Africa. Their most important finding is that over 800 million people still live just above and below the official poverty line.[47] The poorest regions are in Chad, Burkina Faso, Niger, Ethiopia, South Sudan, Nigeria, Uganda and Afghanistan. Inside Afghanistan, poverty rates vary from 25 per cent in Kabul to 95 per cent in Urozgan. Children are most affected. Half of the multidimensionally poor (48 per cent) are children aged 0–17. Nearly half of all MPI poor people – 706 million – are destitute, and so experience extreme deprivations like severe malnutrition in at least one-third of the index's dimensions.

For China's many partners, investment in infrastructure and poverty eradication are inextricably two sides of the same coin, even if Beijing's official discourse has not made poverty eradication its principal message. This disconnect has not dampened Beijing's standing with its many African and Asian suitors. China is in the pole position, 'out-investing' the World Bank and many major powers. Adam Tooze is not far from the truth when he says that the BRI 'is the most spectacular Keynesian promise ever made', though the promise of relentless economic growth brings with it the possibility of environmental catastrophe.[48] Beijing speaks with authority because it has relied on its own resources to lift millions out of poverty. A decade later, its anti-poverty credentials have elevated the OBOR to a leadership role.

[46]Sabina Alkire and Gisela Robles, 'Global Multidimensional Poverty Index 2017', *OPHI Briefing* 47 (2017), p. 6. http://www.ophi.org.uk/wp-content/uploads/B47_Global_MPI_2017.pdf [Accessed October 2018]
[47]Alkire and Robles, op. cit.
[48]Adam Tooze, 'Tempestuous Seasons', *London Review of Books* 40(17) (September 2018), pp. 19–21.

What gives Chinese authorities so much leverage is that the development crisis has deepened since the official aid programmes by Western nations have been slashed. Most in need are the 'eight lower middle income countries, including the most populous in terms of MPI poor, such as Pakistan ($2.30), Nigeria ($1.40) and India ($0.64), [which] receive very low allocations in priority social sector aid from Development Assistance Committee countries'.[49] China's global infrastructure initiative is in no small way a commitment to poverty eradication for the poorest countries in the world, and a majority of nations in Africa and Asia now belong.

So far, Beijing has not been successful in winning the support of global finance to underwrite high-risk, high-employment investment in the countries that need it most. China's model also relies on foreign hedge funds and other investment vehicles to raise capital, share risk and finance the building of pipelines and other costly infrastructural initiatives. The buy-in from global finance has been slow in the last several years. Morgan Stanley, the UK's Standard Chartered, and European banks have partnered with China on different projects. Their reluctance is partly explained by their high fees and expectation of a 10 per cent return on investment. Their lack of interest and scepticism may be changing.

In December 2017, the British government announced with great fanfare that ex-prime minister David Cameron would be heading up a $1 billon private-public investment fund for China's infrastructural projects. With $100 million already secured, this initiative kicks off a new phase in China-UK relations. In the face of Brexit, the British are looking to the future, and thus Cameron and other financial elites are seeking greater engagement with China. The new fund gave China a much-needed platform to work with the global financial sector and also suits British needs in planning for a post-Brexit world. As part of the deal, it provides Chinese financial institutions with a direct channel to trade the 'renminbi in London'. The billion-dollar fund led by London's Standard Chartered may be a game-changer for China,

---

[49]Alkire and Robles, op. cit.

as it could allow China to build much closer ties to global financial markets, with London as a likely anchor.[50]

THE UN TIR AGREEMENT AND THE XI-PUTIN CONNECTION

One major accomplishment embodying the transnational ambition of the BRI is the completion of the freight route linking China's eastern coast to London. It stretches over 12,000 km (7456 miles), linking nine countries through railway cargo. The trip takes only 18 days. By ocean freighter, it takes between 45 and 50 days to send Chinese exports to Europe, so there is a significant saving of time. As a result, shipping over land and rail traffic has grown in importance, though shipping by sea continues to be cheaper, which means it still makes economic sense for many exporters.[51]

Signed in 1975, the United Nations Agreement on *Transports Internationaux Routier* or International Road Transports (TIR) is an international customs transit system to facilitate the movement of goods without constant inspections on long-distance overland shipments. Even though it is a technical agreement, its strategic value is enormous, working in China's favour as a mechanism for Eurasian economic integration.[52] Chronic problems restricting the international movement of freight are multiple border posts and inspections, resulting in costly delays, increased costs and bottlenecks. With its global initiative, China is able to maximise the cross-border regional overland transport, thanks in part to the UN's TIR.

---

[50]Emily Feng and Henry Mance, 'David Cameron takes senior role in China infrastructure fund', *Financial Times*, 16 December, 2017. Beijing has negotiated other financial deals with neighbouring Eastern and Northeastern Asia. In focusing on Mongolia and Hong Kong, China is building and expanding a Chinese commercial security perimeter through investment and development protocols. Such partnerships are transforming China's presence in key markets. In particular, Hong Kong is a major player in the development of new technologies and new markets, and, through its global banking system, links Beijing to other global financial centres across the world.
[51]Andrew Higgins, 'China's Ambitious New "Port": Landlocked Kazakhstan', *New York Times*, 1 January, 2018.
[52]Taxation and Customs Union, 'TIR (*Transports Internationaux Routiers*, International Road Transport)', European Commission, https://ec.europa.eu/taxation_customs/business/customs-procedures/what-is-customs-transit/tir-transports-internationaux-routiers-international-road-transport_en [Accessed October 2018]

Closer to home, China received a helping hand from Russia, a major OBOR bilateral partner, in 2015 to facilitate the transnational movement of goods. Since Russia is an important market for Chinese goods, Russian officials have facilitated the movement of freight through Kazakhstan and Russia without complex customs inspections. Shortly thereafter, Putin banned the import of many European goods in retaliation for Western sanctions over the 2014 annexation of Crimea. Recently, Russia eased many of these restrictions on transiting goods, including food, helping China's credibility in establishing its economic corridor as a major transit superhighway. Bread and wine are transiting through Russia because of Chinese-Russian cooperation.[53]

There is no way to carry out a comprehensive accounting of all the projects and members of the China club of nations that are in different stages of completion without better information. More than 80 countries and five Chinese provinces have signed memorandums of agreement with China (with more on the way) and these countries account for about 70 per cent of the Earth's population and 75 per cent of the world's known energy supplies, according to one business journalist's estimate.[54] The consequence is that China is producing public goods in record amounts.

The point is that China's initiatives are like a two-level chess game: one played very strategically and globally with the US as its primary opponent and a second contest played regionally with a rotating cast of countries. For instance, China is the largest foreign investor in the Suez Canal corridor. Saudi Arabia is China's largest oil supplier, though this could well change. The China-Pakistan economic corridor is a direct challenge to India, linking Pakistan's future more directly to China's with a combination of land and sea routes linking Islamabad by railway to Karachi and then to Gwadar, one of China's string of pearls ocean ports. Another mega-project of strategic importance is the Bangladesh Padma Bridge and Railway, which gives China a foothold in one of the major ports. Its 'bricks and mortar' approach

[53] Andrew Higgins, op. cit.
[54] 'Chinese Spending Lures Countries to its Belt and Road Initiative', *Bloomberg News*, May 10, 2017 https://www.bloomberg.com/graphics/2017-china-belt-and-road-initiative/ [Accessed October 2018]

to development fills real gaps in many partners' development arc. Many (but not all) are feats of engineering.

No one knows for certain the totality of China's foreign direct investment position in the Global North, and, with much of it private, the full extent is likely understated.[55] Chinese banks have a growing presence in global equity, mergers and acquisitions markets worldwide, and its buying spree and investments are predicted to become even larger, even with the regulatory ownership restrictions its citizens are facing in the United States and in Europe.

HINKLEY POINT NUCLEAR POWER STATION: ANOTHER MARQUEE PROJECT

How do all of these investments relate to China's core interests and the practical goals of influence building through its global investment strike force? China is one of the world's major investors in the US, the UK and the EU, with extensive holdings in real estate, energy, cultural industries, information technology, chemicals, green energy, carbon-based energy and the like.

In 2016, Chinese companies invested a record $45 billion in the US, despite the heavy 'China-bashing' of Donald Trump's presidential election campaign. For the first time, investment in physical assets surpassed $100 billion and Chinese companies now employ more than 100,000 people in the US.[56] By no stretch of the imagination is China the largest investor in the United States, the most popular location in the world for foreign investors. The United Kingdom holds the pole position as the largest by a wide margin at $449 billion, followed by Japan with $373 billion and the Netherlands with $305 billion. China is the 11th largest foreign investor in the US and in the last five years has increased its total investment by 500 per cent.[57]

---

[55]Gregor Aisch, Josh Keller and K.K. Rebecca Lai, 'The World According to China', *New York Times* 2015; Dionne Searcey and Keith Bradsher, 'Chinese Cash Floods US Real Estate Market', *New York Times*, 28 November, 2015.
[56]Shawn Donnan, 'Surge in Chinese Corporate Investment into the US', *Financial Times*, 2 January, 2017.
[57]*Foreign Direct Investment in the United States 2017* (Organization for International Investment, 2017), p. 3 http://ofii.org/sites/default/files/FDIUS%202017.pdf [Accessed October 2018]

All of its many diverse American holdings serve to reinforce the belief that China is rapidly ascending the global power ladder.

In the state-run media outlet *China Daily*, when Xi stresses that 'global growth requires new drivers, development needs to be more inclusive and balanced, and the gap between the rich and poor needs to be narrowed', his message finds an immediately receptive audience in Asia, Africa and Latin America.[58] China's strategy has been surprisingly successful in the critical launch period. Xi has reframed and refocused China's alliance-building and put it at the centre of the strategic planning initiative. The global ambition is first and foremost to win diplomatic allies globally, and simultaneously to build a beachhead at the European end of its global infrastructural project. It scored a major victory when Prime Minister Theresa May's government approved, for a second time, the £18 billion project to build the Hinkley Point C nuclear power station in Somerset, England.

Hinkley is the first of a likely new group of nuclear reactors in the UK, with France's EDF acting as the lead partner in the project. Its built-in price guarantees for electricity and budget overruns have raised many questions about the wisdom of public-private partnerships. China has a third of a stake through its state-owned companies, the China General Nuclear Corporation and China National Nuclear Corporation. The Chinese are investing £6 billion and, most importantly, the investment gives China a showcase to promote its nuclear technology to the world. China has 44 reactors in operation and is building 13 more, as well as exporting its technology to other countries. Many regard it as a leader in the field of nuclear technology power generation. As part of the deal, China has won the right to build a subsequent reactor utilising Chinese technology at Bradwell, Essex, demonstrating once again the powerful global ambition behind China's geopolitical strategy.[59]

---

[58]H. L. Bentley, 'Taking inspiration from the friendly emissaries of the ancient Silk Road', *China Daily*, 17 May, 2017 http://www.chinadaily.com.cn/opinion/2017-05/17/content_29376271.htm [Accessed October 2018]
[59]Andrew Ward, 'Hinkley Point: Is the UK getting a good deal?' *Financial Times*, 15 September, 2016.

THE CHALLENGE OF POLICY COHERENCE

Still, a difficult question remains: no one knows if China is spreading itself too thin financially or whether the thousands of projects will have sufficient policy coherence. Its strategy could fall apart and backfire. Without policy coherence, there will be little mutual learning and sharing of common benefits. Will all or any of these traps and constraints deny China the 'policy connectivity' and energy security that it expects to leverage from a new-found coordination with such a diverse group of partners?

The last two decades will be looked back on as a remarkable time. When China joined the global economy in the 1980s, no one could have imagined that, with its star in ascendance, Chinese elites would 'defend the international system as the US, under Donald Trump, goes in the opposite direction'.[60] Robert Hormats, former undersecretary of the American state and vice chairman of Kissinger Associates, a New York-based consultancy firm, adds that Xi's government is embracing a 'responsible leadership role' because '[t]hey see Americans retreating from leadership of the global trading and financial order as harmful'.[61]

To reiterate, China indeed wants a greater say in the global order, but they also do not want the system to deteriorate into US-led protectionism and chaos. No one could have predicted that in 1997 China's economy would be ranked seventh in the world and that, two decades later, it would stand second only to the United States. The dynamic vaulting of China from 11th position in the 1995 world ranking by size of merchandise exports to number one in the year 2015 has been a complex story of an economy driven by exports and domestic growth.

During this period, China's power differential has grown in leaps and bounds in its favour, as it has become a skilled and engaged player

[60]Quotation from Shen Dingli, an American studies professor at Fudan University in Shanghai, cited in 'China's Xi Set for Star Turn at Davos Gathering', *Financial Times*, 15 January, 2017.
[61]'China's Xi Set for Star Turn at Davos Gathering', *Financial Times*, 15 January, 2017.

in international governance institutions. Like any great power, China has more than its share of problems and critics. Imbalances in the economy and the inability of the political system to modernise state and civil society institutions remain large constraints. The visible weakness of the need for reform on the part of Chinese leadership raises serious issues about whether China's open-ended commitment to its global investment strategy will restrict its capacity to adapt to an ever-increasing, complex, fast-changing and demanding domestic order at home.[62]

PUSHBACK, ANGER AND BACKLASH

However effective China's soft power diplomacy has been in the first five years, China faces many boulder-sized challenges ahead. There is no escaping the fact that there will be more pushback, anger and backlash from local populations against China, the 'big money foreign investor' that opposition parties will seize on and exploit for electoral gain. Local political elites cannot prevent the rise of anti-China sentiment nor safely channel it. These entanglements, directed against Chinese investment politics, are likely to increase as China's influence becomes more visible to local populations. Thailand's military dictatorship, for example, signed a deal with China to build a 250 km/155 mile-long railway line linking Bangkok and Nakhon Ratchasima. Since the *coup d'état* in May 2014, the government wants to rethink China's infrastructural project and China has become directly dragged into politics.

Another incipient problem is that many of the projects could go off the rails and fail because administrative oversight is uneven and heavy-handed. Cost overruns could force local politicians to cancel these important projects, thereby putting enormous stress on China's claims about openness and cooperation. For example, in Sri Lanka, following the end of the civil war, the then government borrowed $8 billion from China to build a major new port in Hambantota. The project has roused the fury of local people, to the extent that when

---

[62]Jonathan Fenby, op. cit.

the Chinese flag was raised, it had to be removed. The presence of Chinese workers has also angered the local public. If China expected to use the new investment for economic leverage, it has badly miscalculated. For now, authorities have banned the Chinese Navy from using the port. Sri Lanka is insisting that debt repayments be renegotiated.[63] Significantly, though, it is still part of the BRI and is showing no signs of quitting China's club of nations.

Already, in Africa and Asia, China has had some substantial failures in which projects were cancelled or put on hold. In Pakistan, the current government stopped the enormous hydroelectric project funded by China on the grounds that the debt burden was too great for the economy and that China would end up benefiting more from the power generation than Pakistan. With the 2018 election of Imran Khan, Islamabad is seeking to negotiate a better deal or to cancel its collaboration with China irrevocably. These public quarrels have not prevented China and Pakistan from remaining close collaborators and strategic allies. Indeed, the same is true for many other countries: there have been highly public disagreements with Malaysia, Vietnam, Indonesia, Laos and Bangladesh, but no partner in good standing has quit China's investment club of nations. Many of these countries are signing new agreements.

In September 2018, Ethiopia's prime minister announced that China will restructure its $4 billion railway debt. The repayment has been extended by 20 years. China has invested more than $12 billion since 2000 and neither is ready to abandon the relationship. The message here is clear. Beijing is ready to entertain the same kind of renegotiation to address debt distress with its other bilateral partners such as Nepal.[64] At least, this is what many

[63]Michael Safi and Amantha Perera, "'The biggest game-changer in 100 Years": Chinese money gushes into Sri Lanka', *Guardian*, 26 March, 2018 https://www.theguardian.com/world/2018/mar/26/the-biggest-game-changer-in-100-years-chinese-money-gushes-into-sri-lanka [Accessed October 2018]

[64]Aaron Maasho, 'Ethiopia PM says China will restructure railway loan', *Reuters*, 6 September, 2018 https://www.reuters.com/article/ethiopia-china-loan/update-1-ethiopia-pm-says-china-will-restructure-railway-loan-idUSL5N1VS4IW [Accessed October 2018]

Asian and African countries are expecting. By contrast, crisis-ridden socialist Venezuela has not been one of the lucky ones to get a debt makeover despite their shared ideologies and being an all-weather friend of China.[65] However, they also have received significant financial relief.

Finally, Beijing, like every world power, faces the trap of imperial overreach, undertaking too much, too quickly – a form of 'blind development' – and the question of whether China's high-powered investment blitz will produce very low returns, as many of its Western critics believe, remains paramount. The danger facing the globe is that, as we enter a new period of economic uncertainty and volatility, China's contribution to building a new international order is pivotal, whether or not many Sinosceptics are ready to acknowledge the obvious.

So far, China's elites have not had to choose between domestic priorities and global commitments. But in the future, the critical question is: how will they manage their constant need for strategic leveraging and the emerging legal and financial governance challenges from the China club of nations?

Up to now, Chinese investments have been focused on the single objective of building soft and hard power relationships with their many partners in Asia, Latin America and Africa. Soft power is a favourite contemporary tool of states to build influence with other governments through leadership, values and the transfer of knowledge and resources. Recall Mao's pungent revolutionary words about the essence of hard power: 'power grows out of the barrel of a gun'. US-based China experts are not convinced that Beijing has moved on from Mao's dated maxim and abandoned its appetite for revolutionary change globally, albeit now embracing gradual, incremental change through markets and not liberation movements.

---

[65]Lucy Hornby and Gideon Long, 'Venezuela looks to China for help but gets few promises', *Financial Times*, 14 September, 2018.

Recently, the Middle Kingdom has modernised its army, air force and navy, acquiring the latest in weapons technology, from nuclear submarines to a new generation of aircraft carriers. Sceptics argue that the OBOR is a classic example of blind development and policy overreach that could end in a disastrous 'sino-colonialism'; others see it as 'a civilisational challenge' that needs to be contained, not accommodated; still, for others, it is a 'massive developmental programme' that could fulfil crucial infrastructural demands, which only China is prepared to finance.[66]

The essential question to ask at this critical juncture is: should the countries who have already signed on with Beijing back out of deals because of their suspicions about China's motivation and self-interest? Or would they be better off with the deals? How would China respond? How would the US react? These are the central questions that China's growing band of partners from across the globe are going to have to answer as best they can as they tether their wagons to China's meteoric rise in the world economy.

---

[66]Kishore Mahbubani, *Has the West Lost It?: A Provocation* (Penguin, 2018).

2

Sign on the Dotted Line:
Beijing's Bilateralism Up Close

It is now 40 years ago that China rejoined the world economy. In the last two decades, China has been quite the joiner of global institutions and has developed partnerships with many sovereign states. To give but a few examples, it now supports the UN Security Council, the nuclear non-proliferation treaty, Bretton Woods financial institutions (including the WTO), the G20 and the Paris Global Warming Convention, as well as a host of trade-promoting regional groupings. It is also significant that China, like the United States, has refused to accept the jurisdiction of the International Criminal Court, the Ottawa Landmines Treaty or the Convention on Cluster Munitions, all of which, in the eyes of Beijing, encroach on China's state sovereignty and domestic affairs.[1] So, what does China want from its ambitious infrastructural global project? For certain, it wants respect and global legitimacy.

To many Western ministries of foreign affairs, China is still not seen as a fully-fledged member of the multinational system. The old image of China as insular, rigidly ideological and at the edge of the world governance system still lingers. Beijing is often demonised in the Western mass media and by many private research consultancies as wearing the 'black hat', an archaic stigma signifying the presence

[1]John Eikenberry and Darren J. Lim, *China's Emerging Institutional Statecraft Asian Infrastructure Investment Bank and the Prospects for Counter Hegemony* (Brookings Institute, April 2017).

of a dangerous outsider to world order and stability. This is a crude characterisation and it is a serious error to regard China only as a trading partner, one without a large and growing stake in the stability of the international order.

China's commitment to the international order has been gradual, sceptical, contradictory and persistent. Beijing is signing hundreds of bilateral deals. Its policy banks outperform all Western aid banks as investors by an order of two to one. We do not know if its bilateral partner countries will be disillusioned and fearful of being too dependent on China's investment aid for their development. What is indisputable is that China is resetting relationships in Africa and Asia with its deep pockets, global diplomacy and development strategy aimed at transforming economies, particularly local and regional ones, in a frenzy of infrastructural building. According to Xi Jinping's opening remarks at the 2017 Beijing Forum to officially launch the One Belt, One Road initiative, Beijing is expecting to leverage this gigantic undertaking to build cooperation and peaceful relations for openness and inclusivity.[2]

Twenty presidents and premiers attended and more than a hundred countries sent official representation. It looked as though the United States would boycott the event, but in the end it sent a middle-ranking representative. Only India, China's regional great power rival, boycotted the OBOR Forum, angered over the recently concluded Pakistan China Economic and Partnership Agreement, which, by implication, challenged India's claims over Kashmir. Many Western-based journalists noted that the A-team of dignitaries and heads of state were not present, but the formal launch of the One Belt, One Road initiative was a milestone for Chinese diplomacy. True, there were the 'sad and bad' among the world's least democratic leaders. But the idea to formalise China's global infrastructural initiative and stamp it with Xi Jinping's personal brand gave OBOR a much-needed profile lift in the global media.

---

[2]'Full text of President Xi's speech at Opening of Belt and Road Forum', *XinhuaNet*, 5 May, 2017 http://www.xinhuanet.com/english/2017-05/14/c_136282982.htm [Accessed October 2018]

The true purpose of the high-level launch party in Beijing was to provide the occasion to make many new announcements about China's decision to add more than $100 billion to support new projects and to increase significantly its contribution to the recently created Asian Infrastructural Investment Bank (AIIB).[3] China's strategic idea was to have its policy banks significantly scale up their contributions to finance further projects in the coming two years. Among the many achievements were increased funding to the AIIB, a commitment to work closely with the IMF and the World Bank for greater transparency, and money for food aid, for human development types of infrastructure and, importantly, to promote tourism, cultural events and the movement of people for intercultural individual exchanges at the university level.[4]

Many countries along the 'Belt and Road' are sending students to be educated in China's higher education institutions. The influx of international students to Chinese schools is one of the least publicised aspects of its global education programme. The BRI has a very attractive scholarship programme to draw students to its institutions of higher learning. 'About two-thirds of China's international students – numbering 317,000 last year – come from countries that have partnered with China in the Belt and Road initiative.'[5] The logic behind China's move to attract more international students is to train a workforce that will help many of its Belt and Road partners to become 'good will ambassadors' for China once they return to their home countries. According to the Ministry of Education, China now

---

[3]Henry Hing Lee Chan, 'New Measures to Lessen Negative Effects of Belt and Road Initiative', *South China Morning Post*, 1 June, 2017; 'OBOR: China pledges $124 billion for new Silk Road, says open to everyone', *Business Standard*, 14 May, 2017.

[4]Of the $100 billion initial AIIB investment, 20% is paid in and 80% is callable. China is contributing $50 billion, half of the initial subscribed capital. India is the second largest shareholder, contributing $8.4 billion, meaning that China's voting share at the AIIB (28.7%) is substantially larger than that of the second-largest AIIB member nation, India (8.3%). Martin A. Weiss, 'Asian Infrastructure Investment Bank (AIIB)', (Congressional Research Service Report prepared for members and committees of Congress, 3 February, 2017) https://fas.org/sgp/crs/row/R44754.pdf [Accessed October 2018]

[5]Simone McCarthy, 'Why Foreign Students Along the Belt and Road are Jostling to Enrol in China's Universities', *South China Morning Post*, 27 September, 2018.

recognises scholarly degrees between some of its partner nations and encourages research and other kinds of collaboration.[6] With an extensive scholarship programme, educational goals are likely to become more important in the next phase. So much progress has been made in both economic and non-economic spheres that Beijing was recently confident enough to announce that a second, larger forum is being planned for 2019.

CHINA'S INVESTMENT PORTFOLIO

What does China obtain in return for its trillion-dollars-plus initiatives? Perhaps most importantly, China is in the process of securing an energy supply that would make Beijing less vulnerable to hazardous sea transportation; much of its oil is transported by giant oil tankers shipped through the heavily travelled, chokehold Strait of Malacca. The initiative will also expand China's energy security perimeter in South Asia and Central Asia, with dozens of 'One Roaders' in its own backyard, many of whom are resource-rich in oil, gas and coal. This will also provide its key industries with new access to markets to absorb its surplus production in steel, concrete and transportation. While there is no fixed total for the thousands of contracts and projects currently underway or for those that will begin in the near future, estimates of the final cost of this transformative initiative range from $4 trillion to $8 trillion and the numbers will only trend upwards.[7]

Overall, there is a strategic logic underpinning China's plans. China's elites are building supersized commercial corridors to the Western markets that consume Chinese goods and the Middle Eastern countries it depends on for petroleum. Building railways and pipelines connecting to the Indian Ocean provides an alternative

---

[6]Ibid.

[7]Chris Birdsong, 'OBOR Factors', *SNC-Lavalin's Atkins*, 19 April, 2017 http://www.atkinsglobal.com/en-gb/angles/all-angles/obor-investment [Accessed October 2018]. For a more general discussion see David Ho, 'Cost of funding "Belt and Road Initiative" is daunting task', *South China Morning Post*, 27 September, 2017 http://www.scmp.com/special-reports/business/topics/special-report-belt-and-road/article/2112978/cost-funding-belt-and [Accessed October 2018]

route west, potentially alleviating worries for Beijing's economic and military planners. With strategic importance in mind, the bulk of major Belt and Road projects are in Malaysia, South Asia and Southeast Asia.[8]

Leading projects include the East Coast Rail Link (ECRL) in Malaysia, which tops all BRI infrastructural initiatives at a cost of $14.1 billion; the $8.2 billion Karachi-Peshawar railway in Pakistan; the $6 billion Dhaka-Chittagong railway in Bangladesh; and the China-Laos ($5.8 billion), Thailand-China ($5.7 billion) and Jakarta-Bandung ($5.5 billion) high-speed rail networks.[9] Right alongside these extensive networks of rail links are a series of complexes that make up the Kuantan industrial zones in Malaysia ($8.4 billion), the Kyaukpyu port in Myanmar ($7.3 billion) and the Thar coal projects in Pakistan ($8.1 billion).

While there are certainly strategic and spatial logics to China's investments in these large-scale infrastructural initiatives, there is no standard template Beijing relies on when it cuts deals with its bilateral partners. The debt repayment timeline of our sample initiatives ranges from three to 30 years, and the kinds of investments China is making are highly diverse and far-reaching. We have looked mainly at highways and railways (six projects, $21 billion), power stations (22 projects, $24 billion) and industrial parks (11 projects, $19 billion). In a separate category are a number of ground-breaking projects, including solar parks, hydro-plant complexes, digital OBOR technological development centres and ecological cities.

Moreover, the majority of Chinese energy finance flows into fossil fuel extraction, large hydroelectric projects and coal plants. In some regards this has exposed Chinese policy banks to significant climate change and social risk, but diplomatically, Beijing has become 'the go-to nation' for the Global South. Offering the promise of stimulus spending for all kinds of projects, from logistics systems to

[8]David Fickling, 'Soviet Collapse Echoes in China's Belt and Road', *Bloomberg Business*, 12 August, 2018 https://www.bloomberg.com/view/articles/2018-08-12/soviet-collapse-echoes-in-china-s-belt-and-road-investment [Accessed October 2018]
[9]David Fickling, op. cit.

infrastructure, China hopes to deepen and spur economic integration between neighbouring countries in Asia and Africa.

China finances wind, solar and geothermal power projects in South Asia, Europe, Central Asia, Latin America and Africa as it seeks to strike a hairline balance between renewable energy and investments in fossil fuels.[10] Chinese policy banks are financing more than 59 coal plants across the globe for upwards of $42 billion in financing and 42 per cent of their power generation portfolio, while Beijing devotes 43.9 per cent of its portfolio to renewables.[11] Seen from a different angle, China has provided just 6 per cent of its power generation portfolio for renewable energy sources outside the hydropower sector; so there is enormous potential for China's development banks to diversify into these types of renewable energy investments.[12]

After all, holding assets in coal is increasingly associated with risk. According to a study by Oxford University researchers, over 290 GW of energy produced from coal will need to be eliminated around the world by 2020 to meet climate change and local health regulations.[13] As investors reassess their coal and gas holdings to account for the fact that they may become 'stranded assets', solar and wind energy are becoming increasingly price competitive with fossil fuels, but are hindered by upfront capital costs. Indeed, solar, wind and biomass production could more than double by 2030 if such costs were

---

[10]Many modern mega-sized infrastructural projects, at least in China, are amazing feats of engineering complexity and design. Beijing is building cities in the desert; it is planning to move 250 million people from the countryside to its dozens of newly built cities. It has constructed the West Qinling Tunnel – the longest highway/motorway tunnel in China, measuring more than 17 km (11 miles) – underneath the Zhongnan Mountains. The Hainan power-grid project that runs between the southern island of Hainan to mainland China is getting a second underwater cable. The $900 million Tianhuangping hydroelectric project is the biggest in Asia and plays a vital role in supplying power to eastern China.

[11]Gallagher et al., op. cit.

[12]Gallagher et al., op. cit.

[13]Alexander Pfeiffer, Cameron Hepburn, Adrien Vogt-Schilb and Ben Caldecott, 'Committed emissions from existing and planned power plants and asset stranding required to meet the Paris Agreement', *Environmental Research Letters* 13 (2018): pp. 1–11 http://iopscience.iop.org/article/10.1088/1748-9326/aabc5f/pdf [Accessed October 2018]

addressed.[14] As we discuss in Chapter 3, Chinese development banks are uniquely poised to smooth such cost structures in the future given their longer-term debt horizons and better access to investment capital.

To have a more precise idea of what's happening on the ground, BRI projects can be categorised broadly in terms of energy corridors, transportation projects, public health and green-energy wind farms. As the diversity of the categories shows, not all projects along the BRI are particularly innovative from a developmental perspective. However, none of these infrastructural projects could be built in the recipient countries without Chinese investment dollars.

The first five projects discussed below are impressive in their vision and reach. Scattered across the Eurasian land mass, these projects are attempting to address environmental concerns and secure sustainable energy and water in the coming years. A second group of three demands our attention because they are more typical examples of infrastructural investment with the potential for catalytic effects for the recipient economy.

SOLAR PARKS, RAILWAYS, HYDRO PLANTS AND THE
DIGITAL BELT AND ROAD

We begin in the hinterlands of central China with the Longyangxia Dam, a concrete arch-gravity dam at the entrance of the Longyangxia canyon on the Yellow River in Qinghai Province. Officially part of the BRI, it is typical of China's vision and ambition and includes a solar farm covering 23 square km (9 square miles) with the capacity to power 200,000 households. The solar park, which has been in operation since 2013, is topping an ever-expanding roll call of supersized symbols that underline China's determination to transform itself from climate underdog to green superpower. Its political leadership aims to boost the proportion of electricity

---

[14]'REmap: Roadmap for a Renewable Energy Future', 2016 Edition, International Renewable Energy Agency (IRENA) http://www.irena.org/publications/2016/Mar/REmap-Roadmap-for-A-Renewable-Energy-Future-2016-Edition [Accessed October 2018]

generated from non-fossil fuel sources to 20 per cent by 2030 from 11 per cent today. It also plans to plough 2.5 trillion yuan ($377 billion) into renewable power generation by 2020.[15] Reaching these goals is proving to be very difficult because China is so reliant on coal for the production of electricity.

Built at a cost of about 6 billion yuan ($904 million) and in almost constant expansion since construction began, Longyangxia now has the capacity to produce a massive 850 MW of power and stands on the front line of a global photovoltaic revolution being spearheaded by a superpower that is also the world's greatest polluter.[16] According to a 2017 interview with Anders Hove, a Beijing-based clean energy expert from the Paulson Institute, solar power was shunned as a potential source of energy for China's domestic market as recently as 2012 because it was seen as too expensive.[17] However, solar costs have since plummeted and by 2020 China – which is now the world's top clean energy investor – hopes to be producing 110 GW of solar power and 210 GW of wind power as part of an ambitious plan to slash pollution and carbon emissions. By 2030, China has pledged to increase the amount of energy coming from non-fossil fuels to 20 per cent of its total energy needs.[18]

The massive farm is the latest demonstration that China is serious about its green energy plans. According to projections, China should have 320 GW of wind and solar power capacity by 2022, along with

[15]Josh Ye, 'China's world-beating solar farm is almost as big as Macau, Nasa satellite images reveal', *South China Morning Post*, 24 February, 2017 http://www.scmp.com/news/china/society/article/2073747/powerful-images-worlds-largest-solar-energy-farms-are-china [Accessed October 2018]

[16]Tom Phillips, 'China builds world's biggest solar farm in journey to become green superpower', *Guardian*, 19 January, 2017 https://www.theguardian.com/environment/2017/jan/19/china-builds-worlds-biggest-solar-farm-in-journey-to-become-green-superpower [Accessed October 2018]

[17]'Anders Hove on China's Renewable Energy Challenges', *Paulson Institute*, blog, 24 July, 2017 http://www.paulsoninstitute.org/paulson-blog/2017/07/24/anders-hove-on-chinas-renewable-energy-challenges/ [Accessed October 2018]

[18]'China's Solar Prices Can Fall 38%, Become Competitive With Coal', *Bloomberg News*, 23 May, 2016 https://www.bloomberg.com/news/articles/2016-05-23/china-s-solar-prices-can-fall-38-become-competitive-with-coal [Accessed October 2018]

340 GW of hydropower.[19] But these big targets are by no means contained within China's borders. With its BRI partners, China is exporting its focus on renewable energy investment and growth by bringing its techniques and expertise to bear on projects such as the recently constructed Quaid-e-Azam solar park in Bahawalpur in the Punjab region of Pakistan.

Pakistan is an early and vocal partner in the BRI, and China has frequently expressed concern about the size of its debt burden. After all, Quaid-e-Azam solar park is one of the largest investments in a single country China has made so far. Since its completion in 2015, the park has struggled to maintain full operations in the face of hot, dusty desert conditions and increasing irregularities in the way contract labour on the plant has been distributed.[20] As a former chief economist to the Bank Pakistan admitted, 'Beijing cannot afford to bankrupt Pakistan – in part because of its importance as a counterweight to India, a regional rival of China.' He went on to say that China's primary interest is 'geopolitical rather than strictly economic' as if these two policy areas operate like silos independent from each other.[21]

Several years in, Pakistan is beginning to reap the benefits of Chinese investment in renewable energy infrastructure. To date, Pakistan and China have signed around $57 billion of energy and infrastructure projects under the China-Pakistan Economic Corridor and the Chinese have imported coal brought from coal mines in Pakistan's Thar Desert. Moreover, in January 2017, the government signed loan agreements worth $720 million with the Asian Infrastructure Investment Bank (AIIB) and World Bank, to support Pakistan's hydropower projects.[22]

---

[19]'China to plow $361 billion into renewable fuel by 2020', *Reuters,* 4 January, 2017 http://www. reuters.com/article/us-china-energy-renewables-idUSKBN14P06P [Accessed October 2018]

[20]Khalid Hasnain, 'Irregularities detected in solar plant contract award', *Dawn,* 24 March, 2017 https://www.dawn.com/news/1397108 [Accessed October 2018]

[21]Go Yamada and Stefania Palma, 'Is China's Belt and Road working? A progress report from eight countries', *Nikkei Asian Review,* 28 March, 2018.

[22]Finbarr Bermingham, 'AIIB Extends Clean Energy Push in Pakistan', *Global Trade Review,* January 23, 2017 https://www.gtreview.com/news/asia/aiib-extends-clean-energy-push-in-pakistan/ [Accessed October 2018]

With the opening of the first wind power project constructed as part of the huge CPEC undertaking, Pakistan is drawing upon China's expertise to overhaul not only its solar power but also to develop an entirely new wind power industry in the region. A 50 MW wind farm has been constructed on 680 acres (275 hectares) of land in Jhimpir, near the shores of the picturesque Keenjhar Lake, which is around two hours' drive from the city of Karachi. Jhimpir is part of the so-called Gharo-Jhimpir wind corridor in Sindh province. It is a 180-km (112-mile) stretch of coastal land that the Pakistan Meteorological Department says has the potential to produce 11,000 MW of electricity through wind power, enough for 600,000 homes in an area prone to blackouts.[23]

GLOBAL-SIZED WIND FARM AND CAMBODIAN ELECTRIFICATION

The building of the new wind farm, which opened in 2018, was organised by Sachal Energy Development with financing from the Industrial and Commercial Bank of China. Meanwhile, as part of the BRI, the Chinese government has poured bilateral loans totalling $63 billion into Pakistan. Initially, Pakistan's loan was financed at an interest rate of 3 per cent, but was subsequently reduced to a rate of 1.6 per cent after the government pressured Beijing to reduce interest rates. China's massive loan will fund power plants along the China-Pakistan Economic Corridor, which links China to the Arabian Sea via the Gwadar Port in south Pakistan.[24]

In Cambodia, another long-term BRI partner, a joint World Bank and Asian Development Bank report found that electricity is 'not only more expensive than in most neighbouring countries, but the supply is also intermittent'. In response, Cambodia prioritised the development of hydropower as part of its BRI dealings in the hopes of securing cheaper and more reliable electricity. Since 2015, Chinese

---

[23]Finbarr Bermingham, op. cit.
[24]Rina Saeed Khan, 'In coal-focused Pakistan, a wind power breeze is blowing', *Reuters*, 17 July, 2017 https://www.reuters.com/article/us-pakistan-energy-windpower/in-coal-focused-pakistan-a-wind-power-breeze-is-blowing-idUSKBN1A21B4 [Accessed October 2018]

investments have accounted for 17 per cent of all infrastructure investment across the region.[25]

In a landmark ceremony in Cambodia, Prime Minister Hun Sen and the Chinese Ambassador to Cambodia, Xiong Bo, were present to observe the closure of the water gates of the 400 MW Lower Sesan II Hydropower Plant, Cambodia's largest hydroelectric dam, which commenced operations in November 2017 after four years of construction. The plant construction includes eight turbines each with a capacity of 50 MW; all eight turbines are not yet fully operational.

According to Suy Sem, Cambodia's Minister of Mines and Energy, the estimated cost for the plants is about $2.4 billion and is also part of Sino-Cambodian cooperation in the energy sector under the OBOR initiative.[26] Moreover, the scope of the project will help realise Cambodia's development strategy, including the Rectangular Strategy and Industrial Development Policy (2015–2025).

The plant is expected to be operational for 40 years and is estimated to produce around 1.9 billion kilowatt-hours per year. Electricity production will be sold to the Electricity of Cambodia at the fixed price of 6.95 US cents per kilowatt-hour. Once fully operational, it is expected to generate around $30 million per annum in tax revenues. As a result, the Lower Sesan II Hydropower Plant represents a significant milestone in Cambodia's efforts to develop energy independence. To put this in context, the Cambodian government has now expanded electricity supplies to around 80 per cent of the kingdom's total villages and a total of 2 million households, and 61 per cent of the population have also connected to the grid.[27] Previously,

[25]Chheang Vannarith, 'Belt and Road plan will benefit Cambodia', Khmer Times, 16 May, 2017 http://www.khmertimeskh.com/news/38373/belt-and-road-plan-will-benefit-cambodia/ [Accessed October 2016]
[26]'Cambodia to benefit from China-proposed Belt-Road Initiative: Scholar', XinhuaNet, 16 May, 2017 http://news.xinhuanet.com/english/2017-05/16/c_136288707.htm [Accessed October 2016]
[27]'Cambodia Heralds a New Era in Energy Cooperation with China', Sirius Report, 25 September, 2017 https://thesiriusreport.com/geopolitics/china-cambodia-energy-dam/ [Accessed October 2018]

Cambodia's north-eastern region had largely relied upon electricity imported from neighbouring Laos. The long-term goal of this project is to bring residents in these provinces access to both reliable supplies and cheaper electricity prices.

This project is further testimony to the cooperation that we see under the auspices of the OBOR initiative. China is currently the largest developer of hydroelectric dams in Cambodia, having invested in a total of seven dam projects. The Lower Sesan II Hydropower Plant, however, is seen as a key achievement in energy cooperation between China and Cambodia. According to Cambodian policy analyst Chheang Vannarit, 'The Belt and Road Initiative will also contribute to the realisation of the vision of becoming a middle-income country by 2030 and attain high-income status by 2050.' He added that Cambodia needs about $600 million in infrastructure development and logistic networks annually to maintain the momentum of economic development and to enhance its competitiveness.[28] Whether it reaches its target goal of investment, of course, remains to be seen. The setting of hydroelectric domestic power rates is likely to be controversial and therefore likely to be politicised at parliamentary elections by opposition parties.

THE TRANS-ASIAN RAILWAY PROJECT

The China-Laos railway is another cooperative project currently under construction in the Southeast Asian region, and will commence operation by the end of December 2021. The 414 km/ 257 mile-long railway (over 62.7 per cent of which is bridges and tunnels) will run from the Chinese border in the northern province of Luang Namtha to the capital Vientiane, and will serve as a key link in the land transportation system between southern China and ASEAN. This will be done by extending the railway southward, connecting Thailand and the Trans-Asian Railway, a project designed as an integrated railway network across Europe and Asia, to the larger Chinese railway network. According to the PRC, as

[28]Chheang Vannarith, op. cit.

well as Laotian officials, the project will play a key role in the OBOR and will showcase the enhanced connectivity among China and Southeast Asian states.[29]

Construction of the project is scheduled for five years with investment of some 40 billion Chinese yuan ($5.8 billion), 70 per cent of which comes from Chinese investment, and the rest from Laos. Importantly, the China-Laos railway is the first overseas route connecting with the railway system in China, using Chinese technology, equipment and investment. This is a key reason why both China and Laos agreed to step up efforts to construct a slew of important projects related to completing the railway, according to a joint statement issued by the two sides during Chinese President Xi Jinping's state visit to Laos on 13–14 November, 2017.[30]

The construction of the railway officially started on 25 December, 2016 in northern Laos' Luang Prabang province. In March 2017, during a 100-day dry season, a working competition was launched to speed up the construction process. According to Zhao Xiang, director general of the Laos-China Railway Company, construction units of the project have overcome various difficulties since the launching of the competition to actively promote the implementation of the project. 'In less than six months, site preparation has been completed for the construction of four stations; foundation construction of nine bridge piles have [been] finished; 86 holes for construction of 46 tunnels have been prepared, of which 15 are key tunnels,' Zhao said.[31] Before construction of the railway, there was only a 3.5 km/2 mile-long railway in Laos connecting Nong Khai, Thailand, to Thanaleng outside Vientiane. In this sense, the China-Laos railway project will change the situation by turning Laos from a 'land-locked country' to

[29]Wu Chengliang, 'China-Laos Railway Project Set to be Complete by Late 2021', *People's Daily Online*, 15 November, 2017 http://en.people.cn/n3/2017/1115/c90000-9293209.html. [Accessed October 2018]

[30]Lu Hui, 'Xi meets former Lao president', *XinhuaNet*, 14 November, 2017 http://news.xinhuanet.com/english/2017-11/14/c_136749609.htm [Accessed October 2018]

[31]Li Nan, 'China-Laos Railway to Become a Demonstration Project', *Beijing Review*, 24 October, 2016 http://www.bjreview.com/Business/201610/t20161025_800070105.html [Accessed October 2018]

a 'land-linked country'. Zhao concluded that 'the railway will greatly improve the country's transport capacity, and promote economic and social development'.

Beijing's primary aspiration is to link its mainland with Southeast Asia, all the way down to Singapore. For Vientiane, a pit stop on this ambitious pathway, the impact could be profound. It is an already fast-growing city and the leap towards full connectivity with the region will come faster than most Laotians might imagine. 'Previously we had been talking about the disadvantage of the geographic location of the country. But we are seeing this disadvantage turn into an advantage,' said Dr. Leeber Leebouapao from the National Institute of Economic Research, a key policy advisor to the central government.[32]

INNOVATIVE DIGITAL CONNECTIVITY TOO

Another way in which China is flexing its organising capabilities and technical expertise to overcome geographic limitations in its own backyard of Southeast Asia is the establishment of the Digital Belt and Road International Centre of Excellence Bangkok (DBAR ICoE-Bangkok). In conjunction with seven other international centres around the world (in Pakistan, Italy, Morocco, Zambia, Finland, Russia and the US), DBAR ICoE-Bangkok is part of an initiative led by the Chinese Academy of Sciences for the exchange of expertise and technology in key research areas such as climate change, disaster risk reduction, environmental research, capacity building and mass media telecommunications networks. Leveraging Earth observation and big Earth data from satellites and other sources along these Digital Belt and Road linkages will funnel multiple data streams into an integrated, distributed data repository that decision-makers can reference in the implementation of projects across the BRI.[33]

[32]Jack Board, 'Asia's Future Cities: High-speed rail on track to connect Vientiane to the region', *Channel News Asia*, 23 March, 2017 https://www.channelnewsasia.com/news/asiapacific/asia-s-future-cities-high-speed-rail-on-track-to-connect-vientia-7623230 [Accessed October 2018]
[33]Priyanka Bhunia, 'New centre opened in Thailand as part of China's Digital Belt and Road program', *Bilaterals.org*, 13 March, 2018 https://www.bilaterals.org/?new-centre-opened-in-thailand-as [Accessed October 2018]

In *Nature*, Professor Guo, a researcher at the Chinese Academy of Scientists, identified specific priorities for the programme, such as the development of cloud computing among programme members to accelerate research through the adoption of common standards and methodologies.[34]

According to Steve Lo, Ernst & Young's managing partner for technology, media and telecommunications, potential beneficiaries of DBAR will also include digital marketing professionals familiar with the Chinese digital platforms Alibaba, Tencent and Baidu, as well as the global digital platforms Facebook, Google and WhatsApp – organisations that can deploy business applications for cloud solutions. 'This expertise, along with Hong Kong's place as a cultural and linguistic bridge, will be important to overcome obstacles that could arise in sourcing local talent in Belt and Road countries.'[35]

For Lo, Hong Kong's advantages in tax, financial, legal and infrastructure system design can bridge mainland China and other Belt and Road governments, and are critical to this process. In this sense, the DBAR ICoE-Bangkok is an important link in a digital network of goods and services using WeChat and AliPay. When combined with financial opportunities among OBOR nations, this may contribute to the increased development of nascent industries in Hong Kong, notes Robert Bianchi from Shanghai International Studies University's Middle East Studies Institute.[36] This positions the DBAR to play a critical role in countering challenges arising from large-scale development as well as private sector interests.

---

[34]Guo Huadong, 'Steps to the digital Silk Road', *Nature*, 30 January, 2018 https://www.nature.com/articles/d41586-018-01303-y [Accessed October 2018]

[35]Peter Sabine, 'One belt, one road's digital initiative is full of potential, but Hong Kong firms need to be wary of pitfalls', *South China Morning Post*, 1 November, 2016 http://www.scmp.com/specialreports/business/topics/one-belt-one-road/article/2041881/one-belt-one-roads-digital [Accessed October 2018]

[36]Lars Andersen, Anoush Ehteshami, Mamtimyn Sunuodula and Jiang Yang (eds), '*One Belt, One Road' and China's Westward Pivot: Past, Present and Future* (Danish Institute for International Studies, 2017) http://pure.diis.dk/ws/files/1258174/Durham_OBOR_Conference_Report.pdf [Accessed October 2018]

WHEN THE PLAN DOESN'T LOOK LIKE A PLAN

Specialists in international relations and international economics are both puzzled and divided by the boldness of China's ambitions and its choice of investment projects in Asia, Africa and Latin America. Is there a plan that the Chinese are following, a carefully thought-out agenda? Often it doesn't appear that way, but equally, Chinese planners are not known for their spontaneity. It is a familiar sight that, whenever President Xi Jinping visits, he comes bearing financial gifts for a high-speed transnational railway, a hydroelectric plant or a massive dam.

For the many Global South joiners on the BRI bullet-train spending spree, Beijing's hegemony is premised on a complex agenda of influence-building and targeted investment. China's deep pockets are the only opportunity to develop and modernise their economies. They need reliable electricity, hydroelectric power stations, gigantic dams, clean water, efficient highways/motorways, high-speed railways, green energy, industrial parks and modern ports, among other infrastructure projects. This is what China is offering them and there are many takers, because they are wagering that this kind of development assistance will have long-term productivity effects for regional markets, create employment, make the movement of people easier and generate innovative opportunities for private sector actors.

The BRI projects are difficult to evaluate without full information because many are in the planning stage, while others are not fully completed. For instance, China is building a port in the Haifa Bay in Israel, the new Yalu Bridge in North Korea, Turkey's third nuclear power plant and Kiev's fourth metro line.[37] On top of this, there are thousands of local and regional contracts and projects waiting to be discovered by journalists. The only ones that receive attention from journalists are those in the 'sad and bad' one-party states.

---

[37] Go Yamada and Stefania Palma, op. cit.

Another point to consider is that an evaluation is a very complex process to carry out, one that requires teams in the field to do their work credibly and accurately. Field evaluation may be too costly with so many projects. Finally, we do not know what 'success' means to the Chinese other than that the project is completed more or less on time and within budget.[38] Venezuela, Sudan and Zimbabwe are in a class of their own because China is supporting the regime for political reasons as much as anything else. So, the question is, how many are 'red elephants' as some journalists have insisted? What follows is a discussion of some alternative kinds of projects that are likely to make a significant difference for signed-up regions while also raising many challenging issues for local populations.

AN ASSEMBLAGE OF 'GREEN' INVESTMENTS

Located 150 km (93 miles) from Beijing and 40 km (25 miles) from Tianjin city centre – the site of the Tianjin explosion, one of the worst man-made disasters in Chinese history – the Sino-Singapore Tianjin eco-city represents a new phase in urban development. The ultimate goal of the city is to eliminate all carbon waste and achieve carbon neutrality, by producing energy entirely through renewable resources and drawing a significant part of its water supply from non-traditional sources such as desalinated water.[39] Integrated waste management has also been implemented in the eco-city, with particular emphasis on the reduction, reuse and recycling of waste.[40]

This project, jointly funded by the Chinese and Singaporean governments, was initiated in 2008 on 30 square km (12 square miles) of formerly polluted marshlands, and features solar panels

---

[38]Cost overruns are frequent and due to poor management, corruption, the lowballing of contracts and inexperience. They are the plague of private investment mega-projects as well.

[39]'Tianjin explosion: China sets final death toll at 173, ending search for survivors', *Guardian*, 12 September, 2015 https://www.theguardian.com/world/2015/sep/12/tianjin-explosion-china-sets-final-death-toll-at-173-ending-search-for-survivors [Accessed October 2018]

[40]Derek MacKenzie, 'Green buildings, Singapore's natural ally in climate change fight', *Eco-Business*, 7 November, 2017 http://www.eco-business.com/opinion/green-buildings-singapores-natural-ally-in-climate-change-fight/ [Accessed October 2018]

and windmills peeking through the skyline. While there were early fears that the development may join the ranks of China's 'ghost cities', home sales for the project have gone up substantially since 2016.[41] However, with current residents totalling only 50,000 (less than 15 per cent of the targeted 350,000), and a budget that has ballooned from $9.7 billion (in 2008) to an estimated $16 to $20 billion in the 10-15 years it will take to fully complete construction, much of the city's future rests upon its ability to brand itself as a regional hub for tourism, trade and information technology.[42]

In the summer of 2017, China and Singapore signed further commitments to the Tianjin eco-city, enabling professional exchanges between healthcare professionals from Tianjin and Singapore, and announced that the development is now home to 4500 registered companies with a total registered capital of 200 billion yuan ($40.9 billion).[43] Moreover, a semi-express rail line is currently under construction, and when completed in 2020 it will connect the eco-city to Beijing, Tianjin City and the rest of Tianjin Binhai New Area (TBNA).

According to the Singapore government, this vital infrastructural link will forge closer economic integration with TBNA and the surrounding Jing-Jin-Ji (Beijing-Tianjin-Hebei) region, providing a further boost to the eco-city's growth. The integration is also taking the form of best practice-sharing 'aimed at improving patient care and the healthcare delivery systems,' noted Associate Professor Chua Yeow Leng from SingHealth.[44] Such a knowledge-

[41]Jeremy Koh, 'Tianjin Eco-city residents double in a year despite "ghost city" fears', *Channel News Asia,* 11 August, 2016 https://www.channelnewsasia.com/news/asia/tianjin-eco-city-residents-double-in-a-year-despite-ghost-city-f-7839708 [Accessed October 2018]
[42]Jonathan Kaiman, 'China's "eco-cities": Empty of hospitals, shopping centres and people', *Guardian,* 14 April, 2014 https://www.theguardian.com/cities/2014/apr/14/china-tianjin-eco-city-empty-hospitals-people. [Accessed October 2018]
[43]'Three interesting facts about the Sino-Singapore Tianjin Eco-city', *Government of Singapore,* 29 July, 2017 https://www.gov.sg/factually/content/three-interesting-facts-about-the-sino-singapore-tianjin-eco-city [Accessed October 2018]
[44]Chong Koh Ping, 'Singapore agencies sign 5 pacts for Tianjin Eco-City', *Straits Times,* 26 February, 2017 http://www.straitstimes.com/asia/east-asia/singapore-agencies-sign-5-pacts-for-tianjin-eco-city [Accessed October 2018]

sharing network is a characteristic of the OBOR's larger policy coordination goals.

Equally important to the reconstruction of greener and more integrated cities are the more typical kinds of foundational infrastructural investments that link them. Drifting south from Singapore's eco-city to Indonesia's new overland linkages, China broke ground in early 2018 for the construction of a much-anticipated 142 km/88 mile-long high-speed rail project linking the capital Jakarta to Bandung, its second-largest metropolitan area. According to Indonesian Minister of Trade Enggartiasto Lukita, the project is estimated to cost a hefty $5.9 billion, of which the China Development Bank has committed to fund 75 per cent with loan terms of 40 years and an initial grace period of 10 years at fixed loan rates.[45]

GLOBAL EXPERTISE IN HIGH-SPEED RAIL TECHNOLOGY

China is keen to export its high-speed rail technology and has made its biggest progress on the Indonesian project to connect Halim in East Jakarta to Tegalluar in Bandung, West Java, fending off Japan in 2015 to win the bid to build and operate the line. When construction is completed, it will be the first time another economy has fully adopted Chinese high-speed rail standards, from train carriages to operating systems. According to Xu Liping, a specialist in Southeast Asian studies at the Chinese Academy of Social Sciences, 'countries in the region had less experience of and trust in the Chinese technology compared to that from the West and Japan.'[46]

According to reports, it was China's offer to build the Jakarta-Bandung line with guarantee-free loans that sealed the deal,

[45]Lin Wanxia, 'Indonesia's high-speed rail to start construction early 2018', *Asia Times,* 20 October, 2017 http://www.atimes.com/article/indonesias-high-speed-rail-start-construction-early-2018/

[46]Liu Zhen and Kristin Huang, 'China to get rolling on stalled Indonesian high-speed rail line', *South China Morning Post,* 25 March, 2017 http://www.scmp.com/news/china/diplomacy-defence/article/2081968/china-get-rolling-stalled-indonesian-high-speed-rail [Accessed October 2018]

whereas Japan still requested Indonesian government funding. Full funding allowed China Railway Construction Corporation to enter a joint venture with a consortium of Indonesia's SOEs and commit to cover three-quarters of the project's costs. The deal will be carried out on a business-to-business basis, with Indonesia having 60 per cent interest in the joint venture and China 40 per cent.

The project is scheduled to be completed by 31 May, 2019. Daily passenger flow is expected to be 44,000 with large growth forecasts in later years. These passengers will be spread across four stations: one of the stations will be in Gambir, the executive zone close to Monas, and is expected to witness a huge passenger flow. Manggarai will be another station location equipped to handle a large number of passengers. A station near the airport in Halim will connect the high-speed rail to a planned light rail and will provide easy access to the high-speed rail for passengers in south-eastern Jakarta. Another station will be located in Walini in West Bandung, which is to be a new tourism hub in West Java.[47]

The investment is planned to generate 40,000 jobs a year during construction, creating a positive economic impact. Associated industries such as smelting, manufacturing, infrastructure, power generation, electronics, services and logistics will also receive a boost, thus theoretically leading to a more balanced growth in all sectors. It is projected that stations and their surrounding areas will also experience an increase in activity and development, which will result in new opportunities for the real estate sector. Urban and rural areas along the route are likely to see an acceleration of development as has occurred along the Addis-Djibouti transportation corridor.[48]

[47]'Jakarta to Bandung High-Speed Rail', *Railway Technology*, 2018 https://www.railway-technology.com/projects/jakarta-to-bandung-high-speed-rail/ [Accessed October 2018]
[48]'Indonesia's first high-speed rail project is back on track to meet its 2018 completion date', *SmartRail World*, 21 May, 2017 https://www.smartrailworld.com/indonesias-first-high-speed-rail-project-is-back-on-track-to-meet-its-2018-completion-date [Accessed October 2018]

THE AFRICAN PART OF THE STORY

Shifting focus from Asia to China's linkages in Africa, the year 2017 marked Kenya's inauguration of a $3.2 billion railway linking the capital Nairobi to the port of Mombasa – the biggest infrastructure project since independence more than 50 years ago.[49] The railway is one of China's most important investments in East Africa – 90 per cent of which has been financed by China's Exim Bank and will be maintained and operated by China Road and Bridges Corporation for the next decade – and it follows the opening in January of a $4.2 billion line from Djibouti to Addis Ababa, the capital of landlocked Ethiopia. That line, 759 km (470 miles) long, replaces the 100-year-old French-built railway.[50]

The railway is an integral part of China's BRI initiative, a multi-billion-dollar line that is planned to stretch across the continent, connecting Uganda, Rwanda, Burundi, the Democratic Republic of the Congo, South Sudan and Ethiopia to Mombasa so that the Indian Ocean port can act as a gateway to East Africa for trade with China and other nations. The project has been completed 18 months ahead of schedule, and cuts the journey time from Mombasa to Nairobi to 4½ hours, compared to 9 hours by bus or 12 hours on the previous railway. However, according to Kwame Owino, the executive director of the Nairobi-based Institute of Economic Affairs, the advertised improvement in speed is not important when it comes to cargo. 'The economic benefits for Kenya are exaggerated.'[51]

While the debate over how this benefits Africa in relation to China rages on, Kenya recently secured another $3.6 billion in financing to extend the line by 250 km (155 miles), between Naivasha in central Kenya and Kisumu in the west.[52] According to Deborah Brautigam,

[49]Duncan Miriri, 'Kenya inaugurates Chinese-built railway linking port to capital', *Reuters*, 31 May, 2017 https://www.reuters.com/article/us-kenya-railways/kenya-inaugurates-chinese-built-railway-linking-port-to-capital-idUSKBN18R2TR [Accessed October 2018]
[50]'Kenya's $4bn railway gains traction from Chinese policy ambitions', *Financial Times*, 3 April, 2017.
[51]Ibid.
[52]Lily Kuo, 'Kenya's $3.2 billion Nairobi-Mombasa rail line opens with help From China', *Quartz Africa*, 2 June, 2017 https://qz.com/996255/kenyas-3-2-billion-nairobi-mombasa-rail-line-opens-with-help-from-china/ [Accessed October 2018]

director of the China-Africa Research Initiative at Johns Hopkins University, $2 billion of this is a 15-year loan, while the remaining $1.6 billion is on concessional terms of 2 per cent interest, repayable over 20 years.[53]

'The entire African continent can be connected by Chinese rail, so this Kenya rail is a kind of prototype for all future projects,' notes Wang Dehua, a professor at the Shanghai Institute for International Studies. 'It is a big strategic move for our country.' These new loans have, however, pushed Kenya's debt above 50 per cent of output, raising further concerns that the current government might be building a white elephant. Moreover, as Owino continues, 'Kenya's railway costs [per kilometre] are almost 40 to 50 per cent higher' than some of Kenya's neighbours; 'It's an extremely expensive piece of railway, especially because the technology is more up to date.'[54]

THE SUSTAINABILITY OF CHINA'S GLOBAL DIPLOMATIC REACH: INEVITABLE HEADACHES

China is well positioned strategically to maximise the benefits from these kinds of projects as the world's largest infrastructural environmental investor. Its diplomatic missions cover the globe and it has developed a sophisticated, knowledgeable and dedicated career-oriented foreign service. Many are fluent in local languages. David Pilling reports that China has 52 diplomatic missions, one in almost every African capital, beating Washington's 49. China has more peacekeepers in Africa than any of the other UN Security Council's five members. It has troops in Congo, Liberia, Mali, Sudan and South Sudan. China has many soft power boots on the ground, so many that an eloquent critic of foreign investment, Dambisa Moyo, has now changed her tune. Her book *Dead Aid*[55] attacked

---

[53]Deborah Brautigam, *Will Africa Feed China?* (Oxford University Press, 2015).
[54]'Kenya inaugurates new Chinese-funded railway', *Al Jazeera*, 31 May, 2017 https://www.aljazeera.com/news/2017/05/kenya-inaugurates-chinese-funded-railway-170531113643612.html [Accessed October 2018]
[55]Dambisa Moyo, op. cit.

the enormous amount of money that the EU and the US wasted in pro-market development following the neoliberal Washington Consensus,[56] but today she says, 'African countries need trade and they need investment. To the extent that China, or anybody else – India, Turkey, Russia or Brazil – bring new trading and investment opportunities to Africa, that's good news.'[57]

These 'big ticket', visionary ideas may never materialise to the extent that the Chinese authorities expect, however. Some projects will be cancelled by local opposition political parties and changes in government leadership. Others will be abandoned or renegotiated because they are too costly. It could turn out to be a failed decade of oversold development for many African and Asian members. Beijing has hitched its star to its global infrastructural initiative with the intention of landing at the epicentre of the global economy by the end of the decade. The least controversial thing one can say is that China is well prepared, if not over-prepared, having the bureaucratic resources to plan, execute and support contracts that, according to some estimates, total more than 15,000 – and counting.

However, it should be recalled that developmental economics has never been kind to its grand thinkers at the World Bank and the IMF. On this list, one must include China's planners. The success rate in the field of international development assistance is difficult to measure and many things often go wrong, from low standards and poor construction to the skimming or embezzling of money by global corporations and local elites. According to a survey of 305 IMF programmes by Tony Killick between 1979 and 1993,[58] compliance

---

[56]The Washington Consensus was named accurately after the neoliberal economists that went to Washington to advise the IMF and the World Bank in the 1980s. They called on governments to cut social spending, and deregulate and privatise state enterprises, as well as reduce debt burdens. This set of policies was endorsed in an ideological template and was exported to Latin America and Asia. See Mark Blyth, op. cit.

[57]David Pilling, 'Ports and Roads Mean China is "Winning in Africa"', *Financial Times*, 4 May, 2017.

[58]Tony Killick, 'Principals, Agents and the Failings of Conditionality', *Journal of International Development* 9, 4 (1997), pp. 483–495.

ONE ROAD, MANY DREAMS

with IMF conditionality was no better than 53 per cent, with failure being defined as a recipient not implementing 20 per cent or more of the IMF programmes.[59] In a subsequent study by Ngaire Woods in 2008, similar results were found.[60]

It is too early to tell if China will do better with its own economic model of bilateral infrastructural investments, building on its years of accumulated experience in technologically advanced infrastructural projects domestically. Beijing has in place a tightly controlled planning mechanism and deep pockets that work in its favour. But transferring knowledge from China to more than 80 partner countries and keeping mega-projects on track is another matter entirely.

BEIJING'S KING-SIZED PLANNING MECHANISM

One recent example of China's ability to exercise top-down control over planning, organisation and execution can be found in the background story detailing the China-Pakistan Economic Partnership leaked by *Dawn*, a leading Pakistani newspaper in 2017.[61] It released the actual contract that the Pakistan president had just signed with China, a multi-billion-dollar deal that included an overland highway/motorway linking Pakistan and China, the construction of a new dry port and railway yard in Korgas (a town overlooking the strategic dry harbour and railway yard), industrial parks and too many other projects to name. Even before the deal was signed, China had loaned Pakistan $1 billion to increase its foreign reserves, both as a deal sweetener (a manoeuvre typical of Beijing) and to deepen its relationship with Islamabad.[62]

All these details underline that China has a muscular system in place to plan, negotiate and execute its bilateral deals. Little is

[59]Henry Hing Lee Chan, op. cit.; 'OBOR: China Pledges $124 Billion for New Silk Road, Says Open to Everyone', *Business Standard*, 14 May, 2017.
[60]Ngaire Woods, 'Whose Aid? Whose Influence? China, Emerging Donors and the Silent Revolution in Development Assistance', *International Affairs* 84(6) (2008), pp. 1205–1221.
[61]Khurram Husain, 'Exclusive: CPEC Master Plan Revealed', *Dawn*, 21 June, 2017 https://www.dawn.com/news/1333101 [Accessed October 2018]
[62]Ibid.

left to chance. Before any work commences or any deals are inked on its mega-projects, China regularly conducts feasibility studies that employ hundreds of policy analysts, economists, engineers, geologists and lawyers. They go into the field and carry out an extensive assessment process, visiting sites and interviewing local businesses.[63]

A range of planning and industrial ministries are involved under the authority of the powerful National Development and Reform Commission of the People's Republic of China (NDRC), the key planning commission responsible for macroeconomic planning, structural adjustment, and monitoring and rebalancing the economy. In 2017, the NDRC said in an online statement that it would provide better regulatory guidance on risks to companies investing in OBOR initiatives in order to prevent 'vicious' competition and corruption.[64] The NDRC will 'guide firms to fully consider national conditions and actual needs of target countries, pay attention to mutually beneficial cooperation with local governments and companies, and generate economic and social benefits,' the State Council said in a statement.[65]

In the case of the Pakistan-China Economic Partnership, project planning began three years ago when China sent field teams to conduct onsite interviews and field studies on the suitability of the different sites for the projects proposed. These reports were turned into detailed plans that focused on the opportunities and goals for Chinese state enterprises. This may involve all sorts of concessions, financial undertakings and strategic targeting for each phase of development.

[63]National Development and Reform Commission, *Vision and Actions on Jointly Building Silk Road Economic Belt and 21st-Century Maritime Silk Road* (Ministry of Foreign Affairs and Ministry of Commerce of the People's Republic of China, 2015) http://en.ndrc.gov.cn/newsrelease/201503/t20150330_669367.html [Accessed October 2018]
[64]"China to curb "irrational" overseas Belt and Road investment: State planner', *Reuters*, 18 August, 2018 https://www.reuters.com/article/us-china-economy-odi/china-to-curb-irrational-overseas-belt-and-road-investment-state-planner-idUSKCN1AY0FN [Accessed October 2018]
[65]Ouyang Shijia, 'NDRC: Innovation on the rise in China', *China Daily*, 19 September, 2017 http://english.gov.cn/state_council/ministries/2017/09/19/content_281475869102638.htm [Accessed October 2018]

Since many of the mega-projects may last from three to ten years, or even longer with different phases of work and construction, the plans are very comprehensive – as the China-Pakistan Economic Partnership reveals. China's field assessment teams rely heavily on a technocratic approach under the direction of three or four leading Chinese ministries and powerful bodies such as the State-owned Assets Supervision and Administration Commission (SASAC), which is responsible for the oversight, regulation and supervision of China's state-owned enterprises. In 2017, its companies had combined assets of $26 trillion, revenue of more than $3.6 trillion and an estimated stock value of $7.6 trillion. The key contractors and investors had hundreds of contracts with dozens of China's bilateral partners. Because the amounts of money are so large, the final plan has to be approved by the appropriate Chinese state ministry, which also adds an additional level of bureaucratic complexity to an already steep chain of command.

The planning process then moves to a more overtly political phase of state-to-state negotiations that are complex, multifaceted and difficult. Such negotiations have something in common with those that take place in institutions such as the World Bank, as both have dozens of professional experts conducting complex negotiations between the bank and the recipient.[66] What is different in the case of Beijing's developmental strategy is that the political process is explicit, detailed and conducted at the highest level between China and Pakistan, its bilateral partner. If the account in *Dawn* is accurate, each phase of the planning, execution and development is calibrated, calculated and guided by China's giant bureaucracy and

[66]For a detailed account of the bully-like negotiating process over debt relief and austerity dynamics, see Yanis Varoufakis, *Adults in the Room: My Battles with Europe's Deep Establishment* (Bodley Head, 2017). In Chapter 11, entitled 'Whittling our Spring', Varoufakis explains how Greece intended to concession-bargain with the Chinese, who wanted to expand their investment in Greece's main port of Piraeus. As Finance Minister, Varoufakis requested a loan of €1 billion to supply Greece with much needed liquidity, but the EU vetoed the deal. In the end, the Chinese invested only €100 million, which was insufficient to provide Greece with much-needed breathing space.

political leadership, who negotiate directly with Pakistan's political leaders and top bureaucrats.

THE GAME PLAN: DETAILED PLANNING AND CONCESSION BARGAINING

We have a lot of primary information from the detailed planning documents between China and Nawaz Sharif, then the prime minister of Pakistan, as well as documents from other key government officials. By any standard, the deal signed with Pakistan is complex and challenging, as well as exceedingly ambitious from an engineering point of view. Chinese and Pakistani construction teams are rebuilding some of the most dangerous stretches of the Karakoram, a remote part of Western China bordering Pakistan. According to Tom Phillips, a *Guardian* journalist, the OBOR is improving the world's 'highest transnational highway, a project that took two decades and more than 1000 lives to build'. The Pakistan-China highway-corridor will open this remote region to Chinese businesses and the world beyond.[67]

There are also plans for a railway that would run alongside the Karakoram border, linking Pakistan with the Chinese city of Kashgar and strengthening Pakistan's security perimeter in the Punjab, where it shares a border with India. The core areas where there are knock-on effects include Kashgar, Tumshuq, Atushi and Akto County of Kizilsu Kirghiz in Xinjiang from China, and most of Islamabad's Capital Territory, Punjab and Sindh, and some areas of Gilgit-Baltistan, Khyber Pukhtunkhwa and Balochistan from Pakistan.[68] Already it is setting alarm bells ringing in New Delhi. India has been very critical of this project because it gives China easy access to Pakistan

---

[67]Here is the geopolitical description of the development contained in the leaked Chinese planning document published in *Dawn*: 'The plan states at the outset that the corridor "spans Xinjiang Uygur Autonomous Region and whole Pakistan in spatial range". Its main aim is to connect South Xinjiang with Pakistan. It is divided into a "core area" and what they call the "radiation zones", those territories that will feel the knock-on effects of the work being done in the core area. It has "one belt, three passages, and two axes and five functional zones", where the belt is "the strip area formed by important arterial traffic in China and Pakistan."' Khurram Husain, op. cit.
[68]Ibid.

by means of this difficult route. It is estimated that China is spending $150 billion on infrastructural projects like these.[69]

In the world of infrastructure development, the deal that China struck with Pakistan will be very different from the deals it negotiates with the UK, Russia, Iran and Turkey. The political personalities, processes and contexts all require the bilateral agreements to be tailored to meet the existing regulatory standards, should they exist. Many of China's partners epitomise the 'sad and bad' in the development game, nations that would not qualify for loans from the West's developmental agencies. Hence, China is throwing them a big lifeline to address deep structural problems, such as their lack of transportation infrastructure, around-the-clock electricity and clean water, modern highways/motorways, sufficient resource development projects, and proper sanitation for communities and families. China is a master business negotiator working to expand opportunities for its state-owned enterprises and other investors. It is a tough bargainer, as anyone can imagine when so much money is a stake. Beijing is also a major player at all stages of the construction, service provision, financing and, in particular, post-construction contracts.

DRIVING A HARD BARGAIN

There is little doubt that Beijing is an expert in the diplomatic art of concession-style bargaining. This is premised on the idea that China will invest, develop and modernise a sector or an industry of its bilateral partner, and that, in return, China will obtain further rights and privileges for its investment risk(s). Many of the loans are made at 2.3 per cent financed over long periods, and, for those like Pakistan that cannot pay their debt, China is willing to extend the terms of repayment, reduce the interest rate or, in the worst case scenario, cancel part of it. We need only to think of massively indebted Greece,

[69]Tom Phillips 'World's biggest building project aims to make China great again', *Guardian*, 12 May, 2017 https://www.theguardian.com/world/2017/may/12/chinese-president-belt-and-road-initiative [Accessed October 2018]

Portugal and Ireland to see how atypical China's response is to debt forgiveness in renegotiating loans on a case-by-case basis with high-risk, debt-distressed countries.[70]

Certainly, China uses its massive infrastructural projects to maximise its advantage when it comes to concessionary bargaining. In East Africa's multi-country railway line project, Beijing has been given long-term, highly lucrative service contracts, tax concessions and other business opportunities to build industrial parks in the future. There are reports that China and Kenya are committed to upgrading the construction of the industrial parks along the route while seeking to integrate the Mombasa-Nairobi Railway, the Port of Mombasa and the Mombasa Special Economic Zone. Although these new plans were not part of the original agreement, Beijing and Nairobi are heading back to the bargaining table for another round of negotiations. At this point in time, we do not know if their differences will be resolved.

It is important to recall that concession bargaining is based upon a hard-nosed business principle of exchange that works to the advantage of the investor with the deep pockets – 'you give me this and we will do that', 'you require development and we will finance it, but we will also need something else to seal the deal.' It is this 'something else' that raises the stakes and the recipient's anxiety. It increases the asymmetry between highly unequal partners, with China having more leverage because its negotiating partners do not have the resources to build the projects on their own. Thus, it is not helpful to think of development as the 'win-win' cliché that political elites repeatedly trot out, because the concessions to the Chinese are often very large, costly, unavoidable and long-term.[71]

---

[70]The bitter battles between Greece and the EU with its model *in extremis* of 'no immediate debt relief' is a permanent reminder of the social repercussions and subsequent societal chaos created when debt relief is not an option. See Yanis,Varoufakis, op. cit., for a detailed account of his attempt as Finance Minister to secure a loan of €1 billion from China as one of the conditions for the sale of Piraeus, the main port of Athens. It is an excellent example of the concessions-style bargaining he proposed.
[71]Britain, Belgium, France, the Netherlands, Germany and the United States have regularly extended their economic sphere of influence by using this kind of commercial strategy.

A more realistic metric is whether the infrastructural development is transformative in the medium term, building new institutions and distributing the benefits of regional integration to the poor and other vulnerable publics.

NARROW LEDGE CONTRACTUALISM

Concession bargaining has an additional dimension because it also has a built-in legal or contractual safety net for Beijing and its local partner that protects both parties. In these bilateral agreements, each party has a detailed sphere of operation and well-defined areas of responsibility with respect to all aspects of the investment undertaking, including repayment, construction, sourcing materials, phases of construction, timelines, completion and after-service responsibilities. 'Narrow ledge contractualism' is a fitting term to describe the way the law of contracts is used to shield both parties from the political and economic consequences of their contractual obligation.

They are immunised from any legal responsibility that lies outside of the terms and conditions agreed upon at the outset. For instance, in many jurisdictions corruption in the awarding of contracts is an established part of the public culture. In these individually tailored bilateral agreements, it is the responsibility of the host economy to ensure that the rules of public procurement, protection of the environment and displacement of local inhabitants conform to state laws and practices. Should accountability and transparency not be part of the culture or institutional life of the country, narrow ledge contractualism protects China from any responsibility outside its core infrastructural interests.

Africa has paid a high price for pro-market policies that accentuate the human cost of severe cuts in social expenditures and subsidies, despite infrastructure investment and other forms of developmental aid. Many governments have been unresponsive to citizen needs and the poor have little influence over public policies. The underfunding of social policies and the prioritising of infrastructural development has meant that poverty remains high and growth has not delivered stable, long-term employment. According to one 2010 study, Africa is a low spender of about 3.5 per cent of its GDP on social protection, compared to an average of 4.5 per cent in all low-income countries. The gap between middle-income states that spend 10 per cent of GDP and high-income countries that spend on average 20.6 per cent of GDP seems unbridgeable with the current mix of policies.[72]

In Central Asia, the OBOR initiative opens the door for Chinese companies to expand business opportunities with Chinese entrepreneurs, establishing special zones and tax concessions. Hegemonic powers inevitably put their own interests ahead of those of local firms. For example, expanding local production and raising the demand for locally made goods and services is not a primary concern of Beijing. But it should be of its bilateral partners. It is doubtful that promoting progressive taxation is a key concern of the OBOR's thousand-plus projects in Central Asia. Neither will highly efficient and badly needed infrastructure investment protect local economies from sharp international fluctuations in commodity prices for their leading agricultural exports and in interest rates.

This is not to say that in Vietnam, Cambodia and Laos, local firms are denied business opportunities outright. They could be on a second list of priorities or find themselves on the bottom of the first list of 'best' opportunities. Concession bargaining opens the door to contractually putting the investor in the driver's seat of development. The country with deep pockets promises a great deal to native entrepreneurs, although frequently these futuristic-sounding prospects never materialise because of corruption, bureaucratic red tape, overreach and unrealistic planning expectations. Certainly, China is not alone in demanding concessions for economic and political advantage. This is part of every history of development aid and investment, and the all-important takeaway message in Paul

---

[72]*Policy Innovations for Transformative Change: Implementing the 2030 Agenda for Sustainable Development* (Geneva: UNRISD, 2017) http://www.unrisd.org/flagship2016 [Accessed October 2018]

Collier's classic study of development programmes, *The Bottom Billion*, a 'Sophoclean-like tragedy'.[73]

BUILDING FRIENDSHIP RELATIONS OR A POWER GRAB?

A final objective of concession bargaining consists of a different set of goals. It is the most tangible evidence of soft power being wielded as a diplomatic instrument. It is paradoxically to build relationships for the purposes of politics and solidarity by offering large-scale financing of infrastructural deals at discount rates. Building 'friendship relations' (*guanxi*) in order to be part of China's international community has a different rationale. Every hegemon with deep pockets has adopted the same rationale with both success and failure. For example, in the case of the post-war Marshall Plan, Washington helped rebuild Western Europe post-1945 by initiating a massive 'European Recovery Programme'.

Historians disagree about why the US decided to commit itself to participate actively in European reconstruction. George Kennan's background paper to the Marshall Plan situated American investment in its larger context and emphasised that 'American effort in aid to Europe should be directed not to combating communism...but to the restoration of the economic health and vigour of European society'.[74] As American presence in Europe grew, US help was critical to European recovery – 'every available European dollar was being spent on US food, raw materials, and capital goods'. While many historians note that the Marshall Plan did extend aid to former partners, neutrals and ex-enemies of the United States alike, the USSR denounced the Marshall Plan as a 'capitalist ruse' and ordered the countries in its sphere of influence to do the same.[75]

By characterising the Marshall Plan, as well as the Truman doctrine out of which it arose, as a project whose clear intent was to erect a cordon sanitaire around the USSR, Moscow preferred

---

[73]Paul Collier, op. cit.
[74]Philip Armstrong, Andrew Glyn and John Harrison, *Capitalism Since World War II: The Making and Breakup of the Great Boom* (Fontana, 1984), p. 111.
[75]Norman Davies, *Europe: A History* (Oxford University Press, 1996), p. 1064.

in official parlance to build 'networks of loyalty and friendship' throughout Asia, Africa and the Middle East during the Cold War.[76] While the Soviets initially had considerable success, like many other great power hegemons, their alliances with Global South leaders were difficult to manage and often the material aid had little effect on recipients' development. For instance, the political alliance between India and the Soviet Union proved to be very durable for over three decades after India's independence. India received hundreds of millions of dollars in development aid. Then Soviet-Indian relations unravelled, in spectacular fashion, and India's elites paid a high price developmentally by rigidly following the Soviet model.

Many in the Global North will find it hard to imagine that China, still officially socialist, is poised to become the leading force for continued globalisation and the most committed defender of trade liberalisation.[77] It is worth the effort to identify the logic that has brought the Chinese leadership to embrace hyper-globalisation, regional integration and open markets.

The first piece of crucial information comes from the *Financial Times* article revealing that Chinese lending to Asia has risen significantly since the OBOR initiative was announced in 2013.[78] The most surprising development is that among the 172 loans – with a total value of $100 billion – extended by Chinese developmental banks, 'the lion's share went to Asia', according to recent figures. No better proof is needed that China's geopolitical priorities have shifted away from Africa to a certain degree and that the support for the Asian century is indeed China's top priority.

Government authorities boast about leveraging private firms and investment in these grandiose work schemes, but for the moment there is no clear answer about what constitutes success. The hydroelectric dam that delivers cheap electricity? The tens of

---

[76]Tony Judt, *Postwar: A History of Europe Since 1945* (Penguin Books, 2005), p. 197.
[77]Wenxian Zhang, Ilan Alon and Christoph Lattermann, *China's Belt and Road Initiative: Changing the Rules of Globalization* (Springer, 2018).
[78]James Kynge, 'China's Ambitions for Asia Show through in 'Silk Road' Lending', *Financial Times*, 1 April, 2016.

thousands of kilometres of motorways, stimulating the growth of exports? The bullet trains connecting states, cities and regions? Repayments to China of hundreds of millions of dollars? Generating state revenue to pay for a railway, a deep-sea harbour? Rising health standards resulting from sanitation installation?

The economics are critical to the success of the OBOR because the massive investments are designed to have stimulus effects on economic growth and the betterment of the lives of tens of millions of people. Many economists will argue that Chinese infrastructural investment is likely to have strong multiplier knock-through effects at both the regional level and country level. More debatable is whether this is sufficient to change the course of the world economy as a whole. For starters, its macro-stimulus is too small to have such a global impact.[79] Even domestically, the stimulus effects of its investment blitz are muted given the size of China's $11 trillion economy.[80]

Whether China is able to develop sustainable and more robust governance practices is an open question and one that lies at the heart of this book. Somehow, China has to balance its strong support for Pakistan and Iran with its commitments to work with India and Turkey. Moreover, China faces enormous challenges in its support for Zimbabwe, Kenya, Ethiopia, Djibouti and Sierra Leone. Central Asia and Russia remain unstable political minefields. Of its potential Silk Road partners, many face macroeconomic risks owing to exchange-rate volatility, large debt burdens, poverty and non-diversified, unsustainable economic structures. China's $2 trillion spending juggernaut is hoping to transform Africa and its relations with the rest of the world. Will it succeed? What is the timeline? The answer lies in understanding the complex and crippling effects of crony capitalism.

[79]Francis Cripps, the well-known macroeconomist, did a rough, back-of-the-envelope calculation that is a convincing exercise to demonstrate the limits of China's stimulus spending. He estimates that 'OBOR may be a bigger/better initiative than others around but 1% [increase in world GDP] is hardly enough to change the course of the world economy as a whole.'
(Private communication with Daniel Drache, 2017).
[80]China's GDP per capita (PPP) of $16,676 is way behind the US PPP of approximately $59,609 in 2017.

WHEN POLITICS ARE RISKY AND MISALIGNED

The term 'crony capitalism' made a significant impact in the public arena as an explanation of the Asian financial crisis.[81] What it clarifies is the way public policy and law, as it was constituted, was used for criminal ends and to shield collusion between officials and businessmen, further corrupting state administrations.[82] When economic growth generates such criminality, the biggest issue of our time is, as Martin Wolf writes, that 'corruption ... spreads by enticement, coercion and imitation'.[83]

Corruption has become a global problem driven by multinationals seeking favours and governments hungry for foreign investment. In 2016, the top five Asian countries with the highest rates of bribery were Myanmar, Thailand, Pakistan and Vietnam, with India holding down top spot for the worst record of bribing public officials at a rate of 69 per cent, according to Transparency International. It found that 'in five of the six public services—schools, hospitals, ID documents, police and utility services—more than half the respondents have had to pay a bribe'.[84]

Corruption in India is widespread in its government institutions and political structures, and by no means is China out of the woods. According to a 2017 report by Transparency International, 73 per cent of the mainland Chinese surveyed said corruption has worsened in the past three years. Moreover, the report finds that bribery rates in the country have steadily increased to 26 per cent.[85] Accordingly, a question that requires addressing by the Chinese leadership is how to promote good governance and fight corruption while implementing

[81]Helen Hughes, 'Crony Capitalism and the East Asian Currency and Financial "Crises"', *Policy: A Journal of Public Policy and Ideas* 15(1999), pp. 3–9; The Economist Intelligence Unit, 'Planet Plutocrat: Our Crony-capitalism Index', *Economist*, 15 May, 2014.
[82]George Monbiot, 'Neoliberalism – The Ideology at the Root of all our Problems', *Guardian*, 6 February, 2017 https://www.theguardian.com/books/2016/apr/15/neoliberalism-ideology-problem-george-monbiot [Accessed October 2018]; Minxin Pei, *China's Crony Capitalism: The Dynamics of Regime Decay* (Harvard University Press, 2016).
[83]Martin Wolf, 'Too Big, Too Leninist – A China Crisis is a Matter of Time', *Financial Times*, 13 December, 2016.
[84]Tanvi Gupta, 'Asia's Five Most Corrupt Countries', *Forbes Asia*, 13 March, 2017 https://www.forbes.com/sites/tanvigupta/2017/03/13/asias-five-most-corrupt-countries/#629c21666a98
[85]Coralie Pring, *People and Corruption: Asia Pacific* (Transparency International, 2017).

Belt and Road Initiative projects across Eurasia. The loophole is that there are no Chinese laws that forbid Chinese companies from engaging in illicit activities abroad.[86]

After all, many governments see China as an economic lifeline in places where USAID has been dramatically scaled back in recent years.[87] Of course, what really happens is that ruling parties will often cut a deal on China's terms, opposition leaders then voice strong criticism (based largely on their own electoral ambitions), charging a project as far too costly the Western media comes down on China, and a more financially manageable deal is struck (once again with China). As a result of this ongoing cycle, corruption associated with Chinese entrepreneurship resonates strongly with people in vital BRI regions such as Central Asia, not only in more resource-scarce localities.

For instance, as Kemel Toktomushev, a research fellow at the University of Central Asia, recently pointed out, the malfunctioning of a Chinese-built thermal power plant in January 2018 has already put two former prime ministers from Kyrgyzstan under custody as part of an investigation over alleged graft.[88] Sapar Isakov and Zhantoro Satybaldiyev are currently facing charges of lobbying for the interests of the Chinese company Tebian Electric Apparatus Stock Co. Ltd. (TBEA), which won a $386 million contract to modernise the power plant.[89] The project itself was supported by a loan from China's CHEXIM. Two years earlier, in April 2016, the then prime minister of Kyrgyzstan, Temir Sariyev, also had to step down amid

---

[86]Kemel Toktomushev, 'Corruption and the New Silk Road', *China-US Focus*, October 11, 2018 https://www.chinausfocus.com/finance-economy/corruption-and-the-new-silk-road
[87]Satina Aidar, 'Kyrgyzstan's North-South Road to Corruption', *TOL*, August 9, 2018 https://www.tol.org/client/article/27887-kyrgyzstan-china-infrastructure-one-belt-one-road-corruption.html
[88]Kemel Toktomushev, ibid.
[89]As Fergana.ru reports, the Kyrgyz authorities and Chinese contractor TBEA (which was recommended by Beijing for the modernisation work) signed accounting papers for $600 pliers, $14,000 video cameras and $1,500 fire extinguishers. A parliamentary committee concluded that approximately $100 million was embezzled in the operation. Of course, it is important to remember that the United States has a similar track record: as early as 1980 we have seen oft-reported stories of $640 for a toilet seat or $7,600 for a coffee pot. More information at: https://www.thenation.com/article/only-the-pentagon-could-spend-640-on-a-toilet-seat/

corruption allegations involving a $100 million road construction project carried out by a Chinese construction company.

Of course, widespread corporate fraud, and lying to and cheating regulatory authorities, has reached into the top ranks of the global financial system, as was revealed by the Panama Papers and other investigatory reports.[90] American banks have paid over $300 billion in fines since the 2008 financial crisis (while earning an estimated $1 trillion in profits).[91] Paradoxically, China may have more 'policy buffers' and deep pockets for its global infrastructure spending initiative, because of its massive dollar reserves and the enormous amount of undistributed profits from state enterprises, more than any other Asian superpower.

Moreover, the scale of the Chinese leadership's toolkit to curb corruption on paper is remarkable by current standards and currently extremely invasive of individual rights. It has mandated a powerful new anti-corruption agency, the National Supervision Commission, to investigate any government employee and hold suspects for up to six months without access to a lawyer. China is also piloting a Social Credit System that will ensure Chinese citizens, private companies, public officials and state institutions abide by the rules.[92]

What we know is that development is a complex, fragile process involving the long arc of institutions, markets and technology altering lived experience. In Asia and Africa, dependence on exports is a curse and a blessing, a source of wealth and a cause of crippling dependence. An export-driven economy creates wealth and also

---

[90]The Panama Papers shone the spotlight on where the super-rich hide their wealth from regulatory tax authorities and national regulators. The Panamanian law firm Mossack Fonseca used tropical tax havens to hide billions of dollars. The records were obtained from an anonymous source by the German newspaper *Süddeutsch Zeitung*, which shared them with the International Consortium of Investigative Journalists (ICIJ). The ICIJ then shared them with a large network of international partners, including the *Guardian* and the BBC. The records revealed that more than 140 politicians used these secret networks, as well as 20 presidents and prime ministers. This includes Western elites and top Chinese officials.

[91]Gavin Finch, 'World's Biggest Banks Fined $321 Billion since Financial Crisis', *Bloomberg News*, 2 March, 2017 https://www.bloomberg.com/news/articles/2017-03-02/world-s-biggest-banks-fined-321-billion-since-financial-crisis

[92]https://www.chinausfocus.com/finance-economy/corruption-and-the-new-silk-road

deepens regional inequalities due to the uneven distribution of the resource bounty regionally and globally. So if we give Picketty's core idea a tweak, such that return on 'resources is greater than growth', it tells us something very important, namely that the distorting presence of market forces in many of the poorest countries drains resources away from institutions and discourages much needed investment in human capital.[93]

A lot of empirical evidence points in the direction of harmful negative externalities and it is doubtful that technology on its own will rescue the least developed economies from governance challenges, public corruption, and resource and landlocked traps.[94] Importantly, Collier predicted the limits of techno-determinism more than two decades ago. So far, China has been able to convince its partners to adopt its norms about global development and put them into practice. Indeed, it is trying to redefine what passes for normal and provide an alternative to neoliberal privatisation regimes.

BEIJING'S SIGNAL: MESSAGE IN THE BOTTLE

Still, how did China acquire so much expertise and practical know-how about the virtuous – if done correctly – cycle of infrastructural investment? The answer is anything but simple. A crucial part of the explanation is that after the disastrous policies of the Great Leap Forward and the Cultural Revolution, China's experience with mega-sized infrastructure-centric development accelerated and has been integral to its exponential growth over the past four decades. This experience in constructing the nuts and bolts of a modern economy has entered China's grand narrative gradually in the decades

---

[93]Paul Collier, op. cit.

[94]The least developed countries include: Afghanistan, Angola, Azerbaijan, Benin, Bhutan, Bolivia, Burkina Faso, Burundi, Cambodia, Cameroon, Central African Republic, Chad, Comoros, Democratic Republic of the Congo, Republic of the Congo, Ivory Coast, Djibouti, Equatorial Guinea, Eritrea, Ethiopia, Gambia, Ghana, Guinea, Guinea-Bissau, Guyana, Haiti, Kazakhstan, Kenya, North Korea, Kyrgyz Republic, Lao PDR, Lesotho, Liberia, Madagascar, Malawi, Mali, Mauritania, Moldova, Mongolia, Mozambique, Myanmar, Nepal, Niger, Nigeria, Rwanda, Senegal, Sierra Leone, Somalia, Sudan, Tajikistan, Tanzania, Togo, Turkmenistan, Uganda, Uzbekistan, Yemen, Zambia and Zimbabwe. Almost all are China 'Roaders'.

preceding Xi's 2013 announcement officially launching the One Belt, One Road initiative.[95]

Since then, the prioritising of infrastructural development has taken its place as a foundational notion – hence its remarkable expansion. Much else is needed if it is to be a success. The new Silk Road's massive investment initiative will require shrewd diplomacy to manage its relationships with so many diverse actors, and involve careful planning and successful execution to scale up projects effectively. But what if the local politics and Beijing's largesse are misaligned? That is a much larger systemic challenge for which even Beijing, with all its experience and massive planning machine, has no ready-made answer. Then again, China has built the institutions, possesses the experience and deep pockets, and has the political will to keep its hundreds of projects on schedule, tightly organised and under firm control of the Party's leadership. And yet will this be enough?

[95]For the background and a detailed examination of policymaking, see Nadège Rolland, *China's Eurasian Century? Political and Strategic Implications of the Belt and Road Initiative* (National Bureau of Asian Research, 2017) http://www.nbr.org/publications/issue.aspx?id=346 [Accessed October 2018]

3

China's Multi-layered Banking System: Deep Pockets and their Constraints

According to *Forbes*, in 2018 Chinese banks claimed four of the world's top ten largest public companies.[1] These are: Industrial and Commercial Bank of China, which comes in at number one with total assets valued at $4.009 trillion. Next is China Construction Bank, with assets worth $3.400 trillion. This is followed by Agricultural Bank of China, the fifth largest public company with total assets of $3.235 trillion. And, finally, coming in at ninth, Bank of China has amassed assets worth $2.991 trillion.[2] Such assets, which are the top criteria for establishing bank size, include all resources controlled by these entities as a result of past events and from which future economic benefits are expected to flow.

In 2017, the Chinese banking system broke another record by surpassing all Eurozone banks in size. It is now larger than the entire Eurozone banking system. According to the latest information,

---

[1] These numbers were taken from *Forbes*' Annual 2018 list of the World's Largest Public Companies in terms of market capitalisation – the total value of companies' outstanding common stock (not including preferred shares) https://www.forbes.com/global2000/#23662432335d [Accessed October 2018]

[2] With a market cap of $181.4 billion, China's Ping An Insurance Group takes 10th spot on the list. According to *Forbes*' annual list, Ping An has had an early-mover advantage in mobile apps and underlying technologies from artificial intelligence and blockchain. Spreading across Ping An's vast territory in finance, encompassing insurance, banking, and asset management, are 10 startups spawned by it in the last six years https://www.forbes.com/sites/shuchingjeanchen/2018/06/06/chinese-giant-ping-an-looks-beyond-insurance-to-a-fintech-future/#26403b1d48f3 [Accessed October 2018]

Chinese bank assets hit $33 trillion at the end of 2016, versus $31 trillion for the Eurozone, $16 trillion for the US and $7 trillion for Japan. The value of China's banking system is more than three times the size of its annual economic output, compared with two times for the Eurozone and its banks.[3] Moreover, the country's banking sector hit around $35 trillion in loans in 2017/18, accounting for more than three times the size of China's GDP in dollars.[4]

Such an unprecedented gap in sales, profits, assets and market value between these top four financial titans and their most substantive Western competitors can be attributed to the uniqueness of China's banking system. It has a lot going for it. Top of the list is the unparalleled size and concentration of its banks; multiple, seemingly bottomless pools of capital and revenue streams for the state to draw on; relatively small transfer payments; safety nets for individuals; sufficient top-down regulation effective enough to impose order on its many financial actors; and competing Ministry and Party interests.

Seen from this perspective, China has deep pockets, deeper than any Western economy, to finance all of its infrastructural projects with dozens of partnerships for the next decade, provided that it does not face any major prolonged threats to its domestic stability. Like any concentrated system, distortions and mistakes arise from over-centralisation, lax regulatory practices and off-book debts. Each year, Chinese banks invest billions of dollars in bonds, stocks, hedge funds, corporate acquisitions and pension plans. They finance international mergers and acquisitions worth billions from Boston to Berlin, Bangkok to Beijing.

A NEW CHINA EMERGES

Of the Top 10 global companies ranked by *Forbes*, China and the US are split down the middle at five each. All of the top companies are

---

[3]Gabriel Wildau, 'China Overtakes Eurozone as World's Biggest Bank System', *Financial Times*, 5 March, 2017.

[4]Kenneth Rapoza, 'China's Largest Companies Prove Why It's The World's No. 2 Economy', *Forbes*, 6 June, 2018 https://www.forbes.com/sites/kenrapoza/2018/06/06/2018-global-2000-china-proves-why-its-the-worlds-no-2-economy/#7063d4111791 [Accessed October 2018]

banks, led by the aforementioned Industrial and Commercial Bank of China and China Construction Bank. The US is also bank-heavy, except for Apple, which comes in at number eight on the Global 2000 list.[5] As Kenneth Rapoza from *Forbes* observes, China and Hong Kong account for 291 of the world's 2000 largest companies, up from 262 in 2017.[6] To put things in much-needed perspective, back in 2003, China and Hong Kong had a combined 43 companies on the list. China alone has 232 companies this year. If this trajectory continues, China will pose an even greater threat to the Western-centred multilateral order.

It is worth emphasising that China is a global hegemon because its banks are big – at least within the Top 100 of the *Forbes* list. By comparison, the top US companies are much more diverse. Banks lead the Top 10, and down the list are the tech and energy companies as well as media and telecom firms. In other words, China is bank-heavy. But as Rapoza continues, anyone concerned about China's over-reliance on lending growth needs to look no further than the newest Global 2000 list, which serves as a testament to China's credit-fuelled growth story over the last decade. New banks, such as Guangzhou Rural Commercial Bank and Zhongyuan Bank (numbers 1092 and 1268 on the list respectively), are emerging. Further down the list, one can see a new Chinese economy in the mix. HNA Technology, a tech holding company that owns electronics distributor Ingram Micro out of Irvine, California, and 360 Security Technology are Global 2000 companies today.[7]

In this new environment, the Chinese global strategy is always operating on the borderline between massive OBOR investment projects and funding China's ambitious plans for exponential export-led growth. From any standpoint, it is quite a balancing act. The amount of money that Chinese authorities spend on infrastructure is very large compared to other major countries. The China Development Bank dedicated more than $110 billion to projects in BRI countries as of mid-2018. China's Export Import Bank said it

[5]*Forbes*' Annual 2018 list of the World's Largest Public Companies https://www.forbes.com/global2000/#23662432335d [Accessed October 2018]
[6]Kenneth Rapoza, op. cit.
[7]Ibid.

provided $90 billion. While the United States is a significant player, it committed only $35 billion in economic assistance in 2017 alone. Most was not spent on economic infrastructure, according to the OECD. Only Japan shared an outlook similar to China's. In 2017, Japan provided developing countries over $10 billion in concessional funding for economic infrastructure. The contrast with the US' very small commitment of just over $1 billion speaks volumes about its lack of engagement.[8] At its core, OBOR must navigate carefully between commerce and development. What keeps the financial ship on course is the top-down bureaucracy in control of China's banks. However, there is also a danger that China's huge bureaucratic banking machine cannot be slowed or reversed. As experts at the Brookings Institute have noted, it operates more like 'a non-transparent accelerator' than a brake.[9] In early March 2018, the government announced the creation of a super financial authority, further tightening the Party's leash on competing regulators and aiming to stop turf wars before they start.[10] At least, this is the theory behind the reforms, which bears watching.

Are China's banks up to the task of shouldering its rising economic, cultural and infrastructural ambitions? With China's Belt and Road Initiative gaining more recognition globally, British and US banks are rushing to seize opportunities thrown up by Beijing's vast trade corridors spanning more than 80 partner states.[11] According to *Forbes* senior consultant Mike Reynal, one of the reasons for this banking boom is that Chinese growth is spreading to second- and third-tier

[8]Deborah Brautigam, "Misdiagnosing the Chinese Infrastructure Push," The *American Interest*, April 4, 2019 https://www.the-american-interest.com/2019/04/04/misdiagnosing-the-chinese-infrastructure-push/
[9]Ben Bernanke and Peter Olson, 'China's transparency challenges', *Brookings Institute*, 8 March, 2016 https://www.brookings.edu/blog/ben-bernanke/2016/03/08/chinas-transparency-challenges [Accessed October 2018]
[10]Yang Xiaodu has been appointed head of the National Supervisory Commission. The new anti-graft super agency will have jurisdiction over all public sector bodies. Additionally, the China Insurance Regulatory Commission is to be merged with the banking regulator. See Sidney Leng, and Frank Tang, 'Xi shakes up Chinese government to cut bureaucracy, end turf wars', *South China Morning Post*, 13 March, 2018, http://www.scmp.com/news/china/economy/article/2136939/china-unveils-sweeping-governmental-changes-cut-bureaucracy-and [Accessed October 2018]
[11]Martin Arnold, 'Western banks race to win China's Belt And Road Initiative deals', *Financial Times*, 26 February, 2018.

cities and into services. If this is so, it is likely that China's growth rate is close to the official figure of 6.5 per cent, which should give pause to China sceptics who see only trouble ahead for the Chinese economy.[12]

CHINA'S FINANCIAL REGULATORS

Chinese banks are not faceless bureaucratic entities, as commonly portrayed in the Western press. They have a strong command-control regulatory institution at their apex running the show: the China Banking Regulatory Commission (CBRC) is recognised by Western banking authorities as a key institution.[13] With the reorganisation of the government announced in March 2018 and the creation of a super financial authority, the Party is reasserting its control over its enormous financial sector filled with many independent power bases.[14] The Bank of China has absorbed the Banking and Insurance Regulatory Commissions, once powerful entities in their own right, as part of the recent overhaul of the governance structure in line with Xi's consolidation of power. On the other hand, the National Development and Reform Commission, once the government's most powerful planning agency, has seen its regulatory wings clipped. Other changes are in the works to reinforce effective policymaking, but not at the expense of regional players who will continue to be important stakeholders in China's institutional setup of larger-than-life players.[15]

Surprisingly to its critics, many CBRC practices are gradually becoming more convergent with the standards of the IMF and World Bank, and more reforms are in progress. For example, China's currency has now been accepted by the IMF in its basket of global currencies.[16] China recognises that it has massive unsecured bad debts in the state-owned

[12]Kenneth Rapoza, op. cit.

[13]China Banking Regulatory Commission, 'About the CBRC', http://www.cbrc.gov.cn/showyjhjjindex.do

[14]'China's central bank rises but faces more constraints', EM Squared, *Financial Times*, 19 March, 2018.

[15]Ibid.

[16]'IMF Adds Chinese Renminbi to Special Drawing Rights Basket', *International Monetary Fund*, IMF News, 30 September, 2016 http://www.imf.org/en/News/Articles/2016/09/29/AM16-NA093016IMF-Adds-Chinese-Renminbi-to-Special-Drawing-Rights-Basket [Accessed October 2018]

enterprises, and it has recently introduced capital controls on the record amount of outflow of Chinese investment abroad because of the dangers that capital flight presents. Bank of China is a key actor and is given credit for introducing more financial discipline and other internal safeguard practices during the record-setting, 15-year presidency of US-educated economist Zhou Xiaochuan.[17]

Many experts acknowledge that the bank has adopted more rigorous Western banking regulatory standards that have helped it manage the billions of dollars loaned to China's OBOR club of nations. While American and British governmental regulators enjoy special relations with their banking structures, there are always clear divides in theory between public regulators and private institutions.[18] In China, however, banks function as apparatuses of the government, centralised public institutions resembling a giant, multi-layered, cake-like institution with power concentrated at the apex. The system is based upon a four-pronged approach to banking that is *flexible* within limits and not subject to the same competition of interests as the more decentralised Western banks. It is surprisingly *resourceful,* with direct access to huge amounts of financing from Beijing. It goes without saying that it is bureaucratically and heavily *regulated,* with intrusive oversight coming directly from The People's Bank of China by way of the CBRC. Finally, in a way that is not sufficiently recognised, it is *localised,* as the banking system is controlled at national, regional, municipal and local levels.[19]

Pools of savings, taxation revenue, state-owned enterprises and cash reserves keep China's behemoth banks on the winning side of a seemingly unbridgeable fiscal chasm of bad loans and deficit financing. However, as impressive as this seems, it is far from the whole story with respect to its financial capacity to underwrite the massive investments of the OBOR initiative and the domestic economy's

[17]Gabriel Wildau, Lucy Hornby and Tom Mitchell, 'China names Yi Gang as new central bank governor', *Financial Times*, 18 March, 2008.
[18]Alicia García-Herrero, Sergio Gavilá and Daniel Santabárbara, 'China's Banking Reform: An Assessment of its Evolution and Possible Impact', *CESifo Economic Studies* 52 (2006), pp. 304–363.
[19]Richard Waters, 'Making it big in China requires a large measure of localisation', *Financial Times*, August 20, 2015.

better-than-average performance. So far, Chinese authorities have proven Western experts wrong again about the deep-bench strength of Chinese regulators. In 2017, many economic commentators forecast a dire downturn that did not materialise; investment flows were actually up tenfold from the previous year.[20] Nor did the much-anticipated volatility return, even with higher interest rates. Institutionally, it appears that China has more depth than it seems, and that OBOR has not knocked China off its growth trajectory.[21] At this point, it is difficult to give a frank and accurate assessment of China's capacity to be the world's infrastructural leader and investor without having a much clearer analytical grasp of its financial system, with all its many idiosyncrasies, weaknesses and strengths. The obvious question to pose is: can China have its cake and eat it too?

CHINA'S FINANCIAL MULTI-LAYERED CAKE-LIKE SYSTEM

We do not know if there was a grand design to the system when China became an independent socialist state, but, like many institutional organisations in China, it has evolved over long periods of time. Today, it meets the needs of China's complex financial and socio-political demands through six interconnected layers as detailed in Figure 3.1. These many different, powerful institutional actors, backed by mountains of hard cash, hold the key to the question of whether or not China's financial pockets are deep enough to pay the estimated $2 trillion and counting to fund the OBOR initiative.[22]

DIFFERENT RESPONSIBILITIES AND FUNCTIONS

By any standard, the Chinese banking system has generated seemingly bottomless pools of capital for both domestic and global infrastructural projects. Even more important are the

[20]Eric Platt, 'Hidden Gyrations Underpin the 2017 Global Fund Flows', *Financial Times*, 22 December, 2017.
[21]Kenneth Rapoza, 'Don't Be Shocked When China Stocks Tumble', *Forbes*, 14 November, 2017 https://www.forbes.com/sites/kenrapoza/2017/11/14/dont-be-shocked-when-china-stocks-tumble/#47da83d827cc [Accessed Ocotber 2018]
[22]With so many more potential projects in development, it is important to note that any final figure for total expenditure will be unreliable for quite some time.

The State Council of China
People's Bank of China (PBOC) China Bank Insurance Regulatory Commission (CBIRC)
Policy Banks (3): -The China Development Bank (CDB) -The Export-Import Bank of China (CHEXIM) -The Agricultural Development Bank of China (ADBC)
State-owned Commercial Banks (4): -The Industrial & Commercial Bank of China Limited (ICBC) -The Agricultural Bank of China (ABC) -The China Construction Bank (CCB) -The Bank of Communications (BoCOM) -The Bank of China (BoC)
National Joint-equality Commercial Banks (12): -China Merchants Bank (CMB) -Industrial Bank Co., Ltd. -China CITIC Bank -Shanghai Pudong Development Bank (SPDB) -China Minsheng Bank Co. Ltd. (CMBC) -China Everbright Bank (CEB) -Ping An Bank Co. Ltd. (PAB) -Hua Xia Bank Co. Ltd. (HXB) -China Guanfa Bank (CGB) -Hengfeng Bank Co. Ltd. (EGB) -China Zhejiang Bank Co. Ltd. (CZB) -China Bohai Bank Co. Ltd. (BHB)
Urban Commercial Banks (135+)
Rural Financial Institutions (3500+)

FIGURE 3.1   China's Multi-layered Financial 'Cake'

Source: China Pivot Working Group, Robarts Centre for Canadian Studies, York University, 2018.

interrelationships between the key institutional actors, which create a high degree of system-wide gridlock stability but also facilitate many questionable, off-the-books kinds of relationships that are certainly handy and readily available for its global investment spending spree. From a distance, it resembles a giant layer cake.

On top is the *People's Bank of China* (PBOC), which is operated by the State Council of China in the capacity of China's central bank. This means that the PBOC is responsible for formulating and implementing monetary policy, maintaining the banking sector's payment, clearing and settlement systems, and managing official foreign exchange and gold reserves. From a strategic perspective, the State Council and the

People's Bank of China are responsible for managing a vast portfolio of banks, savings institutions and state-owned enterprises.

It is chaired by the premier and includes the heads of each governmental department and agency. The Vice-Premier Yang Xiaodu formally led the anti-corruption drive at the Politburo against ordinary party members, high-ranking members of the Party, and military and business elites, and is considered Xi's right hand.[23]

Next in the pecking order are *China's policy banks*, which are responsible for financing economic and trade development, state-invested projects and China's global asset management. In terms of the Maritime Belt and Road, they are the most important layer because they work to coordinate the policy process. As a result, their involvement is essential for any large infrastructure projects to get off the ground.

Closely aligned, *China's state-owned commercial banks* are the largest in the world and function as private-public government ministries that directly finance China's complex infrastructural trade agreements. They are fully held by the Chinese Ministry of Finance, administrated by the China Banking Regulatory Commission (CBRC), and their presidents and other senior management are appointed and administrated by the Central Organisation Department of the Communist Party of China. It appears that The People's Bank of China will now have rule-making authority over the Banking and Insurance Commission. This will give the PBOC a more central role in decision-making with respect to the investment needs of One Belt, One Road.

In a class of their own, *China's joint-stock commercial banks* function as intermediaries that work to foster competition within the Chinese banking system, create professional advantages and enhance competitiveness. Thus, they are Western-like financial

---

[23]It is important to note that there was a shake-up on the regulatory side of China's financial institutions in 2018. The Bank of China has absorbed the Banking and Insurance Regulatory Commissions, once powerful entities in their own right, as part of the recent overhaul to streamline the government structure. On the other hand, the National Development and Reform Commission, once the government's most powerful planning agency, has seen its regulatory wings clipped. Other changes are in the works to reinforce effective policymaking, and regional players continue to be important stakeholders in China's institutional setup of larger-than-life players. 'China's central bank rises but faces more constraints', EM Squared, *Financial Times*, 19 March, 2018.

institutions owned by one or two dominant investors. What makes these banks different from all of China's other layers is that these investors may be private companies located in foreign jurisdictions, governments or an individual. A prominent example is the China Merchants Bank (CMB), which was the first share-holding commercial bank wholly owned by corporate legal entities in China. With over 70,000 employees, the CMB has set up a service network that consists of more than 1,800 branches worldwide, including six overseas branches, three overseas representative offices, and service outlets located in more than 130 cities in mainland China.[24]

Big players in China's financial industry are *China's urban commercial banks,* which provide financial support for local enterprises and pave the way for localised economic development. Most city commercial banks have strong ties to their local government and are majority or wholly state-owned. The main purpose of these urban commercial banks is to provide financial support for small and medium projects regionally and in cities. They are also a key source of OBOR funds.

In their own category altogether, *China's rural financial institutions* include rural credit cooperatives, rural commercial banks, cooperative banks, village banks and mutual funds. Rural credit cooperatives have been established with the approval of the People's Bank of China, and are composed of and managed by cooperative members in order to provide personal financial services to local communities. The rural credit cooperatives are independent, enterprising legal entities. Such banks have tens of thousands of branches at the local level. Similar to the European model, with post offices operating as savings banks for local communities, China's rural post office banks are an important institution. They provide an ocean-sized pool of capital from deposits from hundreds of millions of rural Chinese.

Yet the obvious backbone of the Chinese banking system is the policy-centric banks; with their deep pockets and technical professional expertise, they are the workhorses financing China's global initiative. In terms of China's investment frenzy, they are the most important

[24]China Merchants Bank http://english.cmbchina.com/CmbInfo/About/ [Accessed January 2019]

layer working to coordinate the policy process. As a result, their involvement is essential for hundreds of infrastructure projects to get off the ground. In the aggregate, the three policy banks make up 8 per cent of total assets (approximately $15 trillion) and are responsible for taking the lead in funding state-led development projects.[25]

In the past, policy banks were charged with supporting and financing the construction of infrastructure, promoting exports and food production. But, in the last decade or so, the government has steered the policy banks in a new direction and put in motion an intensely driven, dramatic commercialisation movement. A large part of their new responsibility is to negotiate terms and conditions with China's infrastructural partners. They are in the field, frontline representatives of China's global infrastructural projects, inspecting, overseeing and attending to a thousand and one details. Arguably, the term 'policy bank' no longer describes the business operations in which these banks engage. Only the Agricultural Development Bank, with tens of thousands of branches in the Chinese countryside, retains its traditional 'planning era' lustre. The newly directed international scope and scale of these policy banks means that they are the pacesetters financing China's global infrastructural initiative.

For instance, the Export-Import Bank of China has been a global actor since 1995, providing foreign clients with developmental aid and preferential loan services. The following year, CHEXIM took over the distribution of government-backed loans extended to foreign nations.[26]

In 1999, CHEXIM entered the more lucrative market of financing international engineering projects and the export of high-tech products, a perfect match for the dozens of complex and costly projects of the OBOR. The following year, China's Go-Out (*zouchuqu*) strategy

[25]Elliot K. Douglas and Kai Yan, *The Chinese Financial System: An Introduction and Overview* Monograph Series, Number 6 (John L. Thornton China Center at the Bookings Institute, 2013), https://www.brookings.edu/wp-content/uploads/2016/06/chinese-financial-system-elliott-yan. pdf [Accessed October 2018]
[26]Caijing New Desk, 'China's Policy Banks', *Caijing*, 9 September, 2016.

encouraging domestic companies to do business overseas was in full force, and CHEXIM was at the forefront of the internationalisation process. At present, CHEXIM not only holds a giant stake in China's export market but also has regional branches in over 108 countries and financial hubs around the world. It is a perfect fit for China's global infrastructural development initiative and is able to partner with Western banks and hedge funds to finance long-term multi-projects.

THE FINANCING PROCESS: THE CLOSED TENDER SYSTEM

The financing process has to be looked at carefully. There is a special arrangement that facilitates the funding for many of the New Silk Road projects. The hundreds of millions of dollars are drawn largely from internal loans between China's policy banks and its SOEs. China provides 80 per cent of the funding for any given project in the form of long-term loans. The remaining 20 per cent is provided locally through loans from a variety of sources, including China's sovereign wealth fund and the China Investment Corporation, as well as China Development Bank, the Export-Import Bank of China and the State Administration of Foreign Exchange.[27] The Bank of China and the CITIC Bank are heavily committed, as is the Asian Infrastructural Investment Bank.[28] Moreover, in 2017, President Xi pledged another $124 billion for the project, the deals of which have yet to be ironed out.[29]

The second layer of the standard financing model for China's infrastructural projects essentially favours Chinese contractors: with their reserve army of low-paid contract labour, they are able

[27]Susanna Su, 'Risky business: Financing "One Belt, One Road"', *Foreign Brief*, 23 August, 2016 https://www.foreignbrief.com/asia-pacific/china/risky-business-china-standard-obor-financing-model-unpacked [Accessed October 2018]

[28]Michel Aglietta and Guo Bai, 'China's 13th Five-Year Plan. In Pursuit of a "Moderately Prosperous Society"', *CEPII Policy Brief*, 12 (September 2016), p. 2 http://www.cepii.fr/PDF_PUB/pb/2016/pb2016-12.pdf [Accessed October 2018]

[29]Brenda Goh and Yawen Chen, 'China pledges $124 Billion for new Silk Road as champion of globalization', *Reuters*, 14 May, 2017 https://www.reuters.com/article/us-china-silkroad-africa/china-pledges-124-billion-for-new-silk-road-as-champion-of-globalization-idUSKBN18A02I [Accessed October 2018]

to charge cheaper rates than their international counterparts. China has therefore been very slow to adopt the open tender system as an ostensible move towards transparency in order to alleviate international concerns about corruption.[30] The sizeable volume of centrally controlled funding allows Beijing to write lower interest rates and longer grace periods into loan offers, but at the same time it enables Chinese authorities to control the process of negotiating bilateral contracts from start to finish.

Its closed tender system, which draws fire from many Western critics, has advantages, such as shutting out global corporate capital in the bidding system to promote the rapid growth of Chinese enterprises, particularly in strategic sectors. In this regard, critics draw attention to China's discriminatory practices against foreign corporations as a way multinational corporations (MNCs) have to compete in a system rigged against them. It is not only about control, since China partners with a lot of Western firms. It gives state-owned enterprises an edge with access to below-market-rate cheap money.

For example, China outbid Japanese and German competition for Indonesian and Russian high-speed rail projects by offering an attractive package of lower overall costs, lower interest rates and longer grace periods.[31] Furthermore, it bundled fewer liabilities for the host government and ensured flexibility about the ownership structure. At the Beijing global launch party for the OBOR in May 2017, China signed an accord with the World Bank, which commits China to greater transparency in the future in awarding contracts. It remains to be seen how selectively or fully China will apply these World Bank transparency norms.

[30]TASS Staff, 'Russian Railways prefers Chinese offer on Moscow-Kazan HSR construction to German one', *TASS Russian News Agency*, 3 November, 2015 http://tass.com/economy/833886 [Accessed October 2018]
[31]PricewaterhouseCoopers, 'Financialisation: The $9 Trillion Opportunity and What to Do with It', *Global Economy Watch* (July 2014) http://www.pwc.com/gx/en/issues/economy/global-economy-watch/assets/pdfs/global-economy-watch-july-2014.pdf [Accessed October 2018]

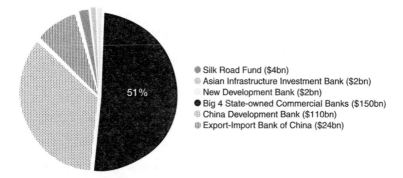

● Silk Road Fund ($4bn)
◐ Asian Infrastructure Investment Bank ($2bn)
  New Development Bank ($2bn)
● Big 4 State-owned Commercial Banks ($150bn)
▦ China Development Bank ($110bn)
▥ Export-Import Bank of China ($24bn)

FIGURE 3.2 China's Deep Pockets: Banks, Special Funds and State Money ($ billion USD)

Source: Adapted from Natixis, Asia Hot Topics, 2017.[32]

Chinese banks derive their financial power from immense holdings, flexibility and their relative international autonomy. Their autonomy comes with many strings attached, both to the Party and to the key ministries. But their colossal-sized resources also give them leverage within the system to defend their interests from encroachment by higher regulatory authorities. As insiders, they also get concessions and compromises that favour their interests and plans.

As a result of this centralised structure, the Chinese have been able to develop powerful shock absorbers to cushion the after-effects of the 2008 global financial crisis and create programmes to fund BRI initiatives (see Figure 3.2). They have been able to build on this decade-long expertise in infrastructural finance to great advantage under very diverse and demanding conditions from countries in Africa, the Middle East and Central Asia. These party-controlled institutions are designed to deal with systemic shocks to the financial system over the short and long term. This enables China to pay for its portion of the OBOR projects and add new projects in this directed, open-ended process with access to

[32] Available at: https://www.research.natixis.com/GlobalResearchWeb/Main/GlobalResearch/ GetDocument/qxYClNbfG8WgxAJS86C99w== [Accessed October 2018]

many different sources of surplus capital, including tax revenue, undistributed earnings of state enterprises and China's foreign exchange US dollar account.[33]

WILL THE CHINESE MODEL IMPLODE? WHAT HAVE THE EXPERTS BEEN PREDICTING?

From a policy perspective, a combination of China's high taxation rates and low transfer payments, as well as $3 trillion in foreign exchange reserves, creates a system of powerful financial buffers. The complex layers of China's banks hold more than $15 trillion in deposits and, in the aggregate, constitute the most important and resilient, powerful shock absorber of the system. Critics are right to point out that China carries the heavy burden of bad debts on its books and that financial reform will continue to be a major priority in the next five years. There are many domestic interests that have slowed the process to a crawl. Notwithstanding these critiques, with its very deep pockets China's financial system should not be underestimated (see Figure 3.3).

In the layered model introduced in Figure 3.1, the Chinese banking system operates like a grey zone of governance in the eyes of the outside world.[34] Chinese banks both make and bend rules to suit their immediate needs. For over 20 years, Western experts have been predicting that the Chinese banking system would implode by becoming chronically laden with debt from state-owned enterprises, state-run deficits and bad loans.[35] In 1998, the *Economist* infamously sounded a 'red alert' stating that 'China's economy is entering a dangerous period of sluggish growth.'[36] In 2003, the *New York Times* warned of a banking crisis imperilling China with 'bad loan bubbles' of extended credit to stimulate

---

[33]Qinqin Peng and Denise Jia, 'China State Banks Provide Over $400 Bln of Credits to Belt and Road Projects', *Caixin*, 11 May, 2017 http://www.caixinglobal.com/2017-05-12/101089361.html [Accessed October 2018]
[34]Daniel Drache and Lesley Jacobs (eds), *Linking Global Trade and Human Rights: New Policy Space in Hard Economic Times* (Cambridge University Press, 2014).
[35]Gabriel Wildau, 'China's state-owned zombie economy', *Financial Times*, 29 March, 2016.
[36]'Red Alert', *Economist*, 22 October, 1998.

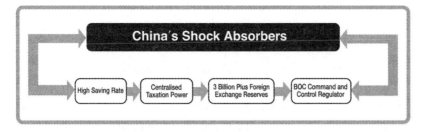

FIGURE 3.3 China's Financial Shock Absorbers

Source: China Pivot Working Group, Robarts Centre for Canadian Studies, York University, 2018.

speculative real estate deals.[37] A year later the *Economist*, followed by *Forbes*, *Fortune* and a host of other commentators, responded in kind, asking whether the country's unprecedented growth rates were culminating in 'The great fall of China?'[38] In 2016, the Economist Intelligence Unit went full circle and once again cautioned that, above all else, 'a hard landing looms in China'.[39]

When Chinese growth is represented statistically, the numbers are often called into question. In 2015, *Forbes* commentators worried over China's 'dodgy statistics'.[40] And according to Brandon Emmerich, a data provider from Wind Financial Information LLC, 'China's control over debt and equity markets and its reliance at times on inflexible rules can also affect the quality of financial data' as companies try to work within the parameters of directly monitored state investments.[41] In 2017, the *Nikkei Asian Review*

---

[37]Gordon G. Chang, 'A bad loan bubble: Banking crisis imperils China', *New York Times*, 19 June, 2003.
[38]'The great fall of China?' *Economist*, 13 May, 2004; Nouriel Roubini, 'Hard Landing in China?' *Forbes*, 6 November, 2008 https://www.forbes.com/2008/11/05/china-recession-roubini-oped-cx_nr_1106roubini.html [Accessed October 2018]; Bill Powell, 'China's hard landing', *Fortune*, 5 March, 2009 http://archive.fortune.com/2009/03/04/news/international/powell_china.fortune/index.htm [Accessed October 2018]
[39]'Hard landing looms in China', *Economist*, 14 October, 2016.
[40]Tim Worstall, 'Don't Believe The Chinese Economic Statistics: Except The Ones About The Crash Perhaps', *Forbes*, 19 July, 2015 https://www.forbes.com/sites/timworstall/2015/07/19/dont-believe-the-chinese-economic-statistics-except-the-ones-about-the-crash-perhaps/#2207e9d06e17 [Accessed October 2018]
[41]'China's Dodgy Data: A Rational Response to a Skewed System, Report Says', *Wall Street Journal*, blog, 20 December, 2016 https://blogs.wsj.com/chinarealtime/2016/12/20/chinas-dodgy-data-a-rational-response-to-a-skewed-system-report-says/ [Accessed October 2018]

alerted investors that if the distrust persists, investors could lose confidence in the Chinese market, in which case the government investors behind the OBOR initiative would have even more difficulty than they do now in stemming capital outflows.[42]

Contrary to some of the more ominous and repetitive predictions – and in spite of the more nuanced ones – the Chinese banking system has proven itself capable of rebounding from severe internal crises that arise from the speculative nature of its currency's fluctuations and the constant problem of corrupt practices. In the sense of both making and managing the rules for stability, the People's Bank of China and the CBRC have proven themselves to be powerful regulators with a reputation for technical professionalism. They have taken the OBOR mega-investments in their stride.

Faced with growing structural imbalances in the economy and mounting risk-management challenges, the banks have yet to face their day of reckoning but may well find themselves on the receiving end of a major financial crisis and meltdown. The evidence is, at face value, contradictory.

China has much institutional financial room to manoeuvre and the financial system is so vast, regulatory oversight is often slipshod. These crises are like ticking time bombs. Through constant monitoring, the State Council is able to fight fire with regulatory muscle as the occasion demands. The possible failures or successes of the 15,000+ OBOR contracts will depend upon the effective oversight, due diligence and regulatory muscle of the CBRC to ensure that the projects are delivered on time, that the costs are kept within manageable limits and that the contracts are not siphoned off for personal gain.[43]

---

[42]Yu Nakamura, 'World suspicious of dodgy data from China', *Nikkei Asian Review*, 16 February, 2017 https://asia.nikkei.com/Politics-Economy/Economy/World-suspicious-of-dodgy-data-from-China [Accessed October 2018]

[43]This technical professionalism was demonstrated by China's response to the 2008 financial crisis. In November 2008, a stimulus package of 4 trillion yuan ($586 billion) was introduced. Acting in tandem, the Central Bank and the People's Bank of China (PBOC) cut interest rates deeply, and the growth rate of credit and of broad money shot up. It seems that the economy started bottoming out as early as the first quarter of 2009, owing to the stimulus package and the extremely accommodating

DEBUNKING KEY MYTHS

There are dozens of misconceptions about China's relationship to market capitalism. Initially, President Xi continued a policy that was a modernised version of Deng Xiaoping's economic reforms, based on the idea that 'Socialism does not mean shared poverty'. Today, China's leaders are proud of the fact that their country is now the largest economy in the world in terms of its 2015 GDP measured on the basis of purchasing power parity (PPP). However, development also becomes a domestic issue when China's GDP *per capita*, upon a PPP basis, ranks only 82nd in the world, far to the back of the pack. Compared to the US, China is squarely a middle-income society. According to Dani Rodrik, the individual share of industrial employment is peaking at a lower level than it did in the past.[44] The manufacturing employment ratio is declining, evidence that deindustrialisation is coming to China. While the West sees China's middle class as the embodiment of three decades of extraordinary economic growth, this is a very large oversimplification.

Much of China is outside the development orbit of the OBOR. China's external commitments coexist uneasily with a very large and demanding domestic agenda of poverty eradication. China remains a rural society for hundreds of millions of people who live at the edge of subsistence and lack the most elemental services. The world looks different from places unknown to Western consciousness, such as Hebei, Tianjin, Chengdu and Chongquin.[45]

monetary policy. Focusing predominantly on this stimulus package, which equated to 16 per cent of the Chinese GDP, you can see the explicit spending breakdown here – Infrastructure: 45 per cent, Post Earthquake Reconstruction: 25 per cent, Rural Infrastructure: 9 per cent, Ecology: 9 per cent, Housing for Low Income Population: 7 per cent, Technological Innovation and Economic Restructuring: 4 per cent, and Medical Services, Culture and Education: 1 per cent. More information can be found here: https://www.cigionline.org/sites/default/files/task_force_2.pdf [Accessed October 2018]
[44]'Out of the Traps', *Economist*, 7 October, 2017.
[45]The *Economist* has a special issue on China, published on 19 April, 2017, which has an excellent up-to-date, interactive map on China's rural-urban income divides, available at: http://www.economist.com/news/special-report/21600797-2030-chinese-cities-will-be-home-about-1-billion-people-getting-urban-china-work

It is important to recall the following quotation because Deng's theoretical justification for allowing market forces into China is more relevant than ever today, a period of rapid financial expansion:

> Planning and market forces are not the essential difference between socialism and capitalism. A planned economy is not the definition of socialism, because there is planning under capitalism; the market economy happens under socialism, too. Planning and market forces are both ways of controlling economic activity. We mustn't fear to adopt the advanced management methods applied in capitalist countries . . . The very essence of socialism is the liberation and development of the productive systems . . . Socialism and market economy are not incompatible . . . We should be concerned about right-wing deviations, but most of all, we must be concerned about left-wing deviations.[46]

What distinguishes China's successes and challenges from other frontiers of capital is that, in post-Mao China, Deng had both the space and the resources to get a strong hold on the liberalisation of the economy, which was simply not feasible in Russia or in the former satellite states. Russia and Ukraine got oligarchs, while, as it turned out, Poland and Hungry got illiberal democracy and weak, ineffective regulation. By contrast, China's banking industry has remained firmly under the control of the Party machinery. As a result, there is no one single power layer in the cake that does not have to answer to the top-level bureaucrats on the Central Committee.

At a 2016 event for major party leaders and executives from big state-owned companies, President Xi Jinping reminded industry leaders that the Chinese Communist Party had the ultimate say over state companies and their vast financial assets. For Xi, loyalty to Party leadership and building the role of the party are the number one

[46]John Gittings, *The Changing Face of China: From Mao to Market* (Oxford University Press, 2005).

priorities for state-owned enterprises. The Party's leadership in state-owned enterprises remains the peak organisational actor in China's governance landscape.[47]

CHINA'S FINANCIAL SAFETY NETS

If the New Silk Road is to succeed, the most important feature of China's financial system is that all six layers move in sync, as difficult a goal as this is. So far, the 300 largest state-owned enterprises in key sectors have played a key role on the ground; their vast resources make them a parallel system of state finance, building, financing and maintaining all kinds of infrastructure. At this point, it is difficult to have a clear and definitive risk assessment as to the viability of all the OBOR projects.[48] In interviews in 2017, we were told that there is a dual process of risk assessment, one made by the bank in question, and one by the Party and the government. Even when a banking economist may not find a project financially sound, government authorities may tell the banks to fund certain projects, which the banks automatically do. They may not expect to make any money on the investment, but all loans are guaranteed by municipal authorities or city authorities. When China's banks invest in infrastructure such as railways, hydroelectric dams, water purification plants and highways, in theory they are shielded against losses by Chinese institutions.[49]

With these financial safety nets in place, Chinese companies have had some notable successes. For example, they have rescued the port of Piraeus in Greece from bankruptcy and have begun to modernise its facilities with new money. But they have also had some notable failures, such as the construction of Poland's A2 highway by the Chinese Overseas Engineering (COVEC) Group. The project,

[47]Emily Feng, 'Xi Jinping Reminds China's State Companies of Who's the Boss', *New York Times*, 14 October, 2016.

[48]David Dollar, 'China's Investment in Latin America', *Brookings Institute*, January 2017 https://www.brookings.edu/research/chinas-investment-in-latin-america [Accessed October 2018]

[49]Authors' interview with bank official, September 2017.

which was supposed to show Europeans the efficiency of Chinese construction companies, turned into a debacle.[50]

If infrastructure is the critical engine of growth in developing economies, then debt financing is the fuel for that engine. Public borrowing to support productive investment is central to the development narratives of today's wealthy advanced economies, and it continues to drive growth in emerging economies. However, there is also considerable evidence indicating significant negative impacts on countries and their people when governments incur too much debt.[51] When government borrowing is not accompanied by enough economic growth and revenue generation to fully service the debt, it can generate a downward spiral that inevitably ends in the need for debt restructuring and possibly the need to put the project on hold or cancel it outright.[52]

On this question of debt borrowing and risk-protection requirements, such as those performed in Poland, many Western China experts are highly critical of the OBOR investment processes. The *Oxford Review of Economic Policy* recently published a report challenging the notion that infrastructure necessarily creates economic value and that China has a distinct advantage in its delivery.[53] Far from being an engine of economic growth, the OBOR

---

[50]In the *Financial Times* article 'China Group Sees Collapse of Poland Ambitions' (14 June, 2011), Jan Cienski points out that, in 2009, COVEC submitted a price bid that was less than half of the planned budget, based upon expected savings from the use of imported equipment and their own financing. The idea of importing construction equipment and building materials was a mistake: China is too far away and its machines are not certified for use in the European Union. Moreover, the Chinese parent corporation did not supply funding as planned and COVEC was forced to look for credit financing. Worse still, the Chinese had not factored in the impact of rising fuel prices, which increased costs by 20 per cent. In 2011, the Chinese company tried to renegotiate the contract, and, failing to do so, left the project unfinished.

[51]John Hurley, Scott Morris and Gailyn Portelance, *Examining the Debt Implications of the Belt and Road Initiative from a Policy Perspective*, CGD Policy Paper 121 (Center for Global Development, March 2018) https://www.cgdev.org/sites/default/files/examining-debt-implications-belt-and-road-initiative-policy-perspective.pdf [Accessed October 2018]

[52]Sadia Shabbir and Hafiz Yasin, 'Implications of Public External Debt for Social Spending: A Case Study of Selected Asian Developing Countries', *Lahore Journal of Economics*, 1 (2015).

[53]Atif Ansar, Bent Flyvbjerg, Alexander Budzier and Daniel Lunn, 'Does Infrastructure Investment Lead to Economic Growth or Economic Fragility? Evidence from China', *Oxford Review of Economic Policy* 32 (2016), pp. 360–390.

infrastructure investments will, they argue, fail to deliver a positive risk-adjusted return:

> Investing in unproductive projects results initially in a boom, as long as construction is ongoing, followed by a bust, when forecasted benefits fail to materialise and projects therefore become a drag on the economy. Where investments are debt-financed, overinvesting in unproductive projects results in the build-up of debt, monetary expansion, instability in financial markets, and economic fragility, exactly as we see in China today. We conclude that poorly managed infrastructure investments are a main explanation of surfacing economic and financial problems in China.[54]

So far there has been no systemic debt crisis among China's club of nations and they are meeting their financial obligations or renegotiating debt relief with Beijing. So these kinds of debt models are too mechanistic and provide no way to look at public policy outside the black box of narrow 'return-on-investment' criteria. The main reason they are in trouble is that many of its partners are struggling to pay back their previous loans. They are faced with the global drop in commodity prices, lower export earnings and slower growth, all of which is largely outside their control pushing their economies into long-term debt traps.

DEBT DISTRESS, A MAJOR CHALLENGE

In a recent report, the Washington-based Center for Global Development looked at 68 states that have agreements with China and found major debt problems in at least eight.[55] One problem is that the availability of easy money can lure politicians to sign up for expensive projects that generate little economic activity. The more pressing issue according to Christine Lagarde, the Managing Director

---

[54]Ansar, Flyvbjerg, Budzier and Lunn, op. cit.
[55]Federico Sturzenegger and Jeromin Zettelmeyer, *Debt Defaults and Lessons from a Decade of Crises* (MIT Press, 2006).

of the IMF, is that 'in countries where public debt is already high, careful management of financing terms is critical'.[56]

China is contributing to an IMF initiative to train officials in the recently created IMF-China Training Centre. The newly established international development cooperation agency will be responsible for BRI decision-making and China's foreign aid. These backstops will meet some of the criticism levelled against China's lack of transparency in public tendering.

Transparency is a very slippery concept. Many Western political elites look the other way and support large development programmes for authoritarian leaders such as Abdel Fattah el-Sisi, King Salman bin Abdulaziz Al Saud, Robert Mugabe and so on. It is hard to point to many examples where Washington or London cancelled a programme because transparency norms were ignored or violated.

For the Global South the world looks very different from Nairobi or Phnom Penh. African delegates at a recent IMF conference were critical of the stringent IMF conditions on debt management. 'When you talk about debt sustainability, that also means low growth. It's about finding the right balance,' one African official stated.[57] For example, the Chinese government has demonstrated a willingness to provide additional credit so a borrower can avoid default in an ad hoc, case-by-case manner. To this end, Beijing's leaders have agreed to write off the debt for diverse partners along the road including Tajikistan, Burundi, Afghanistan, Guinea, Mongolia, Sri Lanka and others through an approach to debt relief that is likely to continue in the absence of full membership of the Paris Club or commitments to some reformed multilateral framework.[58]

For many Western economists, a first-order question for debt sustainability along the OBOR is whether the borrower meets the

[56]Charles Clover, 'IMF's Lagarde warns China on Belt and Road debt', *Financial Times*, 12 April, 2018.
[57]Ibid.
[58]The examples cited have been compiled by the Center for Global Development, which drew primarily on press reports and IMF programme documents because China does not officially disclose information on the details of any bilateral debt agreements.

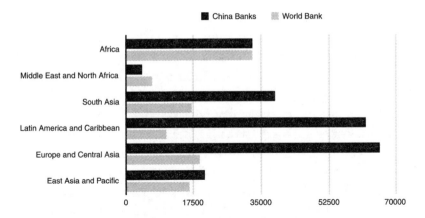

FIGURE 3.4 China and the World Bank: Deep Pockets Compared

Source: Gallagher et al., 'Energising development finance? The benefits and risks of China's development finance in the global energy sector', Energy Policy 122 (2018) pp. 313–321.

tests of transparency, procurement standards and concessionality. These tests are meant to demonstrate the degree to which the One Belt, One Road initiative will be multilateral in character, with a high degree of Chinese government influence, or an initiative that is overwhelmingly directed, financed and operated by the Chinese government outside the purview of World Bank and IMF norms and standards. China's bilateral lending practices have become more important sources of investment since the Belt and Road initiative was established in 2013.

As we can see from Figure 3.4, Chinese banks provided more than two times the amount of energy financing than the World Bank did during the period from 2005 to 2017, and provided more finance to each region of the world except for in the Middle East. When comparing Chinese energy finance for foreign governments with the regional multilateral development banks, CDB and CHEXIM provide more energy finance to Asia as a whole than does the Asian Development Bank (ADB) ($106.3 billion versus $57 billion), more energy finance to Latin America and the Caribbean than does the Inter-American Development Bank (IADB) ($56.2 billion versus $11.6 billion) and more finance to Africa than does the African Development Bank (AfDB) ($26.3 billion versus $14.9 billion).

Kevin Gallagher and Junda Jin of the Global Development Policy Center point out that those nations currently participating in the OBOR have received 55.9 per cent of total energy financing from China's two global policy banks.[59] These banks, China Development Bank (CBD) and the Export-Import Bank of China (CHEXIM), currently hold more assets than the combined assets of all the Western-backed MDBs.[60] CHEXIM and the CBD have more than $2.5 trillion in assets, whereas the Western-backed banks hold just about $1.4 trillion.

Through an open policy of providing non-concessional and concessional finance in virtually every corner of the world, the CDB has amassed more than $2 trillion in assets (with roughly $37 billion overseas), while CHEXIM holds $480 billion in assets, which supports China's overseas development finance. As Figure 3.5 highlights, in just over a decade, China has more than doubled the amount of development finance in the world economy.[61] In this regard, CDB and CHEXIM are truly global development banks, providing finance to all corners of the world in a manner that surpasses the World Bank.

What is masked in the 2017 data is that there has been an *increase* in the dollar amount of loans in the power sector, which almost tripled relative to 2016 and exceeds the 2013–2016 average.[62] China's enthusiasm for new investments in the energy sector can be read as either recklessness on its part, or evidence of its confidence that debt sustainability is not going to be its number one problem. On empirical grounds, debt distress is still a constant worry for the Chinese and has pushed Beijing to develop ways to address systemic debt problems as they arise. This will be done, as it has been, on

[59]Junda Jin and Kevin P. Gallagher, 'Slowing Down, Powering Up: 2017 Chinese Energy Development Finance', *GEGI Policy Brief* 005 (March 2018), pp. 1–5 https://www.bu.edu/gdp/files/2018/03/03.2018_China.Global.Energy.Database_-Jin.Gallagher-1.pdf
[60]Gallagher et al, op. cit.
[61]Gallagher et al, op. cit.
[62]'Developing Countries Lead the Way for Global Economic Governance', *Global Development Policy Center*, 9 October, 2017 https://www.bu.edu/gdp/2017/10/09/new-policy-briefs-developing-countries-lead-the-way-for-global-economic-governance/ [Accessed October 2018]

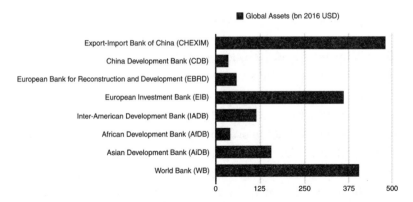

FIGURE 3.5 Bigger than Big: China's Leading Development Banks in Global Context

Source: Gallagher et al., 'Energising development finance? The benefits and risks of China's development finance in the global energy sector', Energy Policy 122 (2018) pp. 313–321.

an ad hoc basis. Ethiopia, Kenya, Malaysia and Pakistan are forcing Beijing to pull back and rethink its approach to investment in Africa and Asia.

In September 2018, China's president criticised what he called 'vanity projects', investments that were poorly conceived and did not address verifiable economic bottlenecks. There is a lot that can go wrong, including local officials accepting bribes in a Kenyan railroad ticket scam to projects that are poorly conceived and do not engage the basic interests of the relevant countries. China is losing money for a variety of reasons, including a foreign exchange crisis in Ethiopia, making it impossible for the government to maintain the repayment of its debts to Chinese state creditors. In this case, Ethiopia's prime minister negotiated easier terms for its $4 billion of railway loans.[63] Even when the results are lacklustre and disappointing, the reality on the ground is that Beijing's big projects have the ability to link markets, raise productivity and spur industrialisation that China's big banks are ready to finance.[64]

[63]David Pilling and Emily Feng, 'Chinese investments in Africa go off the rails', Financial Times, December 5, 2018 https://www.ft.com/content/82e77d8a-e716-11e8-8a85-04b8afea6ea3
[64]Ibid.

WHEN THE ECONOMY EXCEEDS EXPECTATIONS

The degree to which banks occupy the commanding heights of China's modern economy is unprecedented. They are at the pinnacle of the administrative and party hierarchy. Globally, its Belt and Road Initiative is turning up the dial of export-market integration through these bilateral partnerships to integrate China more tightly into the global multilateral trading order.

Where BRI sees itself as instrumental is in realigning the domestic priorities of the China club of nations with diverse, regional, 'opening up' strategies and its core interests. There is nothing hidden in China's goals and its metanarrative is accessible to anyone who cares to be informed. One consequence of so much scrutiny is that it increases the pressure on Chinese elites to reduce non-tariff barriers, including many of its licensing requirements, complex regulations and product quotas for its bilateral partners. (These same contentious issues could also become bargaining chips in the China-US global trade wars.) Chinese industries, such as steel and heavy equipment manufacturers, would also benefit by supplying most of the projects with Chinese-sourced capital goods. The strategic idea is that increased interconnectedness and exchange between China and its partners will be vital to develop closer ties and to tackle the vexing issues of looming slower growth internationally and structural stagnation for many nations left behind by modern technology and badly in need of a capital fix.

The critical point is that the Chinese have a well-articulated, long-term vision for redirecting globalisation driven by their gigantic globally oriented banks with unparalleled resources at their command. As many of the BRI projects are designed for the long term and not for instant market profitability, their viability hinges on whether these investments – in a railway, for example, or a hydroelectricity plant – receive the financial and political support necessary to generate returns over the long run. Other kinds of projects require a lot of post-construction servicing and maintenance, and investment in human capital.

The need for services to be affordable and accessible where the majority are low-income consumers, barely part of a cash economy, will be critical to the long-term viability of the projects, and their ability to improve living standards and lift people out of poverty. In the past, skill acquisition was often poorly funded in showpiece development programmes that showed a bias for status and monumentalism rather than pragmatism and transformative immediacy. Transforming the labour market for employment and significant job creation requires the introduction of disincentives to compete on the short-term advantages of a low-wage economy. Will China's development strategy make a critical difference with such lofty intentions?

Decades of development assistance should drive home the message that 'bricks and mortar' on their own do not have the economic punch needed to support fundamental and uplifting change.[65] Other kinds of small- and large-scale investments can have significant impacts. Clean water for hundreds of communities, 24/7 electricity for an entire country, and young girls being able to go to school with proper sanitation facilities do bring about fundamental change of a different kind to people's lives and communities. The lesson with the policy consequence is that the Global South requires a different sort of infrastructural and institutional makeover – one that is catalytic and which will have powerful legacy effects on the world economy and its structures of global governance. This is the perennial quandary of developmental economics.

So-called infrastructural winners have to be in a position to capture the qualitative value added by structural change, and this usually means the reorientation of the economy over time by building institutions and investing in human capital. What is needed is education, knowledge and skills. Countries that experience deeper benefits must have projects that are community-based and people-centred. They also require infrastructural projects that support creative and productive opportunities and partnerships that were not previously available. Last but not least, governments need infrastructural investment that focuses on modern sustainable or

---

[65] Acemoglu and Robinson, op. cit.

renewable technologies and the green energy needed for planning for a sustainable future with industries to match.

All these bar-raising standards are a tall order by any international measure and progress is often maddeningly slow. As Rodrik et al. explain in a recent paper: 'African countries continue to grapple with the fallout from negative effects of globalisation, job loss and technological change, rising income inequality, unprecedented population aging in richer countries, and youth bulges in the poorer ones.'[66] The only question is whether, over the long haul, Africa will be able to rebound from severe internal structural constraints such as the collapse in commodity prices and corrupt elite practices. In such a volatile global environment, the most important question to answer is whether Beijing's BRI strategic investments are giving many of its partners some badly needed, essential public policy tools that they presently do not have at their disposal. The final chapter returns to look at the macro-conditions that suggest some optimism is in order.

ON THE KNIFE'S EDGE

The big story so far is that Beijing's financial system walks a very fine line between its immense trillion dollar investments in the OBOR and the dangerously high debt levels of China's state-owned banks. In 2018, BOC financial reforms continue to shrink average debt levels in key sectors, including steel, mining, agriculture and food, as well as business services. According to Moody's analysts, Beijing's reform programme is curbing debt growth, a sign of China's regulatory resiliency at a time paradoxically of both stimulus spending and economic tightening.[67] Energy and property firms, two sectors with very high debt levels, are by no means out of the woods and their debt levels are expected to remain high for

[66]Xinshen Diao, Margaret McMillan and Dani Rodrik, 'The Recent Growth Boom in Developing Economies: A Structural Change Perspective' (NBER Working Paper No. 23132, National Bureau of Economic Research, 2017).
[67]Henry Sender, 'The hidden risks of China's war on debt', Nikkei Asian Review, 28 February, 2018 https://asia.nikkei.com/Features/Cover-story/The-hidden-risks-of-China-s-war-on-debt

quite some time. China has a long way to go before it reduces the bad debts on many of its SOEs' books.

A striking example of why China's financial system is so difficult to read accurately is that the most powerful Chinese regulators at the top of the hierarchy have many ways to put out fires rapidly. Beijing's immediate cash injection of $74 billion into its banking system in July 2018 is indeed a sign that China's shock absorbers have the flex to mitigate long-term financial risks. As Gabriel Wildau and James Kynge of the *Financial Times* point out, this injection was the largest ever by the People's Bank of China and used its so-called Medium-Term Lending Facility.[68] Moreover, the PBOC also guided interest rates lower through so-called fiscal deposits, government cash that accumulates at the central bank before being periodically auctioned off to commercial banks, increasing liquidity in the financial system.

This policy tool was created in 2014 to provide loans to commercial banks for three to 12 months. Such a provision for extra liquidity demonstrates that Beijing's banks are moving to sustain growth as a slowdown in housing and infrastructure adds to pressure from the escalating US trade war. China's economy grew at 6.7 per cent in the second quarter in 2018, official data showed, its slowest pace since 2016.[69] By contrast, the slowing of economic growth has not negatively affected the financing for the China club of nations. No 'A list' investments have been cancelled in 2018. China's elites have ambitious plans to add new members and fund many more big-picture infrastructural projects for at least two more decades.

In this sense, Beijing is on the knife's edge, trying to walk a tightrope between staying the course on deleveraging bad debts (to address long-term financial risks) and supporting short-term growth (to appease Party members and the larger population). In a 2018 speech to senior bank executives, Guo Shuqing, PBOC party

[68]'China's $74bn cash injection highlights growth worries', *Financial Times*, 23 July, 2018.
[69]'China GDP growth slips to 6.7% in second quarter', *Financial Times*, 15 July, 2018.

secretary and head banking regulator, urged financial institutions to increase lending to small- and medium-sized enterprises – remarks that were interpreted as a call to balance the need for faster loan growth overall in China, a return to Keynesian stimulus fundamentals.[70]

Nevertheless, Beijing's financial and regulatory reforms are having an impact on troubles in the state-owned financial sector.[71] With the recent entrenchment of the Party's current leadership, the pace of financial reform is likely to accelerate for a very important reason: Beijing has found support from other private sector global banking institutions that will link Asia to Africa and Europe in unprecedented ways.

More shocks and instability could, at some time in the future, prove toxic and precipitate an even larger crisis for maintaining China's trillion-dollar investment in infrastructure at the current levels.

The People's Bank of China and the CBRC have proven themselves to be powerful, slow-footed, effective co-regulators who have earned a reputation for technical professionalism balancing the competing imperatives to spend more domestically and at the same time expand China's global infrastructure footprint. Still, Chinese bureaucracy has been destabilised by paralysing turf wars, where jurisdictional boundaries are unclear and contested by powerful ministries. Faced with growing structural imbalances in the economy and mounting risk-management challenges, China's banks have yet to face their day of reckoning, but may well find themselves again in the near future on the receiving end of a major financial crisis or meltdown.

MACHIAVELLIAN LICENCE OR INSTITUTIONAL RESILIENCE?

So far, China has escaped such a fate. Global markets have been and continue to be on China's side, at least for the time being. But the

---

[70]Shu Zhang and Matthew Miller, 'China to name reformer Guo Shuqing as central bank party chief: Sources', *Reuters*, 25 March, 2018 https://www.reuters.com/article/us-china-banking-pboc/china-to-name-reformer-guo-shuqing-as-central-bank-party-chief-sources-idUSKBN1H105L [Accessed October 2018]
[71]Ibid.

stronger explanation must look to the resiliency of its institutional culture. For instance, the creation of a super regulatory financial commission chaired by a new vice premier in October 2017 after the National Congress is expected to keep SOE indebtedness in check and tackle the explosive issue of bad debt held by Chinese banks.[72] Chinese authorities have clamped down on outflows of money on the part of Chinese investors to make significant acquisitions in the EU, Europe and the UK. The 2017 arrest of the founder of Anbang, one of China's biggest insurance conglomerates, demonstrates Beijing's new-found willingness to curtail big spending as part of a crackdown on high-cost speculative borrowing of foreign acquisitions, which have fuelled concerns about the stability of China's financial system.[73]

Will the robustness of the shock absorbers now in place protect its global infrastructural investments from a trade war, a bout of inflation, massive loan defaults, secular stagnation or currency devaluation? How the Chinese authorities will react is highly unpredictable in each of these scenarios. China's equilibrium point is elusive yet (for the moment at least) sufficiently dynamic, confounding its many critics.

[72]Zhou Xin, 'China's super financial regulator headed by vice-premier more powerful than ministries', *South China Morning Post*, 8 November, 2017 http://www.scmp.com/news/china/economy/article/2119001/chinas-super-financial-regulator-headed-vice-premier-more [Accessed October 2018]

[73]Matthew Miller and Engen Tham, 'China seizes control of Anbang Insurance as chairman prosecuted', Reuters, 22 February, 2018 https://www.reuters.com/article/us-china-anbang-regulation/china-seizes-control-of-anbang-insurance-as-chairman-prosecuted-idUSKCN1G7076

Part II

Beijing's Vaulting Global Ambition

4

Global Image-building:
China's Soft Power Deficit

WHEN CULTURAL FLOWS OUGHT TO MATTER

Why do the Chinese believe that soft power will make others follow its lead and join the OBOR club? This is China's so-called skin in the game, a colloquial expression for China's vested interest in ensuring a positive outcome. At the moment, China is far behind the US in terms of the soft power index and thus it simply cannot challenge US supremacy in the public policy arena. Moreover, it does not have the same global cultural dominance or mass media industries that American power relies upon for global support. English is still the *lingua franca* of a young, transnational class of professional elites, millennials and even social movement actors. Global consumer brands are still largely dominated by American, Japanese and European mass consumption.

Most economists and other experts do not think in any depth about the relationship between China and soft power except to argue that Sino-power is so far behind that of the West that it will not be able to catch up in the near future. China has developed soft power in its own distinct ways, both as a developmental tool and as a form of diplomacy. However, Beijing has no illusions that dynamic change can occur in the economic sphere without major cultural and social consequences. The voluntary giving of aid and the 'unreciprocated giving' have quite different impacts on governments, states and

communities: 'China's net foreign aid has increased from $741 million in 2001 to $3,109 trillion in 2009, to $5,710 trillion in 2012 and to $7,092 trillion in 2013.'[1]

In a primary sense, soft power, like the concept of soft law, is the recognition of voluntary norms and benchmarks without the full legal and institutional authority of the state and courts. It tends to work directly, shaping the cultural and economic policy environment, and can take years to produce the desired outcomes.[2] As a result, the standard view of international relations theorists is that soft power is a more difficult instrument to wield than the traditional show of military force.[3]

Political scientist Joseph Nye coined the much-in-vogue term 'soft power' to describe the processes through which geopolitical actors attempt to shape the preferences of others by means of appealing to shared values and common problem solving.[4] According to Nye, the defining feature of soft power is that it is non-coercive. Its currencies are culture, political values and foreign policies. Soft power can be wielded by all international actors, including NGOs and international institutions, to cultivate a culture that is non-threatening to its neighbours and to political values at home and abroad.

The successful deployment of soft power gives a country's own foreign policy an air of legitimacy. Nye explains that 'a country may obtain the outcomes it wants in world politics because other countries — admiring its values, emulating its example, aspiring to its level of prosperity and openness — want to follow it'.[5] For this strategic reason, Nye particularly emphasises that it is also important to 'set the agenda and attract others in world politics,

[1]Lai-Ha Chan and Pak K. Lee Power, 'Ideas and Institutions: China's Emergent Footprints in Global Governance of Development Aid', working paper, 281/17, University of Warwick, 2017, p. 5.
[2]Joseph S. Nye, *The Future of Power* (Public Affairs, 2011), p. 81.
[3]It is important to point out that soft power can be wielded for wholly nefarious purposes. It is not necessarily any more ethical to twist minds than it is to twist arms. As Nye points out, 'Hitler, Stalin, and Mao all possessed a great deal of soft power in the eyes of their acolytes, but that did not make it good' (ibid., p. 113).
[4]The concept of 'soft power' was first introduced in Nye's work *Bound to Lead: The Changing Nature of American Power* (Basic Books, 1991).
[5]Joseph S. Nye, *Soft Power: The Means to Success in World Politics* (Public Affairs, 2004).

and not only to force them to change by threatening military force or economic sanctions. Such soft power — that is, getting others to want the outcomes that you want — co-opts people rather than coerces them.'[6]

As a concept, it can be difficult to separate the exercise of soft power from hard power. Often soft power masks the strong arm hidden inside the velvet glove. For example, political scientist Janice Bially Mattern argues that former President George W. Bush's use of the phrase 'you are either with us or with the terrorists' was in fact an exercise of hard power.[7] American and economic pressure was used on many reluctant states to join its so-called coalition of the willing, a classic example of the coercive aspects of soft power being used to bring American allies into line.

In her anti-globalisation manifesto entitled *No Logo*, the Canadian social critic Naomi Klein draws on the countercultural thought of the Frankfurt School and Situationists International to explore a more common way that soft power has become an integral part of a mass consumer culture. The hidden persuaders of global advertising and social media have become the dominant influence in people's daily lives – what we buy, what we like, who are our partners.[8] They are so pervasive that new forms and practices have arisen, particularly dangerously volatile identity politics, the rise of populism and the alt-right.

SOFT POWER IN THE CHINESE CONTEXT

While soft power increasingly has many hard edges, it is one of the primary means through which the Chinese leadership has garnered influence with the post-revolutionary independence

---

[6]Ibid.

[7]Janice Bially Mattern, 'Why "Soft Power" isn't so Soft: Representational Force and the Sociolinguistic Construction of Attraction in World Politics', *Millennium: Journal of International Studies* 33 (2005), p. 586.

[8]Naomi Klein, *No Logo* (Random House, 1999); Daniel Drache and Alexandra Samur, *Semiotic Disobedience: Shit-disturbers in an Age of Image Overload* (Robarts Centre for Canadian Studies Counter Publics Working Group, 2006) http://danieldrache.com/publications/semiotic-disobedience-shit-disturbers-in-an-age-of-image-overload/ [Accessed October 2018]

movements in Africa and Asia, which have laid down the gun in return for all kinds of practical and diplomatic support. China does not have Hollywood to spread its message, but it has a long history of supplying massive amounts of material assistance for many of its partners from the Global South – a record that few great powers can equal.

More recently it has run with the message that international cooperation is a potent form of soft power that fits its core interests internationally. In 2011, as Xi Jinping was preparing to take power from General Secretary Hu Jintao, the 17th Central Committee of the Chinese Communist Party devoted a whole plenary session to the issue of culture, with the final communiqué declaring that it was a national goal to 'build our country into a socialist cultural superpower'.[9] Again in 2014, at a Party planning and cultural summit, Xi announced: 'We should increase China's soft power, give a good Chinese narrative, and better communicate China's messages to the world'.[10]

It is a mistake for Westerners to remain entirely sceptical about China's soft power deficit. Contrary to what many Western experts believe, the Chinese leadership has made it a priority to develop soft power in a way that incorporates Nye's thinking to facilitate informal cultural and economic exchange along many Silk Roads. While American and other Western observers fall into the trap of assuming that freedom, civil liberties and democracy are more desired than economic stability, poverty eradication and prosperity, Beijing's soft power influence increases in the regions most devastated by decades of economic exploitation and instability. In countries that have never known democracy and that have been run by authoritarian governments, the democratic process is falsely seen to produce inaction and stalemate. The turn away from liberal

[9]The Economist News Desk, 'China's film industry: The red carpet', *Economist*, 21 December, 2013.
[10]David Shambaugh, 'China's Soft Power Push: The Search for Respect', *Foreign Affairs*, July/August 2015 https://www.foreignaffairs.com/articles/china/2015-06-16/china-s-soft-power-push [Accessed October 2018]

democracy in Poland, Hungry and Turkey offers plenty of support for this dark view of politics by consensus.

Many partners along the OBOR in developing and poorer nations look up to China as a model of political stability coupled with economic growth and prosperity. While larger in scale and ambition than anything China has tried before, the Belt and Road initiative is but the latest and most comprehensive cultural push from Beijing. Since the late 1990s, China has built more than 500 Confucius Institutes around the world to teach the Chinese language and spread Chinese culture, not only in Africa but across other continents as well.[11]

Moreover, China has spent a great deal of money on building soft power through communications, 'investing heavily in its external communication, including broadcasting and on-line presence across the globe.'[12] In 2011, two years after President Jintao announced a $7 billion plan for China to 'go out' into the world, Chinese broadcasting was greatly expanded. China Central Television (CCTV) News' Beijing headquarters dramatically enlarged its bureau of English-fluent foreign journalists to develop a global channel. By 2012, CCTV News was claiming 200 million viewers outside China and broadcasting in six languages, including Arabic. In the same year, CCTV also opened a studio in Nairobi and has plans to increase the size of its overseas staff dramatically.

If soft power is the ability to attract friendly nations into your camp, then China's increasing role as a global economic

---

[11]In 2005, the first Confucius Institute was established in Africa. The institutes are funded by the Chinese government and provide Chinese language and cultural programming to the public. There are 19 institutes today in Africa, and China has planned to spend 20 million renminbi on education projects in South Africa, including the teaching of Mandarin in 50 local high schools. The aim is to make it possible for Africans to live and work in China. In particular, one of the aims of the programme is to provide scholarships to study professional degrees at Chinese universities. It is believed that many Africans at university level are better at learning Mandarin than many Westerners because of the similarity in the phonetic structure of Mandarin and many African languages.

[12]Daya Thussu, *De-Americanizing Soft Power Discourse?* (Figueroa Press, 2014) http://uscpublicdiplomacy.org/sites/uscpublicdiplomacy.org/files/useruploads/u20150/CPDPerspectives2_2014_SoftPower.pdf [Accessed October 2018]

superpower is driving a desire for peripheral economies to link themselves more closely with Beijing. According to a 2014 Global Attitudes survey from the *Pew Research Centre*, China's exercise of soft power receives positive reviews in the poorest sub-Saharan African nations, where many OBOR projects are up and running.[13] Jurisdictions like Burkina Faso, Ethiopia, Ghana, Liberia, Mali and Niger have some of the highest rates of positive views of China's influence, often ranging above 75 per cent.[14] Going further afield, we see the same results in Latin and South American nations. According to data from the Council on Foreign Relations, Chile and Peru held positive views with 66 per cent and 60 per cent of respondents seeing China favourably in 2015, while Argentine and Mexican respondents stood at 53 per cent and 47 per cent, respectively.[15]

XI'S POWER PLAY

It is often ignored that changes in Chinese soft power strategy are also directly linked to political changes in China itself. Since China has globalised to such a degree, the balance between its domestic economy and its role in the world economy today may be indistinguishable and, for all intents and purposes, inseparable. China is the second largest economy in the world, the world's largest exporter (12.76 per cent of world exports in 2017), the second largest importer (10.26 per cent of world imports in 2017), the second largest exporter of capital (12.61 per cent of global outward foreign direct investment in 2016) and holds huge foreign currency reserves

[13]"Chapter 2: China's Image', *Pew Research Center*, 14 July, 2014 http://www.pewglobal.org/2014/07/14/chapter-2-chinas-image
[14]"Global Indicators Database', *Pew Research Center*, 2017 http://www.pewglobal.org/database/indicator/24/survey/17/map/ [Accessed October 2018]; Mogopodi Lekorwe, Anyway Chingwete, Mina Okuru and Romaric Samson, 'China's Growing Presence in Africa Wins Largely Positive Popular Reviews', *Afrobarometer* 6, 122 (2016), pp. 1–31 http://afrobarometer.org/sites/default/files/publications/Dispatches/ab_r6_dispatchno122_perceptions_of_china_in_africa1.pdf [Accessed October 2018]
[15]Eleanor Albert, 'China's Big Bet on Soft Power', *Council on Foreign Affairs*, 9 February, 2018 https://www.cfr.org/backgrounder/chinas-big-bet-soft-power [Accessed October 2018]

($3.14 trillion in 2017).[16] Seen from this perspective, China's soft power packs quite a wallop.

When President Xi Jinping came into office in November 2012, soft power became the primary way to advance China's core interests. Up until that time, China's foreign policy doctrine was one of *tāo guāng yǎng hui*, meaning to hide one's capacities and bide one's time.[17] As Dunford and Liu point out, for the new leadership the primary questions were: how could China constructively and effectively utilise the country's new economic strength and new capabilities; and how could China play a more central role in global development and geopolitics?[18]

However, the consequences of greater neoliberal interdependence and interconnectedness were often negative. In the competitive win-lose context of the economic sphere, the interdependence of globalisation created disruptive asymmetries with losers as well as winners.[19] As political scientist Eric Li writes in *Foreign Policy*, 'the market was never a uniting force—the idea that it could be an all-encompassing mechanism to provide growth, good governance, and societal well-being was an illusion to begin with.'[20] In 2018, Wolfgang Streeck elaborated on this idea, warning that 'soft power globalisation is simply outpacing the capacity of national societies and international organizations to build effective institutions of economic and political governance'. In turn, 'increasing debt, rising inequality, and unstable growth is leading to a general crisis of political-economic governability'.[21]

---

[16]Michael Dunford and Weidong Liu, 'Xi Jinping Thought and Chinese Perspectives on China's Belt and Road Initiative', (Institute of Geographical and Natural Resources Research, Chinese Academy of Sciences, 2018), p. 4.

[17]Zhao Suisheng, 'Chinese Foreign Policy under Hu Jintao: The Struggle between Low-Profile Policy and Diplomatic Activism', *The Hague Journal of Diplomacy* 5(4) (2010), pp. 357–378.

[18]Dunford and Liu, 2018, p. 7.

[19]M. Leonard (ed), *Connectivity Wars: Why Migration, Finance and Trade are the Geo-Economic Battlegrounds of the Future* (European Council of Foreign Relations, 2016).

[20]Eric X. Li, 'The Rise and Fall of Soft Power: Joseph Nye's concept lost relevance, but China could bring it back', *Foreign Policy*, 20 August, 2018 https://foreignpolicy.com/2018/08/20/the-rise-and-fall-of-soft-power/ [Accessed October 2018]

[21]Li, op.cit.

Trade restrictions, restrictive regulations and the freezing of financial assets have fanned the flames of conflict and disagreement in gridlocked institutions, while social media, with its hundreds of millions of users, became a force for political interference and political destabilisation for the global elites. For the past two decades, soft power, compounded by the Internet and social media, at first seemed to be a driving force for a more open society.

THE AMBIGUOUS ROLE OF SOCIAL MEDIA IN THE INFORMATION ECONOMY

When Facebook and Google spread like the wild fire of revolution during the Arab Spring of 2011 and Ukrainian Revolts of 2014, these social technologies were cheered on for their transparent, democratising potentials.[22] A mere two years later however, Russia utilised these same tools in conjunction with mainstream media to manipulate American voters during the 2016 US Presidential Election. This speaks to the inherent ambiguity of such technologies in the ways they can be easily reappropriated by governments and multinationals to serve explicitly undemocratic ends.[23]

In response to sites like Facebook pretending they are not publishers and therefore have no responsibility for what is on their sites, calls for censorship of parts of the Internet are heard routinely in the media and in legislative chambers. Internet giants are now under tremendous political and social pressure from Western politicians and the Western public to better regulate their content. And many, including Facebook, YouTube and Apple, are reluctantly beginning to do so. For the first time since the 2008 global financial crisis, states are concerned about reinforcing national oversight in cyberspace, a major shift in mentality after years of weakening the regulatory capacity of the state.[24]

[22]Eric X. Li, 'The Rise and Fall of Soft Power' *Foreign Policy*, 20 August, 2018 https://foreignpolicy.com/2018/08/20/the-rise-and-fall-of-soft-power/ [Accessed October 2018]
[23]Craig Timberg, 'Russia used mainstream media to manipulate American voters', *Washington Post*, 15 February, 2018.
[24]Harold James, 'Deglobalization as a Global Challenge', *CIGI Papers*, 135 (June 2017).

In his recent book *Has the West Lost It?*, Kishore Mahbubani, a Singaporean academic and former diplomat, highlights what he calls American 'hubris' around soft power.[25] This hubris led to the illusion that the norms of soft power and Western liberalism were somehow irrevocably entangled. As Eric Li concludes, however, the ways in which China has become a key player in soft power serves as a reminder that soft power is actually fragile and contingent.[26]

For Nye, soft power and the values of liberalism are interchangeable. This assumption is based on the notion that soft power is, and will always be, synonymous with liberal values of openness, accountability and democratic institutions. However, places like Iraq, Afghanistan and even China did not become liberal democracies when their economies were globalised. In short, while the West linked soft power and liberalism, that coupling was never guaranteed. As the Western share of the global population and of global power recedes, the West, Mahbubani argues, should recognise its changing status by seeking to influence and collaborate as opposed to coerce and dominate.[27]

IS CHINA WINNING THE SOFT POWER RACE?

As we move into what is being called the Asian century, soft power has lost none of its lustre, however complex it is to exercise effectively. China has shocked many international experts in its ability to rethink its role internationally. A recent report from the Berlin-based Mercator Institute of China Studies found that China's increased involvement in conflict mediation between members of its grand coalition has produced some positive results.[28] The study looked at nine conflicts in 2007, compared to only three in 2012, and

---

[25]Kishore Mahbubani, *Has the West Lost It? A Provocation* (Penguin, 2018).
[26]Eric X. Li, op. cit.
[27]Kishore Mahbubani, *Has the West Lost It? A Provocation* (Penguin 2018).
[28]Sarah Zheng, 'Belt and Road Initiative drives China's growing mediation role in world conflicts but peace elusive', *China South Morning Post*, 23 August, 2018 https://www.scmp.com/news/china/diplomacy-defence/article/2161019/belt-and-road-initiative-drives-chinas-growing [Accessed October 2018]

demonstrated that China is using soft power as its global influence spreads.[29] The Mercator Institute showed that China was better at preserving the status quo through 'short term management' fixes rather than more demanding kinds of resolutions. Should we draw the obvious conclusion that, when it is in its interests to do so, China can be flexible and nuanced as a mediator, having mastered the art of influence-building?

By not forcing others into its own mould, Xi's proposition is presented to the world as more accommodating of difference. In a recent speech, he focused on the global imbalances threatening the international order, or what he refers to as the 'three major deficits' that China's wielding of soft power aims to overcome:[30]

- 'A deficit in peace', which is high on China's agenda, like every other superpower, as conflict, terrorism and the threat of nuclear deployment generate massive flows of refugees and migrants as well as environmental degradation;
- 'A deficit in development', the signature policy and rationale of OBOR because many parts of the world remain mired in poverty. China's leader particularly emphasises that the world is divided by chasm-sized social inequalities; and
- 'A deficit in governance' has become a priority since many global multilateral institutions do not sufficiently recognise the need for a larger role for emerging powers. The pillar of world order has failed to adequately address many global issues such as climate change, poverty and human security.

In numerous ways, the soft power aura surrounding China's OBOR ambitions emerged as a response to the three deficits. The

---

[29]Thomas S. Eder, 'Mapping the Belt and Road initiative: This is where we stand', *Merics: Mercator Institute for China Studies*, 7 June, 2018 https://www.merics.org/en/bri-tracker/mapping-the-belt-and-road-initiative [Accessed October 2018]

[30]Xi Jinping, *Important Speeches at the Belt and Road Forum for International Cooperation* (Foreign Languages Press, 2017).

official line from Beijing is that the OBOR seeks to promote a more open and inclusive model of development and a new system of international relations and global governance.[31] Of course, many China sceptics reject this idea outright. They need to think again. At the centre of this proposed new order is a quest for the familiar goals of economic cooperation and common development achieved through the advancement of connectivity across Asia, Africa and Europe.

Some of what China is proposing is a dramatically reformed, up-to-date model of multilateralism: a reform-minded global neoliberalism with a strong developmental flavour. In this regard, Chinese foreign policymakers are operating with the benchmark assumption that close economic ties will build close political ones. We should think long and hard about this idea – and for this reason, we need to know how China itself stacks up on the Portland Communications soft power index (see Figure 4.1).

THE PORTLAND SOFT POWER INDEX OF CHINA'S AMBITION

The Portland Communications soft power index, which extends Joseph Nye's original idea, compares the relative strength of the soft power resources of a select group of nations by assessing six primary characteristics.[32] In 2018, the top-ranked were the UK in first place, followed by France, Germany, the US and Japan. China ranked 27, just behind the Russian Federation. The index relies on objective metrics as well as international public polling to determine ranking. China scores highest in diplomatic engagement, education, digital capacity and enterprise environment. By contrast, it scores weakest in the area of culture and government.

---

[31]Dunford, Liu and Gao, 2018.
[32]"The Soft Power 30 Ranking', *Portland Communications*, USC Center on Public Diplomacy http://softpower30.portland-communications.com [Accessed October 2018]; interestingly, the rule of law is subsumed within the category of government.

Soft Power Tactics	Description
Engagement	The strength of a country's diplomatic network and its contribution to global development
Culture	The global reach and appeal of a nation's cultural outputs – pop culture and high culture
Government	Commitment to freedom, human rights and democracy, and quality of political institutions
Education	The level of human capital, contribution to scholarships, attractiveness to international students
Digital	A country's digital infrastructure and its capabilities in digital diplomacy, accessibility, as well as free and open social media networks
Enterprise	Attractiveness of a country's economic model, degree of business friendliness and capacity for innovation

FIGURE 4.1 Portland Soft Power Index

Source: Adapted from Portland Communications, 'The Soft Power 30 Ranking', http://softpower30.portland-communications.com.

China has one of the largest overseas populations.[33] The Chinese diaspora is a source of international cheerleaders and critics.[34] Nonetheless, China is building public infrastructure for a modern economy in emerging markets seeking rapid economic growth.[35] To this end, the OBOR initiative is perhaps the most ambitious soft power deployment in history. Despite its democratic deficit and concentration of power in the Party, the question worth exploring is whether these soft Chinese values, ideas and strategies can

[33]Joshua Kurlantzick, 'China's Charm: Implications of Chinese Soft Power', *Carnegie Endowment Policy Brief* 47 (June 2006), pp. 1–7 http://carnegieendowment.org/files/PB_47_FINAL.pdf [Accessed October 2018]

[34]It must also be noted that the rise of China's soft power is coupled with the increasingly convincing argument that American soft power is declining, particularly in East Asia, where, for example, China's enrolment of foreign students has risen, whereas the United States' international student enrolment has declined. In addition, the Trump administration's public disavowal of multilateral institutions has damaged the moral legitimacy of the US abroad, and the failures of neoliberal economics, linked to Washington, in regions such as Latin America have also rebounded against the United States. Using the OBOR initiative as a platform of shared interest, China has moved to reach out to and establish friendly commercial and cultural relations with a number of countries that no longer have strong ties with the US, such as Cambodia and Sudan.

[35]Shaun Breslin, 'The Soft Notion of China's "Soft Power"', *Chatham House* (Asia Programme Paper: ASP PP 2011/03), pp. 1–18 https://www.chathamhouse.org/sites/files/chathamhouse/public/Research/Asia/0211pp_breslin.pdf [Accessed October 2018]

spread, develop and be maintained over the long term. Regardless of what Westerners may think, the OBOR investment in human capital is an integral part of many of these projects. It blunts the stereotypical view that China is interested in economic results only. In fact, China's investments in education, health, sanitation, water and electricity are also investments in human capital and increased quality of life.

Many Chinese experts are less enthralled about the domestic consequences of the OBOR initiative. Internally, there are many questions about whether Chinese stakeholders have the patience to wait for the long-term returns from the OBOR project. If this is the case, the soft power bonus that China is hoping to reap may turn out to be a fleeting chimera. So, what are the Chinese elites planning? How are they intending to develop soft power as a strategic asset?

THE SOFT POWER TO IMAGINE NEW GEOGRAPHIES

China does not have the soft power of its own Hollywood to win millions of passionate, loyal Western consumers to its brands. No country can come close to rivalling the cultural industries, global brands and founding myths of the United States. Along the Silk Road, many languages are spoken and the lingua franca is not Mandarin. At key moments, China has used public policy to bolster its influence through leading by example. According to Joshua Kurlantzick of the Carnegie Endowment for International Peace, the year 1997 was particularly important because Beijing refused to devalue its currency during the financial crisis, a decision that required standing up for Asian markets in the face of Western currency fluctuations.[36] After the crisis, the Association of Southeast Asian Nations (ASEAN) Secretary General Rodolfo Severino announced that 'China is really emerging from this smelling good'.[37]

---

[36]Joshua Kurlantzick, op. cit.
[37]Zhiqun Zhu, 'China's New Diplomacy towards Southeast Asia: Motivations, Strategies and Implications', *International Journal of Global Development and Peace* https://scholarworks. bridgeport.edu/xmlui/bitstream/handle/123456789/268/ub_TheInternationalCollege_ TheJournalofGlobalDevelopmentandPeace27.pdf?sequence=2 [Accessed October 2018]

With Southeast Asian opinions of Washington strained and highly volatile, a window has opened to reveal Chinese soft power to the modern world. China has its own unique approach to soft power. It is more pragmatic than universal, and, like many great ascendant powers, it may also abandon the road of soft power for hardball unilateralism. But, for the moment, China's charm offensive has shown itself to be flexible and attuned to Southeast Asian political realities. Living under China's great power shadow, however, will always pose many questions for Vietnam, Laos, Cambodia, Myanmar and Malaysia. Structural inequalities between countries always produce resentment that comes with the geography.

It is perfectly logical that China's partners look at soft power through a very different lens. It is obvious that building a dam, a hydroelectric power station or a water purification plant will have many positive impacts for local residents and communities. But there is the larger question of whether recipients believe that the Chinese strategy is to reject the win-lose binary behind such unequal power relations. The best-case scenario is that China is working to take this mutually advantageous strategy much further in order to develop powerful geopolitical alliances regionally. In practical terms, China is trying to leverage infrastructural aid as a soft-power tool that builds relationships not only with the leaders, but with the farmers, workers and students transnationally as well.[38]

While China has had a lot of success in its public diplomacy by way of building long-term relationships along the length and breadth of the OBOR initiative, this process of relationship-building is much more complex than such ad hoc agreements demonstrate. When the ancient Silk Road was China's artery to the world, China formed dozens of alliances with its neighbours. It is now forgotten by Westerners that China was a master of alliance-building. It is a stretch to think that there is a close historical parallel with the ancient Silk Road, but it does offer many challenging insights into the collective construction of shared cultural and commercial imaginaries in the present.

[38]Joshua Kurlantzick, op. cit.

THE OLD AND NEW SILK ROAD COMPARED:
DOES IT MATTER?

According to Chinese scholarship, it is often overlooked that the ancient Silk Road was never a centralised collective project of the Middle Kingdom.[39] As Khodadad Rezakhani points out, it was never a single, unified and identifiable road, but a series of trade routes loosely connecting together various regions.[40] In this sense, there were many roads that connected Persia, India, Turkey, China, Afghanistan and Syria. The name of the Silk Road itself was invented by European explorers hundreds of years after the fact. Few remember that the 19th-century German geographer Ferdinand von Richthofen was responsible for coining the term *Seidenstraße* (Silk Roads) in 1877. But every schoolchild recalls Marco Polo's legendary two-decade-long travels on the Silk Road for silk, spices and China's much sought-after porcelain.[41]

Most importantly, no Chinese emperor ever conceived of the Silk Road as a large-scale economic project meant to catapult China to the centre of global trade.[42] Rather, the ancient Silk Road was an ad hoc route, not well travelled, precarious for commerce, and badly maintained by different political, military, cultural, religious and economic state strategies. Some argue that its main purpose was not so much commercial as diplomatic, and that Chinese envoys sent by the emperor would not even have visited the most important 'trading stations' on the so-called Silk Road.[43] There are so many

[39]The English translation of 'Zhongguo' as the 'Middle Kingdom' appeared via the Portuguese in the 16th century. It became popular in the mid-19th century. Some Western writers use the translation 'central kingdom' to imply that China has a deeply rooted, self-centred psychology as the centre of the universe. In *Chinese History: A Manual* (Harvard University Press, 2000), Endymion Wilkinson points out that the Chinese were not unique in thinking of their country as central, although China was the only culture to use the concept for their name. See also: Peter Frankopan, *Silk Roads* (Bloomsbury, 2016).
[40]Khodadad Rezakhani, 'The Road that Never was: The Silk Road and Trans-Eurasian Exchange', *Comparative Studies of South Asia, Africa and the Middle East* 30 (2010), p. 422.
[41]Marco Polo, *The Travels of Marco Polo*, trans. Manuel Komroff (W.W. Norton & Company, 2002).
[42]Ye Zicheng, *Inside China's Grand Strategy: The Perspective from the People's Republic* (University Press of Kentucky, 2011), p. 74.
[43]Khodadad Rezakhani, 'The Road that Never was: The Silk Road and Trans-Eurasian Exchange', *Comparative Studies of South Asia, Africa and the Middle East* 30 (2010), p. 422.

curious pieces of information that are at odds with the mental image that we retain, which is no doubt shaped by Marco Polo's journey and his account.

If the tonnage carried, the number of travellers on it and the monetary value that it generated were all possible to calculate, these indicators would demonstrate that the Silk Road's contribution to China's development has been oversold by generations of Western and Chinese scholars. Caravan commerce was subject to banditry, natural disasters and war. The losses of goods were ruinous for the merchant. It is not possible to give an exact number, but caravan losses could be higher than 60 per cent or even 80 per cent of the value of the goods. Moreover, ordinary people in China had little direct contact with foreign merchants.

Regardless, modern scholarship has established the prominence of the ancient Silk Road as a cultural and economic highway for all kinds of products, persons and ideas. It is celebrated as one of the world's prototypical grand narratives of global commerce, cultural interdependency and exchange. Certainly, the Silk Road is included in historian Ferdinand Braudel's commanding study of the Mediterranean and its system of cultural and economic interchange.[44]

In a more fundamental way, the Silk Road was a unique transcontinental highway of international commerce. Joseph Needham's grand, encyclopaedic study of the history of technology in China also focuses attention on the who, what and why of commodity exchange up and down the length of this monumental trail.[45] China produced tradables, including silk, hides, iron, mirrors, weapons, porcelain, lacquerware, jade, rhubarb, tea, paper, gunpowder, and various medicines and elixirs such as ephedra, Epsom salts and ginseng. Persia sent incense, dates, pistachios, peaches, walnuts, frankincense, myrrh, muslin cloth, wines, glassware, olive oil and silver. Various parts of Asia sold precious and semi-precious stones,

[44]Ferdinand Braudel, *The Mediterranean and the Mediterranean World in the Age of Philip II* (University of California Press, 1995).
[45]Joseph Needham, *Science and Civilization in China*, vol. 3 (Cambridge University Press, 1959).

jadeite, rock crystal and other quartzes, as well as ivory, ornamental woods, spices, horses, flowers, performer-slaves, seashells and pearls.[46]

LUXURY GOODS AND THE INTERPLAY OF CULTURES

From the West, merchants on land routes and Mediterranean ships crewed by people from many regions conveyed wool and linen textiles, carpets, amber, coral, asbestos, bronze, lamps, glass vessels and beads, wine and papyrus, huge quantities of coins and bullion, ambergris, entertainers, exotic animals and, perhaps infamously, opium.[47] It has also been discovered that modern diseases and viruses were other 'dark passengers' on China's artery to the West.[48] Religious ideas also travelled the Silk Road and wandering monks brought Buddhism to China in the second century.

These accounts of the great diversity of traffic on the ancient Silk Road have captured the popular imagination of both Chinese and foreigners in memoirs and travel accounts. They give credence to the fact that China's greatness and contribution to world history placed it at the centre of world civilisation and at its cultural crossroads. A country's political culture is always an essential component of a global image-building exercise, which in the case of China was formed over many millennia.[49] In the popular mind, all the inventions and technological superiority of Chinese civilisation become the legacy effects that reveal a great deal about China's place in the global economy a millennium ago. It is these accomplishments and historical legacies that give China a legitimate claim to what Martin Jacques calls a 'civilisation-state' that predates the modern era,[50] a contentious claim with certain veracity.

[46]Ibid., vol. 1 (1954).
[47]Ibid., vol. 3 (1959).
[48]Cynthia Graber, 'Silk Road Transported Goods—and Disease', *Scientific American*, 29 July, 2016 https://www.scientificamerican.com/podcast/episode/silk-road-transported-goods-and-disease [Accessed October 2018]
[49]Valerie Hansen, *The Silk Road: A New History* (Oxford University Press, 2012).
[50]Martin Jacques, *When China Rules the World: The Rise of the Middle Kingdom and the End of the Western World* (Penguin Books, 2012).

ONE ROAD, MANY DREAMS

For the non-specialist, we need to ask whether China's rise to the centre of global trade via the ancient Silk Road is now repeating itself with the One Belt, One Road initiative. The answer is that in key aspects the parallels are striking but incomplete. The opening of the Beijing-Hangzhou Grand Canal in the fifth century CE, perhaps second only to the building of the Great Wall, represents a history of iconic engineering ingenuity and multiple history-altering infrastructural projects that lets us see more clearly the interplay between periods of domestic stability and a strong, stable, centralised Chinese authority exercising its vast powers with consequences reaching far beyond China's borders.

A BRIEF EXCURSUS ABOUT NATIONAL IDENTITY

Transformative projects such as the Beijing-Hangzhou Grand Canal also had many dimensions other than the narrowly economic. For the first time, the canal fully united the political centres in Central and North China with the economic centres in South China. It led to quantities of silk, porcelain, tea and other goods being transported through the Grand Canal to the two capitals, Chang'an and Luoyang. Pointedly, dramatic improvements in transportation also led to increases in the cultural exchange of various commodities.[51] In this economy, locally produced goods circulated in small quantities. The contrast with the vast transcontinental caravan route made possible the trading of silk as a luxury item over vast areas with many different countries. According to Rezakhani, we need to address where these long-standing ideas about a nation's self-image come from. Why do they survive in the popular imagination over generations and millennia?

Modern historical sociology provides some answers and in *Imagined Communities* historian Benedict Anderson adds much-needed depth to these intriguing questions.[52] In providing the

---

[51]Hansen, op. cit.
[52]Benedict Anderson, *Imagined Communities: Reflections on the Origin and Spread of Nationalism* (Verso Books, 1983).

cultural context to Nye's ideas about soft power, Anderson argues that long-lasting cultural communities form the backbone of the nation at critical times.

Anderson proposes that soft power is a cultural artefact that in the best of circumstances acquires concrete shape through common references in the forms of cultural production, particularly the consumption of music, drama and folk art, and citizen acts of mobilisation of all kinds, from insurgency to mass conscription in armies. For example, Anderson points to the ways in which a codified and standardised language was established through the structural forms of the novel and the newspaper, which revolutionised societies. The result was that they connected people to each other through the shared experience of reading popular news and novels with the spread of literacy and education. Is China now hoping for the same positive outcome along the OBOR by reaching out to its natural constituency of nations?

LEGACY EFFECTS OF IMAGINED GEOGRAPHIES

Anderson's approach tells us something very important. His major contribution to understanding the role of symbols and icons in the formation of political culture is that they are 'capable of being transplanted with varying degrees of self-consciousness, to a great variety of social terrains. [These can] be merged and remerged with a correspondingly wide variety of political and ideological constellations.'[53]

In his ambitious and much-admired study of the history of globalisation as the driving force of human interaction, globalisation scholar Nayan Chanda notes that traders, preachers, adventurers and warriors all acted as agents of cultural dissemination for ideals, practices, goods, artefacts, communities and traditions.[54] The question for us is whether the OBOR initiative can offer its participants all, some or few of these advantages?

---

[53]Ibid., p. 7.
[54]Nayan Chanda, *Bound Together: How Traders, Preachers, Adventurers, and Warriors Shaped Globalization* (Yale University, 2007).

The idea of the special legacy effects created by the long-distance trade between Venice and China continues to gain both followers and critics. It sends the unmistakable message that the OBOR is China's projected destiny in a way that Edward Said might have theorised. Said uses the term 'imagined' not to mean 'false' or 'made-up', but rather 'perceived'. It refers to the perception of space created through images, texts and discourses.[55] It does not take too much effort to understand that this idea of the renewal of the Chinese nation is the hope and aspiration of the current Chinese leadership with their global mega-project.

For Said, imagined geographies have the potential to expand far beyond the spatial and ideological limitations of the fixed borders of the nation state. They are powerfully emotive ideas surrounding community and society, vehicles for spreading shared values of family responsibility, authority and collectivity. Consequently, the more appealing these global cultural flows become, the more easily they can be diffused across cities, nations, continents and even across the world.

It must be interjected that every world power makes a similar kind of claim about its exceptionalism and the universal values of its soft power influence. For example, the United States and France have collectively transformed the singularity and uniqueness of their revolutions into universal truths of individual freedom, rule of law, liberty and equality. It is worth noting that, in contrast, China conceives of the ancient Silk Road as a necessary struggle for collectivity and civilisation, which unfolded over volatile centuries when China was constantly fighting foreign invaders, domestic instability, natural disasters and prolonged wars. Moreover, despite the importance of trade with dozens of empires, Chinese leaders have periodically demonstrated a willingness to withdraw, look inward, disengage from the wider world and revert to isolationism as a safe alternative. For pivotal moments in Chinese history, there was no sanctuary from global capitalism. In this regard, it is important to

[55]Edward Said, *Orientalism* (Pantheon 1978).

remember that neither the ancient Silk Road nor its modern avatar has ever been solely about the narrow economics of trade.[56]

THE DARK PASSENGER OF THE CENTURY OF HUMILIATION

Behind the magnificent silk robes and colourful embroideries, there was another reality. Luxury goods gave way to a debilitating and destructive maritime trade in narcotics.[57] After the first anti-opium edict was promulgated in 1729, 200 chests were imported annually. By 1838, just before the First Opium War, this number had climbed to 40,000 chests.[58] In 1842, at the Treaty of Nanking, Shanghai, along with other cities, was partitioned into ceded zones of British, French and American enclaves. Hong Kong was ceded to the British in the first of what the Chinese would later call 'the unequal treaties' that supported a weak and divided China dominated by the great powers of the 19th and 20th centuries.[59]

Many British banks, such as Mathesons of Jardine, Matheson and Co. and the Hong Kong and Shanghai Banking Corporation (HSBC), made their fortunes in the opium trade, often referred to as the capitalism of misery and soullessness.[60] The Chinese have never forgotten this long period of foreign occupation by both Western powers and Japan between the years 1839 and 1949.[61] Shanghai was occupied and administered by a council largely composed of foreigners – Shanghailanders – and only much later by a few Shanghainese Chinese. It is now all but forgotten in the West that 14 foreign powers benefited directly from the Treaty Ports Rights imposed on the Qing Dynasty. Belgium, Brazil, Denmark, France, Italy, Japan, the Netherlands, Norway, Portugal, Sweden, Spain,

[56]Peter Frankopan, *The Silk Roads: A New History of the World* (Bloomsbury, 2015).
[57]Xinru Lui, *The Silk Road in World History* (Oxford University Press, 2010).
[58]Alan Baumler (ed), *Modern China and Opium: A Reader* (University of Michigan Press, 2001).
[59]Susanna Hoe and Derek Roebuck, *The Taking of Hong Kong: Charles and Clara Elliot in China Waters* (Routledge, 1999), p. 203.
[60]Dong Wang, *China's Unequal Treaties: Narrating National History* (Lexington Books, 2005).
[61]Alison Adcock Kaufman, 'The "Century of Humiliation", Then and Now: Chinese Perceptions of the International Order', *Pacific Focus* 24, no. 1 (2010): pp. 1–33 http://onlinelibrary.wiley.com/doi/10.1111/j.1976-5118.2010.01039.x/abstract [Accessed October 2018]

Switzerland, Great Britain and the United States were powers unto themselves and not subject to Chinese law, only to the laws of their own nation. Foreign merchants were allowed to trade with anyone they wished, particularly in the lucrative opium trade that was the source of so much Western wealth and Chinese misery.[62]

What this meant was that an American, French or British citizen could be tried before their national court housed in the settlement, all justified by the principle of extraterritoriality. The scourge of the opium trade became the dark passenger of the 20th century and this legacy 'to eat bitterness' (*chi ku*) was a primary factor in the rise of the Communist Party, the ensuing revolution for independence and China's international insularity post-1949 from a largely hostile West.

FOUNDING MYTHS, THE ANCIENT SILK ROAD AND NOSTALGIA: IMPOSSIBLE ENTANGLEMENTS

In the ensuing years, modern China rediscovered an important role for the ancient Silk Road, as historian Valerie Hansen points out: '[They] planted their cultures like seeds of exotic species carried to distant lands through a network of routes that became the most famous cultural artery for the exchange of religions, art, languages and new technologies.'[63] Even a rudimentary dirt road such as the ancient Silk Road was a magnet for the political intrigue and power politics of the time.[64]

Not unlike China's current global infrastructural initiative, politics have always been at the forefront of commerce. What remains indisputable is the iconic importance of the ancient Silk Road in the historical metanarrative of modern China. Contemporary historians, however, are much clearer about the latter's modest but significant

---

[62]Paul French, *City of Devils: The Two Men Who Ruled The Underworld Of Old Shanghai* (Picador, 2018).

[63]Hansen, op. cit.

[64]Goods were not exchanged on the Ancient Silk Road in terms of buying and selling. Instead, most (around 80 %) of the goods exchanged along the ancient Silk Road were attributes and gifts; in most cases, they were not exchanged for money, but camaraderie, something that was deemed more important.

accomplishments for China and world history. The final irony is perhaps that, according to claims made by modern historians, 'the Silk Road was one of the least travelled routes in human history and possibly not worth studying if tonnage carried, trade or the number of travellers at any time were the sole measures of a given route's significance'.[65]

Even China's claim to be the world's first producer of silk is now in doubt as recent discoveries of silkworm production well outside China's borders in Transoxiana, Parmirs and Turkestan require us to rethink our nostalgic concept of the ancient Silk Road. But does any of this really matter? Indeed, it does.

China has more than one founding myth. For a billion Chinese today, modern China emerged from independence and revolutionary socialism. Much further back in the collective consciousness, the ancient Silk Road occupies a prominent place that has been actively promoted and reaffirmed in the modern Chinese cultural imagination. Yet, strictly speaking it is not comparable to that of the American founding myth of the transformative, restless, unstoppable North American frontier, the French founding myths of *egalité, fraternité, liberté* from the French Revolution, or the United Kingdom's Lockean-Hobbesian revolution of possessive individualism and constitutional monarchy. Louis Hartz, a distinguished 1960s' Harvard political scientist, was powerfully drawn to the notion that many societies have shared political fragments in which their sociocultural formations continually reproduce politically influential legacies long after their formative moments.[66] Is this not what makes China's global initiative so richly compelling, an initiative with a long historical tail conflating past and present?

[65]Hansen, op. cit.
[66]Louis Hartz, *The Founding of New Societies: Studies in the History of the United States, Latin America, South Africa, Canada, and Australia* (Harcourt Brace Jovanovich, 1964).

5

The Messy Business of Governance

SYNCING THE GLOBAL AND THE LOCAL

The OBOR is not a bloc of nations with a unity of purpose or much of a shared ideology. Even poverty eradication is not their single common agenda. Countries in Latin America and Asia often desperately need sizable foreign exchange reserves as a buffer against international crisis. China's foreign aid is a lifeline Beijing extends without IMF austerity-driven conditionality such as cutbacks to social spending, privatisation of public firms or slashing electricity subsidies. Even its internationalism is not a call to arms, but rather is a product of hard-headed realism.

For definitional purposes, it is enough to list all New Silk Road members – currently there are more than 80, with another 30–40 expected to join in the coming years. At some point it will have enough members to be a mini United Nations of the Global South as it keeps on adding new supporters to the BRI. In 2018, it added Panama and the Dominican Republic to its growing list of Latin American and Caribbean nations, offering the promise of major infrastructural funding.[1] Its structure is more elusive, a consensus without institutions and with no commitment on the part of China or any of its members to come to the aid of a fellow member if attacked.

---

[1]Jorge Heine, 'Chinese inroads in Panama: Transport hubs and BRI in the Americas', *Global Americans*, 26 June, 2018 https://theglobalamericans.org/2018/06/chinese-inroads-in-panama-transport-hubs-and-bri-in-the-americas/ [Accessed October 2018]

Officially, the sales pitch from the Chinese leadership is that they are building, in the often repeated expression, 'a community of common destiny'. Certainly the words have vision and pluck. It is more likely that China's partners give new meaning to the Chinese expression 'same bed, different dreams'. This applies to many of China's partners because they have their own motivation to accept China's investment loans. In the larger scope of things, China is laying the foundation for a Sinocentric order in Asia and beyond. So where do transparency, accountability and responsibility fit in China's grand scheme of things?

To date, China has not publicly proposed an international architecture with an agreed-upon set of rules and common institutions to coordinate its many-sided global initiative. In the absence of a recognised legal umbrella, it plans to rely on the China Development Bank, the Export-Import Bank of China and other policy banks, as well as powerful SOEs working with regulatory authorities to coordinate, finance, service and build the railways, ports, wind farms and industrial parks in its various partner nations.

To recall once again, Beijing supplies the workers (if needed), the financing and management (always) and the material inputs (obligatory) for all the high-speed trains, major infrastructural projects, massive generators for hydroelectric stations and so on. So far, officially, it is keen on the idea of working collaboratively to build parallel global governance institutions for its growing infrastructural coalition alongside the WTO, World Bank, IMF and others, even if this is not immediately realisable. China is cautious, steering clear of confrontation with the globe's multilateral institutions. It is not a usurper of the IMF's mandate – at least, not at the moment – but rather is an active challenger from outside its institutional framework. Its intention is quite clear: China seeks to reduce the influence of the IMF in the domestic affairs of an aid recipient, for the IMF may offer financial assistance during a crisis but it does so with what many regard as punitive conditions.

It comes as no surprise that China's grand coalition does not have a formalised voice in decision-making. At least publicly, Beijing has not provided a mechanism of consultation and cooperation. China sits at the centre of a global switchboard and all communication, coordination and cooperation are routed through its administrative and political structures. OBOR could evolve into some loose-knit economic association. To date, Chinese authorities have shown no interest in forming a new kind of umbrella organisation with a collective voice and member responsibility for limited joint action.

For the time being, the BRI prefers playing the role of a 'pure' bilateralist. A new order of multilateralism could come later, and that would require an original way to balance national interest with the foundational principles of international economic law (including fair process, national treatment and investor protection) without crossing the red line of national sovereignty.

As a general rule, China's infrastructural projects do not have a resident Board of Directors for each project to provide governance oversight. One exception is that projects financed by the AIIB are vetted by an international board of directors reporting to the bank. Importantly, Beijing set up the AIIB to conform loosely to World Bank governance norms by way of an independent board of directors and styled as an embryonic international organisation. However, as Professor Greg T. Chin argues, it still remains to be seen whether these projects actually meet the official transparency norms with respect to public tendering and financial oversight that are normatively associated with international standards and safeguards.[2]

FLEXIBLE BILATERALISM: A CORE PRINCIPLE

In all cases, China's partners are defined by their government-to-government bilateral agreements, and China is not alone in relying

---

[2]Greg T. Chin, 'Asian Infrastructure Investment Bank: Governance Innovation and Prospects', *Global Governance* 22 (2016), pp. 11–25 http://journals.rienner.com/doi/pdf/10.5555/1075-2846-22.1.11?code=lrpi-site [Accessed October 2018]

on bilateralism for a variety of purposes.[3] It is very popular with the US, UK, India, Mexico, the EU, Japan, Australia and South Korea – to cite this widely accepted practice in the area of investment treaties. Hundreds of bilateral investment agreements have been negotiated in the last decade or so.

Cynically, transparency is always 'in the eye of the beholder', and the details of many investment agreements worldwide are not easily accessible. In most cases, they are secret and the final agreement totally out of reach to the general public.[4] Importantly, public intellectuals such as Noam Chomsky, Michael Lewis and Naomi Klein have much to say critically about this relationship between the concentration of power, 'transparency' and the dangers posed by unregulated financial institutions in the global system.[5] It is indeed worrisome for globalists that there are so many critical public intellectuals and activists in the United States who are attacking the multilateral order that has served Western interests so well in the past. A more cunning Washington is trying to create alliances and behaviour that has a messianic impulse to change the order of the world.

China is by no means unique in cloaking its core interests behind a veil of secrecy. The Canada-EU Trade Agreement and ill-fated Trans-Pacific Partnership trade and investment negotiations that covered a multitude of commercial and non-commercial subjects, including the environment, generic drugs, intellectual property rights and food security, were all negotiated in secret, excluding the public interest. There were no adequate public consultations, nor were accountability norms generally respected. Negotiating these global trade agreements

[3]Derek Scissors, *The Double-Edged Sword of China's Global Investment Success* (American Enterprise Institute, 2016).
[4]These investment treaties are available on the Internet, but the dispute resolution proceedings are secret and not accountable to the public.
[5]Others include, but are by no means limited to: Edward Said, *Orientalism* (Pantheon, 1978); Benedict Anderson, *Imagined Communities* (Verso, 1983); Partha Chatterjee, *The Nation and its Fragments* (Princeton University Press, 1993); Ha-Joon Chang, *Kicking Away the Ladder* (Anthem Press, 2002); Dong Wang, *China's Unequal Treaties* (Lexington Books, 2005); Acemoglu and Robinson, op. cit.; Piketty, op. cit.; and Wolfgang Streeck, *How Will Capitalism End?* (Verso, 2016).

have become flashpoints of anger and mobilisation, with large parts of European public opinion hostile or suspicious of investment treaties protecting the rights of multinational corporations (MNCs) in the guise of free trade agreements.[6]

SECRECY, TRADE DEALS AND REALISM

Increasingly, since the 2008 global financial crisis, dozens of governments find themselves on Transparency International's list of states with 'deplorable' practices. It is accepted practice to rely on the secret hearings of the investor state dispute mechanism to resolve a state's conflicts with MNCs about money, contract disputes and due process. A version of this legal ordering mechanism has been incorporated into Chinese law and, unlike in Western practice, the state has an oversight role in the mediation and arbitration proceedings.

Importantly, China has its own system of commercial arbitration, which hears disputes and makes nonbinding awards. For Westerners, the system is very different from commercial arbitration because the state intervenes through the courts in accordance with Chinese legal provisions. Such provisions, enforced by the Party rules and discipline, take into consideration the validity of the arbitration award, the making of arbitration procedures and the enforcement of awards in accordance with local laws and regulations.[7] The difficult issue is to give foreigners legal standing with rights and privileges, and already there have been proposed changes to Chinese commercial law in this direction.

The system is expected to evolve further, and China is likely looking at the need for reforms being proposed as part of an EU-China free trade agreement. Pressure is also being exerted by the World Bank to change many of its regulatory practices

---

[6]Daniel Drache, 'Post Brexit and the Crisis of Trade Multilateralism: Heartbreak or Mess? Ought We Be Worried?' (conference draft, *TLI Think! Paper 84/2017*, 10 December, 2017) https://papers. ssrn.com/sol3/papers.cfm?abstract_id=3046810 [Accessed October 2018]

[7]'Arbitration System of China', *China International Trade Lawyers*, 17 January, 2012 http://www. cn-linked.com/en/view.php?id=237 [Accessed October 2016]

with respect to public contract awards. The obvious areas are at the constitutional level, to strengthen the rule of law, and at the administrative level, to combat corruption and give non-state actors greater voice.

It is unlikely that China would agree to such sweeping changes in its domestic affairs. On the other hand, there could be important practical reforms to its commercial mediation and arbitration measures, which, like in most jurisdictions, require voluntary compliance servicing corporate needs for arbitration and mediation when business deals go bad.[8] Evidentiary rules could be tightened, arbitrators better trained and legal thresholds raised. Foreign ownership restrictions that require a foreign investor to find a Chinese counterpart could be relaxed or abolished. Beijing is actively changing its foreign-ownership rules in the auto industry and Elon Musk is the first to benefit from the change, setting up a factory to manufacture his electric car without a Chinese partner.

China also relies on administrative secrecy as a dominant part of its political culture. Not unlike their Western counterparts in the Middle East and Southeast Asia, Chinese officials often turn a blind eye to corruption and human-rights violations in countries where they have infrastructural projects on the ground. As we emphasise in Chapter 2, narrow ledge contractualism of the law is a highly flexible legal concept that creates a convenient legal shield for Beijing's negotiators. As China becomes more involved in global governance through the multitude of One Belt, One Road projects, it is facing new kinds of formidable challenges. Chinese authorities are already drawn into the domestic cultural, social, political and religious entanglements of their partners. In Kazakhstan, Turkmenistan and Uzbekistan, private security companies are, with China's approval, guarding different sections of the 10,000 km/6210 mile-long gas pipeline and its investments.

---

[8]Lai-Ha Chan and Pak K. Lee, op. cit. p. 8.

In 2018, China launched another round of infrastructural projects. The Boston University Global Policy Development Center has compiled the following list for a two-week period ending 8 May. It makes the point that Beijing's minimalist approach to critical governance practices has not dampened the enthusiasm of China's bilateral partners to join up. What is immediately apparent is that, on paper, all the new projects are individually important and going ahead full steam; China continues to fund big-ticket items, but many cost well under $1 billion. The very least one can say is that the Belt and Road initiative is firing on all cylinders.

GLOBAL DEVELOPMENT POLICY CENTER'S CHINA
GLOBAL ROUND UP
- AIIB approves Papua New Guinea and Kenya as new members, making the total number of OBOR members 86
- AIIB considers financing Lumpur-Singapore High Speed Rail
- Padma Rail Link: Bangladesh Railway (BR) to finally ink deal with CHEXIM Bank
- Indonesia wants to speed up China's high-speed rail project
- Abu Dhabi industrial zone attracts $1 billion FDI from China
- China and UAE move a step closer to opening a 'Belt and Road' exchange
- Turkish minister attends tourism event in China
- Romania to pay $6.12 million in first contribution to Asian Infrastructure Investment Bank
- Czech Republic signs memorandum of understanding with China's CITIC Group
- China-CEE Investment Cooperation Fund II closes after $800 million pours in
- Estonia joins Chinese 'New Silk Road' plan

However, it is also true that there is a political rationale driving China's investment largesse. We can see the geopolitical design of

China's world divided into different zones: neighbouring South Asia, Russia and its former satellites, the Middle East and Africa. Some, such as India and Pakistan, are regional rivals and China's lucrative relationship with the latter will certainly irritate and antagonise the former. Many in China's orbit are liberal democracies, but many others are ruled by authoritarian leaders – 'the sad and the bad' – and all dealmaking is designed to enhance China's diplomatic leverage and undermine a US presence or complicate US military operations. Many 'One Roaders' in China's expanding coalition are small fish politically without vast influence or geopolitical importance. Others, such as Russia, Turkey, India, Vietnam and Indonesia, will never be comfortable depending exclusively on Beijing for aid and development. So, there will always be grey areas in the governance of OBOR, conflicts over which Beijing cannot exercise control or guarantee favourable outcomes.[9]

ALTERNATIVE TO FINANCIAL GLOBALISATION?

Beyond the cluttered details of dealmaking, the Belt and Road Initiative has a much bigger global agenda to pursue. The Chinese leadership is in the middle of a very carefully orchestrated balancing act between the status quo and the gradual reform of the international financial system. China's national development banks, such as the all-important China Development Bank and its Export-Import Bank, have the economic muscle and international scope to transform global financial institutions. This would be a major step towards changing the criteria of private investment in the way that Western banks allocate capital. It would also create new norms and conditions to support the Chinese authorities' priorities for the resurgence in infrastructural spending to promote social inclusiveness and green energy.

The financial demands of its massive infrastructure investment initiative are forcing Beijing to give special attention to developing

[9]Daniel Drache and Les Jacobs (eds), *Grey Zones of Governance: Linking Trade and Human Rights* (UBC Press, 2018).

an alternative system of financial globalisation to shoulder the costs and the risks. While the Chinese authorities have been very circumspect, they are reluctant to openly criticise the World Bank and the IMF. In fact, China would like more cooperation between itself and these global bodies in order to share the risks in financing its massive infrastructural projects. China's long-term goal is, however, to back the creation of a multipolar monetary system with a much larger role for China's policy banks. The main challenge is to ensure that, in the words of Aglietta and Bai, 'such investments are aimed at producing positive externalities for the economy'. These kinds of investments are often high risk and cannot be financed by a framework bounded by market-finance logic.[10]

Under the rules and practices of the Washington Consensus, the US dollar is the reserve currency, and integration is driven by market efficiency and the financialisation of the firm, which results in a focus on optimising shareholder value. In this model, investment banks are at the centre of the system and private capital flows are the linchpin of all asset markets in the world. In the view of the Chinese authorities, China and other developing countries are disadvantaged, particularly when they are forced to accumulate significant reserves in order to avoid large insolvencies and contain the possibility of systemic risk.

One of China's goals is to provide an alternative to integration via infrastructure finance with countries being granted special drawing rights with their choice of multilateral currencies. In the Beijing Consensus, market-driven globalisation would be counterbalanced by global public goods and positive externalities largely financed by development banks such as the AIIB, which can borrow from international bond markets at low cost. Certainly, it can borrow at lower interest rates than from private wealth funds, hedge funds or pension funds. The important idea from Aglietta and Bai is that developing economies would no longer have to

[10]Aglietta and Bai, op. cit., p. 15.

The US-led Washington Consensus + US Dollars as the Central Currency	Integration via Infrastructure Finance + Special Drawing Rights (SDR) with Multilateral Currencies
Key concept: market efficiency	Key concept: systematic resiliency
Financialisation of the firms (emphasis on shareholder value)	Driven by short-term Return on Investment (ROI) of firms and growing importance of public ownership
Globalisation through capital flows linking all asset markets worldwide via arbitrage and speculation	Globalisation through global public goods and externalities; finance structured through long-term investments
Intermediation through financial markets under dominance of investment banks	Intermediation through development banks (national and multilateral)
International Lender of Last Resort (LOLR) through the US federal government's swap network	International LOLR through International Monetary Fund's SDR loans account
Developing countries forced to accumulate USD reserve as self-insurance	State investment funds release savings for productive investing
Major shortcoming: inability to escape the trap of short-term investments and therefore to finance real long-term investments	Major shortcoming: risk of political conflicts in selecting, monitoring and executing investment projects

FIGURE 5.1 Two Models of Financial Globalisation

Source: Adapted from Aglietta and Bai, CPEII, 2016.

rely on the American dollar as the sole reserve currency. Instead, national developmental banks would increasingly play a counter-cyclical role in protecting the Global South against 'external shocks and natural disasters'.[11]

China signed the 2015 Paris Climate Accord, along with 174 states and the EU, committing to reduce its greenhouse gas emissions incrementally. The first evaluation to monitor compliance is set for 2025. China wants to take the lead in global infrastructural development which includes greener policies for its own needs and population. In West Africa, for example, China's appetite for exploiting the world's fisheries now collides with Senegal's need to protect its fishing grounds from China's massive offshore fishing fleet subsidised by Beijing.[12] It is now estimated that two-thirds of these

[11]Aglietta and Bai, op. cit., p.14.
[12]Andrew Jacobs, 'China's Appetite Pushes Fisheries to the Brink', New York Times, 30 April, 2017.

boats contravene either local or international laws with the tacit approval of China's ministries. Whether sustainable development will be an integral part of the OBOR project long-term is less than clear. The need is overwhelming to enforce sustainable policies with its bilateral partners. Its record up to now leaves a lot of room for improvement.

CHINA: FUTURE LEADER OF THE GLOBAL GREEN MOVEMENT?

Much Asian infrastructure is substandard, inadequate and unable to withstand natural disasters, which range from mudslides to earthquakes. According to a recent report entitled 'Natural Hazards and Disaster Risk in "One Belt, One Road" Corridors', these natural hazards can be grouped into four major categories: the geophysical (earthquakes, landslides and volcanic activity); the hydrological (floods, debris flow and wave action); the meteorological (storms, extreme precipitations and fog); and the climatological (droughts, glacial lake outburst floods and wildfires).

Southeast Asian countries are prone to earthquakes, landslides, floods and wave actions such as tsunamis. Similarly, most countries in Central and Western Asia are high-risk regions for earthquakes, debris floods and also landslides. On the other hand, South Asian states in the proximity of the Himalayas experience earthquakes, landslides, outburst floods and wildfires, while those in the southern parts of Bangladesh and Sri Lanka are prone to floods and wave actions.

The Middle Eastern and African project countries are already suffering from extreme temperatures, floods and wave actions, while the Central and Eastern European ones in the OBOR initiative are mainly affected by devastating earthquakes, horrific floods and terrifying mudslides.[13] China's partners along the OBOR do not wish

[13]Cui Peng, Amar Deep Regmi, Zou Qiang, Yu Lei, Xiaoqing Chen and Deqiang Cheng, 'Natural Hazards and Disaster Risk in "One Belt, One Road" Corridors', in Matjaž Mikoš, Binod Tiwari, Yueping Yin and Kyoji Sassa (eds), *Advancing Culture of Living with Landslides* (Springer International, 2017), pp. 1155–1164.

to become environmental dumping grounds for China's 'ecological civilisation', but Chinese policy elites have yet to push for the adoption of transnational social and environmental standards across what could be called its China club of nations, a term that is more descriptive than a reflection of realpolitik.[14]

The urgency to act cannot be underestimated. For example, the Global South has become a dumping ground for 50 million tonnes of electronic waste generated worldwide every year. The problem is very difficult to regulate, as the European Environment Agency admits. It estimates that between 250,000 and 1.3 million tonnes of used electrical products are shipped out of the EU every year, mostly to places with weaker environmental protection standards in West Africa and Asia.[15]

WEAK ENVIRONMENTAL OVERSIGHT

As a result of these environmental concerns, all projects should be subject to strategic assessments through extensive stakeholder consultations with the communities and groups potentially affected by these development projects. So far they are not. The goal is to monitor and assess these projects routinely, from their inception to their planning and, finally, to their implementation. There is also an important role for future multilateral environmental agreements to play, which could promote the adoption of standards in projects involving more than one country.

China is a laggard in carrying out rigorous environmental monitoring. It needs to develop a coherent strategy on climate change and environmental review. Beijing is in a position to make environmental sustainability a priority through the AIIB. Its newest

[14]Elena F. Tracy, Evgeny Shvarts, Eugene Simonov and Mikhail Babenk, 'China's New Eurasian Ambitions: The Environmental Risks of the Silk Road Economic Belt', *Eurasian Geography and Economics* 58 (2017), pp. 56–88.

[15]European Environmental Agency, 'Waste', 18 February, 2015 https://www.eea.europa.eu/soer-2015/europe/waste [Accessed October 2018]; John Vidal, 'Toxic "e-waste" dumped in poor nations, says UN', *Guardian*, 14 December, 2013 https://www.theguardian.com/global-development/2013/dec/14/toxic-ewaste-illegal-dumping-developing-countries [Accessed October 2018]

bank will provide a large share of the financing of China's ambitious overseas projects. The bank's ongoing capital injections can play a key role in pushing for effective environmental standards on all the parties applying for these funds.

Leveraging these capital investments, the AIIB could become a leading institution in the promotion of green regulatory standards. Its ranks have increased from 57 to 84 members and it is successful in mobilising almost $20 billion from public and private investors.[16] If there is a strong European presence on its governance board with positive experience in building local capacity and supporting the need for independent environmental review processes, that could make a big difference. One idea is that the AIIB would be open to establishing stronger environmental priorities for the bank. It could give Chinese leaders greater confidence to promote a greener agenda by supporting the need for obligatory public interest and an arm's-length review process.

Fossil fuel development remains a dominant part of China's needs as well as an integral part of its global infrastructural initiative for many partner nations. Beijing's 13th five-year plan makes it abundantly clear that China will continue to support an open multilateral global economy as part of its drive to be the leader *primus inter pares* in Asia. It needs to protect its global supply chains from any external threat, because it relies on fossil fuel imports. How much a green leader China will turn out to be in the 5,000+ projects of its global infrastructural strategy is anyone's guess.[17] China faces demanding and difficult structural change if it is to meet its ambitious carbon-cutting goals.

[16]Daniel Poon, 'AIIB: Experiments in scaling-up development finance', *World Financial Review* (UNCTAD, March–April 2018) http://unctad.org/en/pages/newsdetails.aspx?Original VersionID=1704 [Accessed October 2018]

[17]It is important in this regard to distinguish between OBOR contracts and OBOR projects. Journalists and economists discuss somewhere between 5,000 and 7,000 projects along the road, whereas Nadège Rolland argues that there are approximately +15,000 contracts (there can be multiple contracts per project).

HARD AND SOFT POWER ENTANGLED: AN UNEXPECTED RESPONSE FROM THE WORLD BANK

Beijing's global investment blitz faces many other governance challenges. The China model is an example of the potent combination of both 'hard and soft power' exercised by China's political class. Dangerous security issues continue to resurface. A case in point is that militants have killed more than 40 Pakistani workers near OBOR project sites since 2014.[18] In order to protect the $57 billion economic corridor that China is building through Pakistan, Beijing has brought in private security contractors (such as DeWe Security) to secure the safety of its workers. OBOR is never very far from national security concerns either on land or on China's 'string-of-pearls' sea lanes. Perhaps the most disturbing example of the entanglement of security and Chinese infrastructural ambitions is a domestic one.

For years, the ethnic Muslim Uighurs from the western Chinese region of Xinjiang have been targeted as a security threat to Beijing. Already, hundreds of thousands have been placed in internment centres while mosques have been closed, with the express aim of eradicating the distinct Uighur identity in the name of countering terrorism. The authorities argue they are tied up with radical Islamist groups in the Middle East and Syria accused of killing Chinese diplomats in Central Asia.[19] However, it is no coincidence that China's crackdown on Xinjiang comes as Xi is promoting the region as a core overland route for the transportation of goods.

As China steps into a more prominent global leadership role, Beijing is trying to stabilise the situation by taking pre-emptive measures that traditional state-to-state diplomacy cannot easily

[18] Gul Yusufzai, 'Ten gunned down near China "Belt and Road" projects in Pakistan', *Reuters*, 13 May, 2017 http://uk.reuters.com/article/uk-pakistan-militants-idUKKBN18908I [Accessed October 2018]

[19]Ryskeldi Satke, 'Uighurs in Kyrgyzstan hope for peace despite violence', *Al Jazeera*, 8 January, 2017 http://www.aljazeera.com/indepth/features/2016/09/uighurs-kyrgyzstan-hope-piece-violence-160915133619696.html [Accessed October 2018]

handle. Yet it is susceptible to public opinion and international criticism. According to Lily Kuo, the *Guardian's* Beijing Bureau Chief, this is likely why the PRC launched a publicity campaign, changing its tactic of denying the existence of re-education camps by reframing them as 'humane' job training centres.[20] For James Leibold, a scholar of Chinese ethnic policies at La Trobe University in Melbourne, these are deeper signs that China is attempting to legalise, standardise and ultimately normalise this process: 'I think the ultimate aim is the creation of a vocational, patriotic education system for adult minorities in Xinjiang.'[21]

Despite mass arrests, Beijing is moving ahead with its global police containment design and removal policy. Countries expecting to benefit from increased development along the route should be aware of the potentially destabilising effects of China's crackdown in the region. Some will see this strategy of bilateralism as a looming alternative to the template-driven austerity focus development of the World Bank. They would not be mistaken even if Chinese authorities present their financial investment strategy in non-confrontational language.

In the investment development wars, the World Bank has turned increasingly to Wall Street to finance global infrastructure investments under Jim Young Kim, its former president. In terms of global lending, no Western institution can match China's terms. In 2016, the bank invested just $61 billion in loans and investment.[22] In 2017, the bank loaned even less, only $43.9 billion, a far cry from competing with China head-to-head.[23]

The bank has also formed private-equity partnerships with some of Wall Street's investment giants. Private investors have committed a

[20]Lily Kuo, 'From denial to pride: How China changed its language on Xinjiang's camps', *Guardian*, 22 October, 2018 https://www.theguardian.com/world/2018/oct/22/from-denial-to-pride-how-china-changed-its-language-on-xinjiangs-camps
[21]James Leibold. 'Mind Control in China Has a Very Long History', *New York Times*, 22 November, 2018 available at: https://www.nytimes.com/2018/11/28/opinion/china-reeducation-mind-control-xinjiang.html
[22]Landon Thomas Jr., 'The World Bank is Remaking Itself as the Creature of Wall Street', *New York Times*, 25 January, 2018.
[23]Daniel Poon, op. cit.

very modest amount by international development standards of only $1 billion to emerging markets, not all of which is for infrastructure. Such stakeholders have very shallow pockets when it comes to public investment in poor countries.

Already China has had an impact on the World Bank's loan practices to African nations. According to economist Diego Hernandez, interviewed by the BBC, 'when an African country is also assisted by China... the World Bank provides fewer conditions attached to its loans'. For every 1 per cent increase in Chinese aid, Hernandez found that 'the World Bank lessened its typical demands for things like market liberalisation or economic transparency by 15 per cent'.[24]

Of course, we still have to assess comprehensively the range of tangible benefits from China's highly malleable form of development diplomacy, including the regulatory competition between aid agencies. There is also an insufficient number of reliable independent studies identifying the inherent risks when China's regional partners become dependent on a single benefactor.[25] It is worth repeating that China's comparative advantage is that it offers highly attractive low-interest loans of 1 per cent to 3 per cent, which accounts for much of its rapid acquisition of new members.

With its minimalist contractual architecture, Beijing's infrastructural initiative is a blend of incremental pragmatism and self-interest. Chinese authorities do not the hide the fact that it is uniquely designed to support the Chinese economy by utilising its excess capacity in many industries such as steel, construction and heavy machinery. American economists, who have tried to estimate the impact of these investments on China compared to the benefits flowing to other countries that have accepted the deal, are divided in their answers. On the one hand, through enhanced access to new markets and opportunities for strong export growth, China's domestic

---

[24]Celia Hatton, 'China's secret aid empire uncovered', *BBC News*, 11 October, 2017 https://www. bbc.com/news/world-asia-china-41564841 [Accessed October 2018]

[25]Greg T. Chin, 'Asian Infrastructure Investment Bank: Governance Innovation and Prospects', *Global Governance* 22 (2016), pp. 11–25 http://journals.rienner.com/doi/pdf/10.5555/1075-2846-22.1.11?code=lrpi-site

economy will reap many benefits.[26] The danger of debt diplomacy, however, is this: if successful, it leaves countries facing financial difficulties and a growing dependence on China. On the other, the value added for emerging economies is that China's hundreds of millions of investment dollars will free up scarce financial resources for cash-strapped governments that could never fund these projects without China's help. For the least developed countries in the world, whose economies have stagnated and which lack the basics of a fully developed modern infrastructure, China's offer is too good to refuse. In a postcolonial age, this has to be their choice – neither Washington's nor Beijing's.

THE 'CHINESE DREAM' AND ITS IMPACT ON DOMESTIC POLITICS

A lot of what happens in the future to China's global initiative depends on the Chinese leadership. President Xi has used the catch-all phrase 'the Chinese dream' to convey a rudimentary kind of social contract between the Party and the people in promising them a brighter future, which now includes the big-ticket, capital-intensive OBOR.

According to recent public opinion polls, many Chinese do not accept the idea that they are part of a good society.[27] There is a lot of dissatisfaction with the way the Party has tried to solve quality of life issues for the average Chinese citizen. These include public housing shortages, access to services and China's pollution crisis, and have led President Xi to admit that the reforms he has initiated have entered 'deep waters'. By this he meant that, under his leadership, China has to 'venture along a dangerous path to break through barriers to reform'.[28] At the Central Committee

[26]David Dollar, 'China's Rise as a Regional and Global Power: The AIIB and the One Belt, One Road', Horizons, 4 (Summer); Hoffman, Bert, China's One Belt One Road Initiative: What we Know Thus Far (World Bank, 4 December, 2015), cited in Edwin Truman, 'Governance Challenges', in China's Belt and Road Initiative Motives, Scope, and Challenges (Peterson Institute, 2016).
[27]'China: Building the dream', Economist, Special Report, 19 April, 2014.
[28]Ibid.

meeting in November 2016, Xi singled out, in the strongest terms possible, the central role that market forces must play at this critical juncture.

Conceivably, China could lose control over its world vision of infrastructural beachheads if many of its bilateral partners exit as the Chinese economy continues to slow. So far, this has not happened. No country has quit the BRI up to now, but this could happen in the future. India would be the obvious leading candidate. It relies on AIIB to finance many infrastructural projects and yet views Beijing's dominant presence with a great deal of suspicion. Recently, India refused to sign the final communiqué of the high-level 2018 Shanghai Cooperation Organisation, the Chinese-led initiative with other Asian states to promote closer ties and cooperation.

Getting a handle on corruption is an ongoing battle. Some Chinese officials have spoken publicly about the institutional graft surrounding such projects. It represents a liability for China, inflates costs, leads to social unrest and raises the bar needed for profitability. President Xi acknowledged this worry in a speech last year, saying, 'We will also strengthen international cooperation on anticorruption in order to build the Belt and Road Initiative with integrity.'[29] Many experts are sceptical that China will take an assertive leadership role in enforcing the multilateral transparency and accountability norms that so far its political elites have downplayed.

OBOR AND THE INTERNET

How the BRI global vision will impact Chinese domestic politics is another entanglement requiring careful analysis. State censorship on the Internet and foreign news sites has increased dramatically since Xi became China's leader. Paradoxically, the global information

[29]Maria Abi-Habib, 'How China Got Sri Lanka to Cough Up a Port', *New York Times*, 25 June, 2018 https://www.nytimes.com/2018/06/25/world/asia/china-sri-lanka-port.html?rref=collection%2F sectioncollection%2Fasia&action=click&contentCollection=asia&region=stream&module= stream_unit&version=latest&contentPlacement=2&pgtype=sectionfront [Accessed October 2018]

revolution has legitimised a growing belief in freedom of expression for the 800 million Chinese users on WeChat and other social media platforms. If, on the world stage, China projects an image of domestic confidence and national pride, the government still needs to come to terms with the growing alienation among its millennial generation.

MILLENNIALS, OBOR AND GOVERNANCE TROUBLES

Presently, the millennials make up almost 30 per cent of China's population, are better educated, more technologically savvy on Weibo and WeChat, and possess more advanced digital-surfing and information-gathering skills than previous generations. They are a huge consumer market and distinct political demographic. Certainly if their Internet life is any indication, they are more individualistic thanks to their ability to access information despite state censorship and a recent crackdown on 'unofficial' dissent pushing the boundaries. Connectivity via the cell phone is immediate and ubiquitous, and 92 per cent of Chinese millennials own a cell phone and have increasingly exhibited a different mentality about hierarchy and authority.

Compared to their parents, Chinese millennials have more freedom to travel and educate themselves abroad in record numbers. In 2016, more than 500,000 studied abroad, according to the Ministry of Education.[30] New studies emphasise that their principal preoccupation remains focused on work, careers, education and family.[31] One reason they are so different is that they have come of age during three decades of high-speed economic change and the doubling and tripling of family incomes for the middle class.

---

[30]'Annual Report on Education', Ministry of Education of the People's Republic of China, 2016.
[31]For more on the rise of China's millennials and the implications of their coming of age on the Chinese and world economies, see: R.L. Moore, 'Generation Ku: Individualism and China's Millennial Youth', *Ethnology* 44(4) (Autumn 2005), pp. 357–376; R.L. Moore and Z. Chang, 'From Balinghou to Jiulinghou, China's Millennials Come of Age', *World Politics Review* 105 (2014).

Yet, many young, ordinary Chinese do not share the idea that China is a leading world power as of yet. They are patriotic and nationalist, but are more focused on domestic issues of housing, pollution, poverty and, first and foremost, jobs. They have their doubts and might tell you, 'Yes, China is important, but it is a developing economy far behind the West.' If this perception gap about the sustainability of its 'great leap outward' widens, Chinese leadership may have to change its lending standards and the financing of its agenda. It is unclear whether the rising Chinese middle class will support – at any cost to themselves – the economic sacrifices demanded by Xi's dream of building a global coalition of common interest.[32]

CHINA'S SPATIAL FIX: CHALLENGING ONE WORLD ORTHODOXY

How then should we think theoretically about the way diplomacy, governance and power intersect and interact? As the global economy has become visibly multipolar, driven by regional actors, the OBOR represents a *new form of diffuse regionally based multi-polarity of competing Asian countries*. Some readers will immediately make the analytical connection with the 'varieties of capitalism' perspective, well known in Western academic circles, which explains the great diversity in the way markets, states and societies are organised within a universal framework of global capitalism.[33] China's party-state market system is another powerful and unique variant as we have already seen with the BRI, one of its recent pillars.

Notionally, the Anglo-American, German, Chinese and Scandinavian market economies have well-known characteristics explaining the sharp differences in the domestic role of social

---

[32]With, for example, China bullying the Philippines over possession of disputed islands in the South China Sea, the Confucius Institute that China established in Manila to teach Chinese culture can win only so much goodwill. As Nye (2005) points out, the consequences of the country's foreign policy can be seen in last year's anti-Chinese riots in Vietnam following the positioning of a Chinese oil drilling rig in waters claimed by both countries.
[33]Robert Boyer and Daniel Drache (eds), *States Against Markets* (Routledge, 1996).

welfare, state spending, public goods, rule of law and labour market practices. Internationally, there are equivalent varieties of trade and investment agreements. At one end, we find the EU with its ambitious, but elusive, goal to transform itself into the United States of Europe. At the other is the new NAFTA, now renamed USNCA, and the Canada-Europe Free Trade Agreement, with their invasive deregulatory ambition and myriad legal rules.

For students of international relations, China's infrastructural offensive does not fit into any pre-existing model. Yet its geopolitical importance for Beijing as well as India cannot be underestimated in the Asia-Pacific region.

The point is that countries are looking to form regional trade alliances and there are as many models as countries. India continues to cold-shoulder much of the global vision of China's BRI, but is busily engaged in Southeast Asia in a variety of groups with different aims and ambitions, including ASEAN Defence Ministers Meeting, the Bay of Bengal Technical Initiative and the Mekong-Ganga Economic Corridor. The number of regional coalitions to address specific problems and issues has exploded in recent years. India has mirrored China's bilateralism, signing trade deals with Singapore, Japan and South Korea as well as ASEAN and Thailand.[34] However, there is no other regional power broker with the resources, determination and strategy to match China.

The controversial hypothesis that needs testing and requires careful watching is that Beijing is in the process of acquiring its own rival system of trade and development alliances and institutions. China is looking to construct 'a spatial fix' that reflects its core interests and political culture. It assumes a synchronicity of interests between itself and its bilateral partners, a contested proposition that frames much of the economic activity it sponsors. The Middle Kingdom's international, political and economic governance capabilities have

[34]"Prime Minister's Keynote Address at Shangri La Dialogue (1 June, 2018)", *Ministry of External Affairs*, Government of India http://www.mea.gov.in/Speeches-Statements.htm?dtl/29943/Prime+Ministers+Keynote+Address+at+Shangri+La+Dialogue+June+01+2018 [Accessed October 2018]

evolved in ways few predicted. Increasingly, countries are distancing themselves from crisis-prone multilateralism as new opportunities arise. How the BRI will evolve is another matter, with its unlimited ambition and drive. Whether it will coalesce into a major global actor is still an unknown with its 'light' governance norms and practices. In the meantime, the Chinese people's commitment to a 'spatial fix for a new century' will be tested as never before.

6

Incremental Pragmatism, Success Stories and Self-interest

THE GROOVES OF HUMAN AND PHYSICAL GEOGRAPHY

China is conscious that it has many different ways it can leverage its ascendant power to redirect the grooves of commerce to capture new markets and build stronger, more sustainable economies. Some critics are troubled by the fact that it is difficult to separate the special deals of loans, investments and financial agreements from their political dimensions up and down the Road. China is buying friendships, loyalties and influence in exchange for financing regional development projects of every description on a scale that has never been tried before. Human and physical geographies have always been intertwined. From a geopolitical perspective, there is no mystery in what China is doing. It is connecting the underdeveloped, rapidly growing Asian region to China's southern provinces through ports and railways, with global markets in Rotterdam and surrounding European countries as the ultimate Eurasian market destinations.

In comparison to other infrastructure programmes, the OBOR does not appear to have fixed boundaries of membership, and it supports highly eclectic and diverse kinds of activity. China's global infrastructural initiative is open-ended and expansionary with new bilateral investment opportunities being signed with each batch of freshly recruited participants. Certainly, the OBOR project has grown remarkably in a very short span of time. Howard French, whose book *China's Second Continent* is about Chinese investors and entrepreneurs who settled in Africa, says that Africa has been 'the workshop of ideas', and, within less than two decades, Chinese investments have increased tenfold. In the year 2000, China-Africa trade was only $10 billion; today, it is more than $220 billion.[1] Is this the future for Europe, Latin America and Asia? Being a recipient of a non-stop flood of infrastructural dollars to build many more trade corridors?

In the case of Africa, a continent of 1.3 billion people, it is hard to fully grasp the scale of China's presence. It is a major investor, pouring billions of dollars into Egypt, Nigeria, Algeria, South Africa, Mozambique, Ethiopia, Angola, Niger, Zambia and Morocco. It supported independence movements in 34 African countries and its ties remain strong, even seven decades later. According to a recent Johns Hopkins School of Advanced International Studies Report, Chinese direct investment in 2015 was equally divided between mining and construction. Manufacturing, financial services, and science, research and technology services each received 5 per cent of the total. In their report, close to 20 per cent of foreign direct investment covered a variety of other sectors.[2]

In Asia, we see much the same pattern, where small and large countries negotiate one-on-one for their infrastructural investment projects (such as a hydroelectric plant, an industrial mall for development or a wind farm). There are also mega-projects such as pan-Asian high-speed railway systems linking economies together in ways that have never been tried before. Some of these projects are controversial with local populations, and the promise of the latest in modern technology and connectivity are insufficient to overcome local opposition and the anti-China sentiment lurking beneath the surface. Nonetheless, China is the world leader in infrastructure development and many heads of state find partnering with China's BRI an attractive option.

---

[1] Howard W. French, *China's Second Continent: How a Million Migrants are Building a New Empire in Africa* (Alfred A. Knopf, 2014).
[2] David Pilling, 'Chinese investment in Africa: Beijing's testing ground', *Financial Times*, 13 June, 2007.

IS THE PRIVATE SECTOR STEPPING UP TO INVEST?

The dilemma for Western strategists is that poor countries cannot afford to pass up the economic benefits of this railway-building age. High-speed rail is expensive and the engineering side of these once-in-a-generation projects is also complex and high risk. For example, investing in high-speed railway projects across Southeast Asia breaks new ground regionally, and possibly globally, by involving some of capitalism's biggest and most advanced firms, specialising in mammoth-sized transportation networks. It will take a decade or longer before commercial and passenger traffic will be sufficient to offset the sunken costs of construction. A recent 2018 study of the high-speed trans-European train network found that the European railway systems, after decades of operation, often miss their financial targets long after they are supposed to and are supported by governments because they are a public service.[3] Regardless of the continent, investment in modern rail systems always remains risky with difficult-to-predict returns on investments.

Chinese companies are working with Japan's Kawasaki Heavy Industries, Germany's Siemens and France's Alstom, all of which bid for projects and supply top-tier equipment and technology.[4] In the Chinese model, sharing risk and investment opportunities with private global multinationals is also part of the story, although it is less well known in the United States. Chinese lenders are already starting to syndicate participation in some of the top One Belt, One Road projects to international global investors and lenders.[5]

Western companies are particularly attracted to the high-technology opportunities and potential attractive rates of return on

[3]Josh Spero and Rochelle Toplensky, 'Europe's high-speed rail network "slow, expensive and ineffective"', *Financial Times*, 26 June, 2018.
[4]'Chinese Consortium Prepares for Singapore - Malaysia Rail Bidding', *China Daily*, 14 May, 2016.
[5]James Kynge, 'How the Silk Road Plans will be Financed', *Financial Times*, 9 May, 2016; *Meeting Asia's Infrastructure Needs* (Asian Development Bank Institute, February 2017) https://www.adb.org/sites/default/files/publication/227496/special-report-infrastructure.pdf [Accessed October 2018]

OBOR projects. It comes as no surprise that Morgan Stanley, Deutsche Bank, JPMorgan Chase, HSBC, Credit Suisse and other leaders in global private investment banking are very interested in being part of the Chinese global consortium and are already financing projects. They are waiting to bankroll others; they will not be lead players but they certainly will have a larger place at the table.

In its most recent report, the Asian Development Bank highlighted the fact that only 3 per cent of infrastructural development has been financed by the IMF, the World Bank, the Asian Development Bank, the African Development Bank and the European Investment Bank. For the risk management side of these infrastructural projects, Western firms are very important in some instances. Still, it is doubtful that they have the funds to meet the challenge posed by the world's development deficit.[6] The state-backed China Development Bank and Export-Import Bank of China have close to $500 billion in assets, and thus twice as much capital to invest, and they outperform all Western global finance institutions combined in the aid and development field. China's biggest and most successful banks are spearheading China's infrastructural commercial engagement.

What is different is that China places a special emphasis on a new type of great power relations to find alternative ways to coexist with major powers. This element remains more of an aspirational goal than a concrete plan of action for the Chinese leadership and may become better defined in the future. In reality, the Chinese authorities attach special significance to their notion of the existence of the China club of nations and have adopted the BRI formally into the Party Constitution, giving it more clout and political legitimacy.[7] It underlies China's growing desire to take a leading role in global

---

[6]*Meeting Asia's Infrastructure Needs* (Asian Development Bank Institute, February 2017) https://www.adb.org/sites/default/files/publication/227496/special-report-infrastructure.pdf [Accessed October 2018]

[7]Brenda Goh and John Ruwitch, 'Pressure on as Xi's "Belt and Road" enshrined in Chinese party charter', *Reuters,* 24 October, 2017 https://www.reuters.com/article/us-china-congress-silkroad/pressure-on-as-xis-belt-and-road-enshrined-in-chinese-party-charter-idUSKBN1CT1IW [Accessed October 2018]

affairs. We need to be clear – this is not a coalition of the willing, nor is it an economic bloc with a fixed goal. Rather, it is a simple description of membership in an investment club where China's deep pockets pay the membership fees.

WINNING NEW FRIENDS AND GAINING INFLUENCE
Beijing realises that the biggest prize is successfully building a Eurasian superhighway for commerce, which would require deep integration with new commercial structures and the movement of people and goods between China and more than 30 European countries. Many, like France, Germany and Italy, are among the richest in the world. The EU is already China's largest trading partner, not the United States. Closer to home, more than half of China's trade takes place with countries in the Asia-Pacific region. Beijing has made the Northeast, Southeast and South Asian regions priorities for infrastructural investment by putting special emphasis on building communities of cooperation through infrastructural projects.[8]

Take China's example of strategic targeting. How threatening are such strategies to Indian, Japanese and Australian interests? In order to understand this process, one must follow China's money trail across Asia and Africa. Through financing complex energy projects and underwriting a massive modernisation of the existing transportation systems, China is winning friends and gaining influence. The estimated costs and expenditures have recently been documented by Boston University's Global Economic Governance Initiative's global energy database.[9]

Since the year 2000, 60 per cent of the $165 billion in energy finance provided by Chinese banks has been concentrated on the

[8]Jin Kai, 'Can China Build a Community of Common Destiny?' *The Diplomat*, 28 November, 2013 http://thediplomat.com/2013/11/can-china-build-a-community-of-common-destiny [Accessed October 2018]
[9]Kevin Gallagher, 'China Global Energy Finance: A New Interactive Database' (GEGI policy brief 002, March 2017) https://www.bu.edu/pardeeschool/files/2017/03/China-Global-Energy.-Gallagher.Finaldraft.pdf [Accessed October 2018]

Asian continent, an enormous amount of development assistance for the expansion of oil, gas and coal investments for China's industries and domestic consumption.[10] Indeed, it is not all going to Asia: $42 billion has been invested in Latin America and over $23 billion has gone to Africa. The bulk of the financing has been earmarked for power plants, coal and hydroelectrical – channelled through 27 natural power hydroelectric stations. The major countries and regions on China's 'A list' included Brazil ($25.4 billion), Indonesia ($6.7 billion), India ($7.8 billion), Pakistan ($18.8 billion), Russia ($39.5 billion) and Central Asia ($50 billion) in 2016, all of which are energy-rich states. The important element that they share in common is that each is a pivotal actor in a major region and all are of strategic importance to the Middle Kingdom's global infrastructural initiative.

Nonetheless, it is disheartening to realise that fossil fuel development plays such a large role in China's developmental strategy. 'So much of China's overseas energy portfolio is heavily concentrated in fossil fuel operations that accentuate climate change, especially in coal.' Kevin Gallagher, who made this point and is in charge of the Boston University Global Economic Governance Initiative, also strikes a more optimistic tone in pointing out that the Chinese development financial model often makes 'swift, decisive changes in policy direction'. In Gallagher's view, 'Beijing could easily use the same model to globalise its world-class solar and wind industries.'[11] There are signs that sustainable energy is moving up China's policy ladder since the Paris Climate Accord was signed and endorsed by Beijing.[12] Even so, Chinese elites still have a steep hill to climb in order to realign their priorities to green.

In 2016, at their meeting, the G20 made green finance and climate finance major commitments, but it remains an open question whether China will be able to combine all its many different

[10]Ibid.
[11]Ibid., p. 2.
[12]Charlie Campbell, 'Why an Unlikely Hero like China could End up Leading the World in the Fight against Climate Change', *Time Magazine*, 1 June, 2017 http://time.com/4800747/china-climate-change-paris-agreement-trump [Accessed October 2018]

forms of sustainable-energy financing under the big tent of their policy banks.[13] Certainly, Chinese banks face fewer institutional and political constraints than their Western-backed competitors. China's mega-banks have to get the green light from their political masters to close thousands of existing coal-fired hydroelectric plants, cancel plans for bringing new ones online and aggressively invest in green energy.

A MARITIME SUPERPOWER WITH A STRING OF PEARLS

It would be a mistake to ignore the maritime section of the One Belt, One Road initiative. In fact, it has been a very large part of China's global ascendancy, changing the pattern of global commerce in fundamental ways. On the oceans of the world, China has created a transnational network of modern ports that is redrawing the maritime maps of commercial shipping and the movement of goods. China is looking for new acquisitions to build the Euro/Asia land-sea corridor. COSCO Shipping Ports and China Merchants Port Holdings, China's mammoth MNCs, have just purchased another 'pearl', the port of Zeebrugge, Belgium's second largest port.[14]

Since 2014, the second pillar of China's global infrastructural strategy is to become a major sea power. Investments have poured into strategically located, ocean-accessible harbours across the world, which have made China a world power with access to secure sea lanes. Most of these ports are for civilian use, but some serve a dual purpose as they are also for military bases. Abhijit Singh, a senior fellow at the Observer Research Foundation in New Delhi, stressed that China's much vaunted 'string of pearls' of new ports could be easily upgradable for important military missions in the South China

[13]Aldo Caliari, 'China Leads G20 into Green Finance Reflection: To be continued?' *Sustainable Development Goal Knowledge Hub,* International Institute for Sustainable Development http://sdg.iisd.org/commentary/guest-articles/china-leads-g20-into-green-finance-reflection-to-be-continued [Accessed October 2018]
[14]Keith Johnson, 'Why is China Buying Up Europe's Ports?' *Foreign Policy,* 2 February, 2018 http://foreignpolicy.com/2018/02/02/why-is-china-buying-up-europes-ports/ [Accessed October 2018]

Sea and in the Korean Peninsula. 'They are great for soft projection of hard power.'[15]

The port of Gwadar, Pakistan, bordering the Strait of Malacca where 60 per cent of the world's oil is transported by mega-sized ocean tankers, will give China powerful security leverage over this key waterway. It is one of the templates that Beijing has pioneered, relying on its commercial know-how, financial muscle and diplomatic skills to secure ownership of this critically located trading base with military convertibility.

The maritime strategy of the OBOR project is less well known in the West, but its rapid implementation has enabled China to emerge as a commercial superpower on the world's oceans and seas. The Chinese Navy has expanded and is one of the fastest-growing segments of China's military. As China has become a maritime superpower, it has largely followed the Western example of acquiring a bigger, stronger navy with tactical capacity for rapid response, a merchant shipping fleet second to none and a modern Coast Guard equipped with the latest technology to patrol the thousands of kilometres of its coastline.

The *Financial Times* reported that the five biggest Chinese shipping lines quoted on the stock exchange controlled 18 per cent of all container shipping handled by the world's top 20 companies in 2015. This is much higher than the next closest country, Denmark, the home nation of the Maersk Line, the world's biggest container shipping group.[16] Add to this the fact that China's deep-water ports now encircle the globe. With climate change and the rise of global temperature, China is looking to expand its presence in the Arctic to be able to trans-ship goods from China through the Northwest Passage to Europe via the world's longest underwater tunnel from Finland to points beyond.[17]

[15]James Kynge, Chris Campbell, Amy Kazmin and Farhan Bokhari, 'How China rules the waves', *Financial Times*, 12 January, 2017 https://ig.ft.com/sites/china-ports/?mhq5j=e3 [Accessed October 2018]
[16]Ibid.
[17]Emily Feng, Alice Woodhouse and Richard Milne, 'China reveals Arctic ambitions with plan for "Polar Silk Road"', *Financial Times*, 26 January, 2018; Sebastian Murdoch-Gibson, a post-doc at the Asia-Pacific Foundation, kindly shared his research findings on the Polar Silk Road.

Alfred Thayer Mahan, a prominent American strategist in the 19th century, said that: 'Control of the sea by maritime commerce and naval supremacy means predominant influence in the world; because however great the wealth of the land, nothing facilitates the necessary exchanges as that of the sea.'[18] We can see that his strategic counsel has lost none of its appeal for China's authorities. They want to be key players in all spheres of commerce and, for geopolitical advantage, have been highly proactive in using Chinese yuan diplomacy, deep financial pockets and SOEs to transform themselves into the global maritime superpower.

Chinese companies now handle over 60 per cent of global container volumes, and two-thirds of container traffic is moved through Chinese-owned ports or those where Beijing has invested significant amounts of money. From a geo-economic point of view, Chinese port construction and maritime investment, which includes some of the world's largest ports, also includes many of the world's smaller ports such as Walvis Bay, Namibia. This is another example of Beijing's intermediary approach. China's regional maritime strategy with its global reach is a mirror image of its intensely concentrated regional infrastructural railway and energy investments in Central and South Asia, East Africa, Brazil and elsewhere.

CHINA'S INTERIM REPORT CARD

What does the scorecard look like to date for China's global infrastructure initiative? Are the grooves of geography bending to its will? Are there green shoots of positive structural change? The process of vetting projects in Asia, Africa and Latin American countries is, to say the least, obscure. One recent study by *Nikkei Asian Review* is unique. It sent a team of reporters to assess how well China's One Belt, One Road initiative is proceeding in eight countries. The story reads like a smart student's report card for 2018. Completed projects include: Hungary, Huawei logistics centre, $1.5

[18]Alfred Thayer Mahan, *The Influence of Sea Power upon History: 1660–1783* (Little, Brown and Co., 1890), p. 158.

billion; Iran, Rudbar Lorestan hydropower dam, $570 million; Kazakhstan, Khorgos Port, $245 million; Pakistan, Gwardar port construction of breakwaters, $123 million; Sri Lanka, Hambantota sea port – phase 1, $1.3 billion; Cambodia, National Road number 214, Stung Treng-River Bridge, $117 million; Indonesia, Sumsel 5 power plant, $318 million; and North Korea, New Yalu Bridge, $350 million. Many other projects are under construction. In Bangladesh, China is building the Paya power plant at a cost of $1.65 billion, and in Israel a Haifa Bay port at a cost of $1.16 billion. Other projects are under negotiation in Mongolia, Turkey and Ukraine, and the nuclear power plant in Turkey is estimated to cost $25 billion when completed.[19] For this group of reporters, the BRI has acquired a strong record of achievement.

BENEFIT SHARING, REMORSE AND DEBT DISTRESS

So where have China's elites invested the bulk of their money? In a new report on troubled infrastructure projects by Bloomberg's investigative reporters, the top two preferred states are Malaysia and Pakistan, which are both part of Beijing's regional investment push.[20] There are few surprises as China moves to invest billions within its close geographic sphere. As Figure 6.1 makes clear, none of these partners are middle-income countries. Other top partners include Cambodia, Laos, Vietnam, Bangladesh and Indonesia, all of which face crippling infrastructural deficits from past international lenders, are unable to provide round-the-clock electricity services to their rural populations or sufficient commercial opportunities for business elites. As a natural constituency for China's promise of stronger economic growth and poverty eradication, the BRI seeks to overcome the political instabilities that bookend their infrastructural and developmental needs.

British researchers have also made a study of debt distress among BRI partners and are more pessimistic. China has been lucky so far with its relatively minimalist governance structures. It has not signed

[19]Go Yamada and Stefania Palma, op. cit.
[20]David Fickling, op. cit.

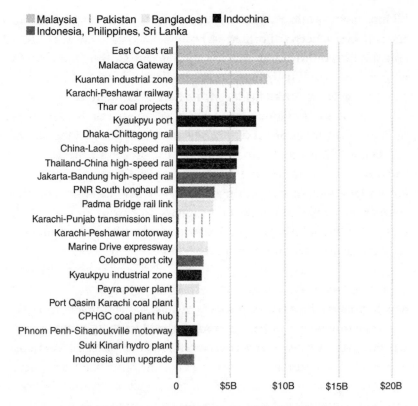

FIGURE 6.1 China's Investment Blitzkrieg in Malaysia, South Asia and Indochina

Source: Nomura Securities, AIIB, China-Pakistan Economic Corridor, news reports, Bloomberg Opinion calculations.
Note: Indochina includes Myanmar, Thailand, Loas and Cambodia. We've broken Malaysia out separately and no projects in Vietnam are large enough to show on this chart.

on to World Bank standards in addressing debt problems, and does not share the bank's focus on austerity and spending cutbacks. In the eyes of many American commentators, this laxity raises many questions about multilateral standards being ill suited to the needs of poor countries and the way debt burden is assessed.

China's elites have had more than their share of disagreements, cancellations and fights about benefit-sharing with their partners – to be expected when so much money is involved and local elites have so much at stake. However, there have been no governance meltdowns leading to a permanent diplomatic rupture. China's very public, messy disagreements with Pakistan, Russia, Turkey, Indonesia, Vietnam and India have been controlled and managed. One reason that these BRI conflicts did not spin out of control is found in a major study on debt sustainability by the Sussex Centre for Global Development. 'Looking at the entire range of countries in the initiative, the risk of debt distress among China's partners is not widespread.' It went on to say, 'The majority of BRI countries will likely avoid problems of debt distress due to BRI projects.'[21] In any event, loans by China's policy banks do not incorporate public tender transparency as a condition of the loan. Loans are generally secured only by the project and the country in question is on the hook in case of a default.

There is not a great deal of information in the public domain regarding the final criteria used by Beijing to invest in a region. As a general rule, China's investments are based on strategic considerations such as geopolitics and influence-building. Recipients inevitably have concerns about loss of sovereignty, ballooning deficits, the mass displacement of local inhabitants, contract skimming, and institutional corruption and project delays. But look at hundreds of projects and one thing is certain: Chinese state-owned enterprises reliably deliver the projects as contracted most of the time, a surprising difference between China's and India's performance in infrastructural investment projects.

Still, we know that Beijing is reviewing its due diligence practices and is more focused on getting reasonable rates of return on its investments. But since political factors are often as important as strictly narrow economic criteria in the Chinese narrative, building friendships between China and other countries is always a primary consideration in its decision to sign a bilateral trade agreement. For the Chinese authorities, the OBOR initiative is very differently marketed in comparison to the World Bank or the IMF, both of which claim to provide fair and unbiased aid based on an ideological

[21]John Hurley, Scott Morris and Gailyn Portelance, 'Will China's Belt And Road Initiative Push Vulnerable Countries Into A Debt Crisis?' *Center for Global Development*, 5 March, 2018 https://www.cgdev.org/blog/will-chinas-belt-and-road-initiative-push-vulnerable-countries-debt-crisis [Accessed October 2018]

doctrine of 'economy neutrality'.[22] Or as A.W. Clausen, President of the World Bank from 1981 to 1986, put it: 'Our ideology is economics... We should not address political questions and we don't.'[23]

In sharp contrast, the Chinese authorities have a higher tolerance for risk than the World Bank or other Western-sponsored global financial institutions.[24] For this reason, they take higher exposure in their overseas lending portfolio than the World Bank. The OECD has ranked the default risk of the Top 10 borrowers of Chinese overseas development loans. China's average risk rating was 5.33 and the World Bank's average risk rating was 4.35, a full point lower. What this means, of course, is that these numbers are not particularly great for loaning large sums of money to a country that is already troubled. In short, it is a 'flashing amber light' warning countries of the danger of a crushing debt burden in the billions of dollars.

In real terms, this means 'the weighted average of the OECD risk ratings on the top 10 borrowers shows that the Chinese overseas development loan portfolio is about 20 per cent riskier than that of the World Bank'.[25] Can the 20 per cent differential be explained by the politics of relationship-building, making riskier loans in the short term for longer term political gain?

WEIGHING THE COST OF POLITICAL ADVANTAGE VS.
THE POLITICS OF ECONOMIC RISK

China's policy banks, according to one official, 'assess risk differently from Western agencies because we look at the potential for

[22]As Richard Swedberg examines in detail, the two major assumptions of the doctrine of 'economic rationality' include: 1) that politics can be kept out of the IMF and the World Bank; 2) that decisions can be made on neutral, economic grounds, both of which must be considered in terms of the ways in which they provide an ideological smokescreen for Western nations to intervene in the domestic affairs of developing countries (*Journal of Peace Research*, vol. 23, no. 4, 1996, pp. 377–390).
[23]Altaf Gauhar and Alden Winship Clausen, 'A. W. Clausen', *Third World Quarterly*, Vol. 5, No. 1 (Jan., 1983), pp. 1–5.
[24]Brook Larmer, 'Is China the World's New Colonial Power?' *New York Times*, 2 May, 2017.
[25]Ibid.

development of the country.'[26] Indeed, it is standard for China, having very few ironclad rules, to make investments in highly unstable and conflict-ridden countries such as Venezuela and South Sudan, which Western global governance institutions would be reluctant to support, for either financial or political reasons.[27]

China's investment and willingness to make significant loans to Pakistan, Brazil, India, and many other countries not considered safe bets on the OECD risk-scale has a significant political component for the Chinese authorities.[28] In Figure 6.2, the World Bank is shown to have loaned money to Pakistan and Ethiopia even though they were high-risk bets, as well as Nigeria, Vietnam, Bangladesh and Brazil, which are middle-risk economies.

For many recipients of China's investment in infrastructural dollars, there is a political dimension that is difficult to calculate with precision. What seems obvious is that high-risk countries in Africa, Central America and Asia are also the most likely to have the highest poverty rates. There are more than 40 countries designated the 'least developed countries', with low per capita incomes. For example, Guinea Bissau had a per capita income equivalent to 8 per cent of the world's average in 2016, and averaged $552.30 from 1970 until 2016, reaching an all-time high of $730.80 in 1997, 30 years ago!

MONEY TROUBLES: FALLING OUT BETWEEN FRIENDS

China's highly flexible approach has not meant that its lending practices are trouble-free even with its closest 'all-weather' partners. Throughout Africa, there is a good deal of anti-Chinese sentiment,

[26]The Big Read, 'China rethinks developing world largesse as deals sour', *Financial Times*, 13 October, 2016.

[27]Clifford Krauss and Keith Bradsher 'China's Global Ambitions, Cash and Strings Attached', *New York Times*, 24 July, 2014.

[28]In the past, the World Bank applied its own political calculus to make significant loans to Chile and Argentina, and subsequently, to impose severe programme cuts in social welfare and political conditions as the price for the loan. 'General Conditions for Loans', *International Bank for Reconstruction and Development*, World Bank http://siteresources.worldbank.org/ INTLAWJUSTICE/Resources/IBRD_GC_English_12.pdf [Accessed October 2018]

Risk of default	World Bank, 2011-15		China, 2013-15	
Higher		$bn		$bn
7	Pakistan	7.5	Venezuela	9.0
	Ethiopia	5.6	Pakistan	7.8
			Argentina	7.6
			Ethiopia	5.8
			Sudan	4.0
			Zimbabwe	3.6
6	Nigeria	6.4	Ecuador	9.3
5	Vietnam	8.6		
	Bangladesh	8.4		
4	Brazil	11.4	Russia	15.7
	Turkey	5.2	Brazil	5.0
3	India	18.9	Indonesia	10.3
	Romania	4.7	India	5.0
2	China	8.0		
Lower	World Bank average risk rating* **4.35**		China average risk rating* **5.33**	

* Weighted average
Sources: World Bank, OECD, Grisons Peak, China Centre for Contemporary World Studies

FIGURE 6.2 Lifting the Curtain on China's and the World Bank's Risky Lending Practices to Precarious Economies

Source: Financial Times, *13 October, 2016, from World Bank's OECD risk classification (0-7).*

particularly from local populations, against the aggressive business practices of Chinese small merchants and traders. There are more than 1,000,000 Chinese immigrants in Africa and they are a visible target for different kinds of systemic racism. Its diasporic communities have grown larger and more visible as the BRI has expanded across the globe. In the Middle East, there are more than 70,000 recent Chinese immigrants. After five years of operation, China has encountered some major setbacks in different parts of the globe. There is no common trigger point and all reflect highly localised conflicts between China and its partners. These are important to look at, even briefly, because China has responded to each in quite different ways and they explain why China is likely to become increasingly embroiled in local issues over which it has no control.

LOCAL ANGER AGAINST BEIJING

China and Pakistan have recently had a falling out over the $14 billion infrastructure agreement to build the Diamer-Bhasha Dam. The head of the Pakistan water and power development authority said, 'The project was not doable and against our interests.' The Pakistan government stressed that it would finance the project itself. The truth is that since China is one of Pakistan's so-called bankers, Islamabad could be using the dispute to negotiate better terms.[29] Imran Khan, Pakistan's new prime minister, has promised a public examination of the agreements for the China-Pakistan economic corridor made by the last government, to determine whether they were poorly negotiated as well as the result of corrupt practices.[30] The *South China Morning Post* then reported that Beijing had agreed to a $2 billion emergency loan to help Pakistan weather its economic crisis, dispelling any doubts that China and Pakistan would work out their differences.[31]

In Venezuela, where China has invested massively, there is a full-blown crisis, as reported in the Western press.[32] The government of Maduro cannot meet its huge financial obligations because of a deteriorating political situation and the collapse of oil revenues. For political reasons, China, like any emerging superpower, has had to weigh the political costs of abandoning Maduro against its promised return on investment. Like many superpowers faced with a crisis-ridden government held together by 'a long-time friend', the Chinese authorities have chosen to cancel part of the debt and reschedule repayment at very low interest rates.

[29]Liu Zhen, 'Pakistan pulls plug on dam deal over China's "too strict" conditions in latest blow to Belt and Road plans', *South China Morning Post*, 16 November, 2017.

[30]Tom Hussain, 'Where does Imran Khan's government stand on China's Belt and Road?' *South China Morning Post*, 12 August, 2018.

[31]'China agrees US $2 billion loan to Pakistan, report says, as Beijing seeks to keep Imran Khan close', *South China Morning Post*, 2 August, 2018.

[32]Andres Schipani, 'Venezuela hit by more violent anti-government protests', *Financial Times*, 21 April, 2017; Andres Schipani, 'Venezuela's PDVSA makes $2.2 BN bond payment', *Financial Times*, 12 April, 2017.

Officially, China often reverts to the practice of elite policy accommodation, accepting whoever is in power as its partner. Beijing defends its practice on the grounds that it does not interfere in the domestic affairs of countries. China is not the first global power to change the repayment rules for a friendly regime. Western development aid has poured in billions of dollars to support corrupt authoritarian regimes in Latin America and Africa. As Paul Collier points out, very few of these projects improved the lives of ordinary people, built the infrastructure that was promised or fundamentally kicked away the ladder of dependency.[33] In all cases, the aid and support vital for these authoritarian regimes in Central America, Latin America and Africa keeps flowing. In Venezuela, if there is a regime change, there is every indication that China will negotiate a continuation of the existing loan with Maduro's replacement.

Many of the regions showing strong anti-Chinese sentiments are in China's own backyard: Vietnam, Laos, Cambodia, Myanmar, Thailand and Malaysia. Despite Chinese rhetoric about building a 'community of common destiny', there are a lot of obstacles to China's leadership. In June 2018 the Vietnamese government faced quite unprecedented street demonstrations against China's investments. In Cambodia, the establishment of 30 Chinese casinos has created a lot of resentment from locals complaining about the arrival of jumbo jets and thousands of Chinese tourists.[34]

SEARCHING FOR ALTERNATIVES: ARE THERE ANY?

In Sri Lanka, the incoming government is reviewing the controversial and highly favourable financing that China negotiated for itself in building the giant port of Hambantota. The deal has left Sri Lanka massively in debt and, as part of the financial rescue package, China

---

[33]Two classic studies of Western aid and development incompetence are Paul Collier, op. cit., and Ha-Joon Chang, op. cit.

[34]Sheridan Prasso, 'Chinese Influx Stirs Resentment in Once-Sleepy Cambodian Resort', *Bloomberg News*, 21 June, 2018 https://www.bloomberg.com/news/features/2018-06-20/chinese-casinos-stir-resentment-on-cambodia-s-coast-of-dystopia [Accessed October 2018]

is now the outright owner of the port, as reported by the *New York Times* in-depth analysis.[35] Sri Lanka is still meeting its financial obligations and the port, despite initial difficulties, continues to turn a small profit. The Chinese investment promised to transform the port into a bustling industrial park, generating revenue and jobs for the government. Violent protests broke out when the government announced its deal with China. With local inhabitants and public opinion so strongly against it, the future of the maritime hub is under review.[36]

Thailand and Malaysia are looking actively at ways to reduce their dependence on China. Thailand has proposed a regional investment infrastructure fund to back projects for development. This initiative is part of the Mekong cooperation strategy and would also include China, a significant builder of dams on the Mekong River. Countries do not want to trade off their economic freedom for development, and a regional fund would give them more leverage with China, Japan and the Asian Development Bank, another player in the region. Still, it is hard to imagine that Thailand's initiative will come anywhere close to equalling China's investment – in the region of $1.5 billion in concessional loans.[37] Yet, China's natural constituency is about to get a lot larger.

For China watchers, it is important to remember that China has not been passive in the face of protests. It has promised job training for local people and the opportunity to learn Chinese. It is difficult to ascertain whether China has made good on its promises and, moreover, whether any of these promises will provide satisfactory compensation. Public opinion still has a very strong anti-Chinese element and there are likely to be more protests against Chinese mega-infrastructural investments in other countries. Sri Lankans

[35]Maria Abi-Habib, op. cit.

[36]Jessica Meyers, 'Sri Lankans who once embraced Chinese investment now wary of Chinese domination', *Los Angeles Times*, 25 February, 2017.

[37]Yukako Ono, 'Thailand plans regional infrastructure fund to reduce China dependence', *Nikkei News*, 4 June, 2018 https://asia.nikkei.com/Politics/International-Relations/Thailand-plans-regional-infrastructure-fund-to-reduce-China-dependence [Accessed October 2018]

are hardly unique in believing that China is getting too powerful in the economy and being suspicious of its motives. Environmentalists are worried about protecting wildlife habitats, local people fear losing their homes to development, and even the political party that originally wanted Chinese investment is now opposing it as too invasive, too costly and a threat to Sri Lankan sovereignty.[38]

WHEN WILL THE BENEFITS ARRIVE?

The most important question remains: are Beijing's billions invested in transport and technical structures, which will increase the interconnections between peoples, a positive catalyst for deeper transformative change? In ten years' time, the large and yet to be proven assumption is that many of these countries in Asia and Africa will become global players when the multiplier effects of infrastructural spending and efficiency gains from building cost-cutting and time-saving transportation systems kick in. They expect to see many of the tangible benefits from the continuous supply of electricity in urban and industrial areas that communities and families never enjoyed before. Many other sectors will benefit, including education and health, where electrification has demonstrable positive impacts on school attendance, personal hygiene, prenatal care and schooling for young girls. This is a different concept of connectivity and is often found at the forefront of Xi's formal speeches.

It comes as no surprise that many of China's economic beachheads are driven by local needs. In South Asia, China is not acting alone. Recently, a group of policy experts from Himalayan countries such as India and China, as well as from the Asian Foundation, met to discuss regional infrastructure coordination. All commerce always has strong geographical dimensions because the region is landlocked. The aptly named Himalayan Consensus is anchored in the idea that the glacier and river support systems constitute a fragile ecosystem under assault by unsustainable economic growth. 'Without infrastructure connectivity, none of the provinces in the region

[38]Jessica Meyers, op. cit.

can potentially benefit from mainstream economic development elsewhere. Rethinking the prevalent economic model is required'[39] so that economic empowerment of communities around the region is a tangible option, not a theoretical one. The idea is that Beijing's many infrastructural investments have been catalysts for India and others to launch initiatives of their own.

Initiatives like the Bangladesh, Bhutan and India Network (BBIN) are looking to develop land-based transportation corridors to fill the gaps in hard and soft infrastructure. They are taking a page from China's global infrastructural playbook and, under the leadership of Prime Minister Modi of India, they have begun to create an alternative policy discourse about the potential of inland waterways and the greater Bengal Bay region and river system. Thinking large, Sri Lanka, Myanmar and Thailand would also be part of a larger network of policy coordination; Iran too, as well as tiny Nepal. All parties recently reaffirmed their commitment to building the International North South Transport Corridor (INSTC).

The region witnessed a number of positive developments in late 2017 and early 2018, which bode well for the future of the INSTC. Writing in *The Diplomat*, Roshan Iyer warned that the Trump administration's tough stance 'on Iran has made private sector investors jittery about the INSTC'.[40] There are very large technical issues of differing railway gauges between the railways in each country in the region, and these have so far proven to be an insurmountable obstacle for building 'seamless' railway connectivity – now little more than a pipe dream without the construction of new rail lines. India's pockets are not anywhere as deep as China's, preventing it from financing such an undertaking. New Delhi would have to be

[39]'Event Report: Unleashing Connectivity for Inclusive Growth Leveraging Himalayan Consensus to Further India's Act East Policy' (India International Centre, New Delhi, 23 January, 2018) http://www.icsin.org/uploads/2018/02/26/1923dd64f6a6ccbd84b55e95582d46c4.pdf [Accessed October 2018]

[40]Roshan Iyer, 'Filling In the North-South Trade Corridor's Missing Links', *The Diplomat*, 28 February, 2018 https://thediplomat.com/2018/02/filling-in-the-north-south-trade-corridors-missing-links/ [Accessed October 2018]

the lead investor ready to commit hundreds of millions of dollars, but its financial ability to form a dynamic coalition with major resources is obviously very limited.[41]

The countries of East Africa, recipients of billions of US dollars of Chinese infrastructural investments in railways, ports, roads and other facilities, may be in a category of their own, on the edge of a development breakthrough of some kind. The African Union is hoping to abolish visa restrictions imposed by member states as well as introduce a common passport at some point in the future. In any event, member countries will be required to cooperate multilaterally and to develop cooperative strategies to profit from the value added by an infrastructure-led approach to export markets that could support the growth of local industry rather than being positioned as resource exporters of raw materials for global markets.

The question that no one can answer is whether Chinese infrastructural investment will provide the much-needed catalyst to trigger powerful, long-term legacy effects for specific sectors and the domestic market. At the very least, one can say that this group of East African countries have opportunities that never existed previously – and a debt burden to match. Another question is, will elites, and more importantly, local communities, feel empowered to modernise the economy and develop new institutions promoting sustainable growth?

EASTERN EUROPE BILATERALS

The countries of Central and Eastern Europe are high-value assets in China's global strategy and are not only crucial for their markets and resources, but also because of their strategic geopolitical position. For China, these hundreds of bilateral agreements are one of the lynchpins upon which Beijing relies to deepen regional security arrangements. The high-speed train that will link Moscow to Beijing is part of the plan. In a separate development, another high-speed train will connect Budapest to the cities of Bratislava, Vienna

[41]Ibid.

and Sarajevo before extending on to Slovakia. Train travel from Moscow to Kazan, the capital of the Republic of Tatarstan, will be shortened to just three or so hours, instead of the more than 14 hours that it takes now. These examples are an essential part of Beijing's strategy for deepening China's Eurasian bridge to the heartland of Western Europe. China has many negotiations underway for new investments and projects in Hungary, Slovakia, Serbia, Russia and Poland.[42]

There is no clear answer about whether the projects will automatically bring about creative business opportunities and partnerships in the different regional economies. Nor is the impact of the OBOR projects on communities or the degree to which they are people-centred self-evident. In our database, there were some significant investments in clean water, sanitation and green energy, but hardly enough to meet the Asian Development Bank's recent report on the human development deficit in infrastructure.[43]

A more definitive answer would require that we systematically explore the comparative advantage benefiting countries along the Road and China itself. For instance, we do not know to what extent regions and countries will be stimulated by the direct investments made by China. But the analytical exercise is valuable because it establishes some preliminary benchmarks about the capability of the OBOR initiative to stimulate economic growth and, in the process, accelerate regional development transnationally. The proposition to test is whether export growth in China and its partners is a one-way street or a highway of commerce flowing in both directions. If we were to take aerial photographs of China's export growth with African and Asian countries, what are the lessons to be learned?

---

[42] A useful news source on the Balkans and Caucuses is Francesco Martino, 'China goes to Serbia: Infrastructure and politics', *Osservatorio Balcani e Caucaso Transeuropa*, 23 January, 2018 https://www.balcanicaucaso.org/eng/Areas/Serbia/China-goes-to-Serbia-infrastructure-and-politics-185401 [Accessed October 2018]

[43] *Meeting Asia's Infrastructure Needs* (Tokyo: Asian Development Bank Institute, February 2017) https://www.adb.org/sites/default/files/publication/227496/special-report-infrastructure.pdf [Accessed October 2018]

DEVELOPMENT GAPS: ARE THEY GETTING SMALLER?

What we would see are very large development gaps that are responsible for the instability and turmoil that have arisen in Africa, Southeast Asia and Latin America. Particularly in sub-Saharan Africa (SSA), the polarisation of income and the crippling effects of single-commodity production have led to a cycle of low growth in low- and middle-income regions. Per capita income needs to increase from $2 a day to $30 a day if Africa is to leave behind its postcolonial globalised past. Francis Cripps, who has analysed these developmental gaps, reminds us that: in West Africa, comprising 14 countries, per capita income is $1690; in the 12 countries in East Africa, $1347 is the per capita income; and in the eight other sub-Saharan African countries, the per capita income is $3664. The reader can draw the obvious conclusions from Figure 6.3 that the picture is daunting. While Africa is home to more than one billion people, the per capita income PPP was a mere $2603 in 2005. South Africa sticks out as a strong but increasingly troubled performer. In the recent period Ethiopia is seen as the 'one growth miracle'.

While other regions have enjoyed some success, there have also been many failures. It is the case, Cripps says, that 'development may be polarised around Ethiopia, Kenya and Tanzania, and Southern Africa'. This bloc of countries may become a different kind of beachhead than the one China is attempting to establish. The mountain-sized obstacles in the way of African development remain huge. Cripps has created an 'Africa first', imaginary macro-scenario of what is needed for countries in SSA to dramatically boost their commodity exports and investment in order to gain a share of markets for manufacturers across the African continent and in other world regions. How this would happen, he says, has to be based on the formation of a pan-African common market with a global agreement to put Africa first without imposing outside agendas.[44]

[44]Francis Cripps, 'Narrowing the Development Gap: Africa, Europe, ASEAN in the World to 2040: Macro Perspectives' (Seminar: 'Narrowing the Development Gap', Ismeri-Europa, Poggio Mirteto, 18–20 June, 2018).

REGION	BASE LINES		AFRICA FIRST	
	Per Capita GNP Growth REGION 2018–40 (%per annum)	GNP Index 2040 World = 100%	Per Capita GNP Growth 2018–40 (% per annum)	GNP Index 2040 World = 100%
Africa SSH	1.9	20	5.9	50
Nigeria	−0.6	13	6.5	61
Ethiopia	5.7	37	6.9	48
Congo DR	0.1	4	5.9	14
Tanzania	4.9	33	6.8	50
South Africa	1.2	69	5.9	196
Kenya	4.2	30	6.4	49
Uganda	3.5	18	6.3	34
Sudan	2.3	17	5.3	33
Ghana	1.8	24	7.3	80
Gulf of Guinea	1	23	4.9	56
Other W Africa	3.8	20	6.8	39
Other E Africa	−0.9	6	4.3	18
Other S Africa	0.6	21	5.2	60

FIGURE 6.3 Africa's Steep Climb out of Poverty?

Source: Francis Cripps, *Ismeri Europa*, Poggio Seminar, 2018.[45]

In the meantime, there is no guarantee that the shift from export-based to more domestic consumption-based growth with the rise in technology-driven services manufacturers will be the primary beneficiary in new investment and consumption centred transport infrastructure. It may not be sufficient for securing Chinese trade and FDI or to change the current mix of top-heavy, resource-led exports. High growth rates, driven by commodity prices, are always a powerful incentive for governments to rely on these resource-intensive, exports-oriented industries when prices are high. Hence they become inevitably self-reinforcing processes, locking producers into their past export structures.

[45]In this framework, 'World = 100%' refers to the projected global average GNP for 2040. Africa SSH is a term utilised by Francis Cripps to refer to the average GNP for African countries. Specifically, for Cripps, the SSH signifies that this research was compiled under the 'socio-economic sciences and humanities' research cluster.

According to Alice Sindzingre's important research, there are grounds for some optimism that SSA is on the trajectory to break free from its resource curse.[46] She demonstrates that many of China's infrastructural projects positively impact growth and structural change. 'We are very far from resolving these fundamental issues, but the success or failure of China's global infrastructural initiative will depend on how successful it is in reducing these intractable developmental gaps of income polarisation, the absence of market diversification, resource dependency and social inequality.'[47] In the Cripps scenario, transfers need to average 3–4 per cent of GDP and reach as much as 7 per cent in a select number of countries to help targeted groups provide a development pillar. The first step is to raise the baseline per capita income from $10 a day to $40 a day and, for Cripps, the dream would be $100 a day PPP to guarantee success for the entire Africa first story.

In top OBOR markets in Vietnam, Kenya, Ethiopia and Tanzania, regional development has accelerated wherever Beijing invested in significant ways. Demand in overseas markets has picked up, led by growth in major OBOR partners, but China's export composition has also changed. African countries still remain trapped by the resource curse and other structural obstacles. During the downturn in global trade, as a *Bloomberg* overview points out, China's exporters moved away, quietly but rapidly, from traditional labour-intensive goods to machinery and electrical products.[48] This has allowed the economy to benefit from the cyclical upturn in trade markets since mid-2016.

Trade patterns among Beijing's regional partners support a highly integrated cross-border flow of intermediate, unfinished goods. Importantly, in this sense, China's export dividends have been highly profitable to its industries. Diversification in Africa's industries

[46] Alice Sindzingre, 'The Detrimental Consequences of Dependence and Externalisation: Sub-Saharan Africa's Mixed Prospects' (Seminar: 'Narrowing the Development Gap', Ismeri-Europa, Poggio Mirteto, 18–20 June, 2018).
[47] Ibid.
[48] 'China Signals Robust Growth as Factory Gauge Hits Five-Year High', *Bloomberg News*, 29 September, 2017 https://www.bloomberg.com/news/articles/2017-09-30/china-factory-gauge-rises-to-highest-since-2012-on-robust-output [Accessed October 2018]

south of the Sahara has been slow and uneven. A lot of the empirical evidence underlines that China has just begun to scratch the surface of the diversification quandary. There is strong empirical evidence that China's 'spatial fix' has been an accelerant for key Chinese sectors, but less so for its African partners. Moreover, Beijing's export market share in emerging markets has risen from 16.7 per cent in 2012 to 20.8 per cent in 2016, demonstrating that although the country plays a key role in the trade for intermediate goods, it is not confined to Asian trade relationships. It maintains a large volume of purely bilateral trade with more distant partners as well.

Business is thriving between China and Ethiopia, Vietnam, Kenya and elsewhere. Unquestionably, resource exports are booming, but manufactured goods make up less than 4 per cent of all exports destined for China despite massive inflows of China's investment dollars.[49] The distorted composition of trade remains a stubborn problem for much of Africa.

CHINA-ASIA EXPORT RELATIONS

Despite this pessimistic assessment, the Asia-Pacific trade network is now a global driver. According to a 2011 IMF report on the changing patterns of global trade, supply chains in Asia extend 'across several countries, with goods-in-process of final assembly crossing borders several times before reaching their ultimate destination'.[50] The strength of this supply chain network is shown through Asia's export composition: nearly 70 per cent of Asian trade growth in the 2000s was attributed to intermediate Chinese goods. Of course, there are many different kinds of intermediate goods, but usually the term refers to partially assembled manufactured goods not yet ready for consumption. Intermediate goods thus move between various production sites with greater frequency in

---

[49]Sindzingre, op. cit., slide 17.
[50]Tamim Bayoumi, *Changing Patterns of Global Trade* (International Monetary Fund, Strategy, Policy, and Review Department, 15 June, 2011) https://www.imf.org/external/np/pp/eng/2011/061511.pdf [Accessed October 2018]

REGION	Population 2017 (millions)	GNP Index 2017 World = 100%	Per Capita GNP Growth 2018–40 (% per annum)	GNP Index 2040 World = 100%
Other E Asia and Pacific	290	252	2.7	279
Europe	606	244	2.2	241
Malaysia, Singapore, Brunei	38	194	2.1	188
World	7,553	100	2.3	100
China	1,410	98	4.5	162
Thailand	69	91	4.2	139
ASEAN	648	55	3.3	70
Philippines	105	45	26	48
Indonesia	264	44	27	49
Vietnam	96	43	6	98
India	1,339	38	5.1	71
Other S and Central Asia	537	29	1.3	24
Lao PDR and Cambodia	23	26	1.3	21
Myanmar	53	19	3.9	27

FIGURE 6.4   ASEAN's Long Road to Prosperity?

Source: Francis Cripps, Ismeri Europa, Poggio Seminar, 2018.

Asia.[51] These goods often flow through China, which serves as a regional hub. Back in 2000, China made fewer than 15 per cent of Asia's total exports. In the years that followed, however, the Middle Kingdom's share surged – peaking above 40 per cent in 2015. As China's primary trade and investment strategy, One Belt, One Road has yet to reach its full potential. As we can see in Figure 6.4, ASEAN has success stories, but far too few. Many countries are trapped in poverty and low growth.

The same 2011 IMF report found that lowered export growth in China appears also to lower Asian exports to China, reflecting its

[51]Olaf Unteroberdoerster, 'Implications for Asia from Rebalancing in China', in *China's Economy in Transition: From External to Internal Rebalancing*, edited by Papa N'Diaye, Malhar Nabar and Anoop Singh (eds), (IMF, 2013), p. 111.

centrality in the regional trade network. This is supported by research from the Paris School of Business, which shows that other East Asian currencies tend to react in fear of appreciating strongly against the Chinese currency.[52] While the numbers suggest that China's RMB currency has played an ever larger role in Asia's movement of currency in the last decade, Beijing's trade network both sources and exports to its global partners with goods more likely to cross borders and exit through China.

According to a note by Louis Kujis, economist at Oxford Economics, other economies have been making gains at the expense of China's manufacturers and boosting their share of Asia's exports since 2015, thanks in large part to the OBOR.[53] For example, rising wages in China have driven manufacturers relying on low-skilled labour to relocate to Vietnam and other developing economies in the region. At the other end of the OBOR value chain, global demand for labour-saving technologies like AI and robotics have helped buoy trade in advanced electronics and semiconductors from Hong Kong and South Korea.

Then again, it comes as no surprise that China has not lost its competitive edge in manufacturing, Kujis notes. Instead, Chinese labour now focuses more on manufactured goods than it once did, allowing partner countries to focus more on low-skilled labour. For the time being, this has to be considered a small step in the right direction, but clearly it is not an answer to South Asia's deeply rooted structural problems.

China's massive investment programme has contradictory effects as well, which gives some hope for optimism and a soft landing. Vietnam is an important case study of the transformation of Asia's export markets. In total, China exports more goods to Vietnam

[52]Benjamin Keddad, 'How Do the Renminbi and Other East Asian Currencies Co-Move? New Evidence from Non-Linear Analysis', SSRN (December 2016) https://papers.ssrn.com/sol3/papers.cfm?abstract_id=2850421 [Accessed October 2016]

[53]Louis Kuijs, 'Research Briefing, Asia: The short, medium and long-term outlook for Asian FX', Oxford Economics, 8 August, 2016 http://www.ioandc.com/wp-content/uploads/2016/08/1-Oxford-Ecos-paper.pdf [Accessed October 2018]

than any other destination in Southeast Asia, sending textiles to be made into shirts and sneakers, and electronic components for mobile phones and large flat-panel displays. Those completed products are exported around the world, as well as back to China. For Vietnam, these subcontracts are seen as an opportunity to begin a new trajectory in the global economy, but for critics they are also seen as a new form of dependency. One hypothesis is that Vietnam will evolve from its role as a cheap-labour contractor to an industrial force in its own right. It might become another Asian Tiger – or some domesticated version. However, this may take another decade.

According to Chinese customs data, Beijing exported about $72.1 billion worth of high value-added products such as advanced components goods to Vietnam in 2017, up 49.8 per cent from the previous year. Moreover, experts predicted that bilateral trade between the two countries would reach a record high of $100 billion in 2018, after reaching $93.69 billion the previous year.[54] Beijing strategically invests in Vietnam because of its geographical advantage – 'closer to China and hence lower cost on materials, transportation and relatively shorter production lead time,' said Bosco Law, chief executive of the Hong Kong-based Lawsgroup.[55] But is it a model for other countries?

AFRICA: A CORE CONSTITUENCY

China-Africa relations are so complex because China has such extensive relations with the entire continent. China has a core constituency of countries that were part of colonial independence movement struggles. Part of the reason for this is that in its ideological battle with the Soviet Union, Africa became a primary battleground between Beijing and Moscow. To name but a few

---

[54]"VN-China Trade likely to Reach $100 Billion', *Việt Nam News*, 21 January, 2018 http://vietnamnews.vn/economy/421539/vn-china-trade-likely-to-reach-100-billion.html [Accessed October 2018]

[55]Tostevin, Matthew, 'Despite strains, Vietnam and China forge closer economic ties', *Reuters*, 1 September, 2017 https://www.reuters.com/article/us-vietnam-china/despite-strains-vietnam-and-china-forge-closer-economic-ties-idUSKCN1BC3S2 [Accessed October 2018]

examples, China gave military aid and training to revolutionary movements in Tanzania, Algeria, Kenya, Ethiopia, South Africa and Zimbabwe. No one should be surprised when China gave the African Union the gift of a stunningly modern, permanent headquarters in Addis Ababa. This serves as a permanent reminder of China's leading role in anticolonial and postcolonial struggles in the region after the Second World War, and embodies the Chinese view of soft power infrastructural influence.

The OBOR has formalised China's relationships with many African countries. According to the John Hopkins China-Africa Research Initiative, bilateral trade between the two regions has been steadily increasing for the past 16 years, punctuated by a slight slump and quick recovery from the 2008 financial crisis.[56] Economically, trade networking and technology transfers have dramatically increased. It is still unclear whether China has received the lion's share of the benefits from its recent high-growth performance, or whether African countries are on the verge of overcoming the lingering effects of colonialism.

Thousands of news articles have been written about China's export engagement in Africa, but much of the information in these articles does not hold up under scrutiny, as Brautigam has pointed out.[57] According to Brautigam's analysis, the academic literature on Chinese investment in Africa is thin, especially in terms of rigorous empirical studies. Whether popular or academic, most of these articles tend to describe China's export relationship with Africa as neo-imperial; far less benign than it should be, with many trade imbalances.

As Tufts University economist Margaret McMillan points out, China's interest in Africa is directly linked to the renaissance of economic growth across the continent.[58] Average annual GDP growth

[56]'Data: China-Africa Trade', *China-Africa Research Initiative*, Johns Hopkins School of Advanced International Studies, December 2017 http://www.sais-cari.org/data-china-africa-trade/ [Accessed October 2018]

[57]Deborah Brautigam, *The Dragon's Gift: The Real Story of China in Africa* (Oxford University Press, 2009).

[58]Margaret McMillan, 'Chinese investment in Africa', *International Growth Centre* (blog), 15 August, 2017 https://www.theigc.org/blog/chinese-investment-africa/ [Accessed October 2018]

in 38 African countries was 4.9 per cent between 2000 and 2015; in resource-poor Ethiopia the average was just under 10 per cent. In fact, only seven of the 17 countries in Africa that had annual GDP growth rates above the continental average of 4.9 per cent are considered resource rich. If anyone has doubts, they should take a second look at Figure 6.3, *Africa's Steep Climb out of Poverty?* Economists are still debating how much of this is due to Chinese investment and how much is due to structural change, particularly the shift away from low-productivity agriculture and towards high-productivity industries. The fact that growth has been rapid in many resource-poor countries, and has continued past the collapse in highly volatile global commodity prices, calls into question the notion that Africa's recent performance is intimately and primarily tied to Chinese demand for its importing commodities.[59] There are many other local factors in play.

GREEN SHOOTS OF DIVERSIFICATION: SOME GOOD NEWS AT LAST?

What is unexpected is that Beijing is diversifying exports to Africa, both in terms of sectors and location. China accounted for only around 5 per cent of global foreign direct investment into Africa in 2015,[60] hardly a banner year for Chinese investors. In contrast, roughly 25 per cent of Africa's global trade in 2015 was with China. The two sectors most affected are mining and construction, undoubtedly the lingering effects of what is known as Africa's resource curse – its dependence on the global demand from this single sector, and the urban development boom, clearly visible in Africa's major cities and still accounting for 54 per cent of exports. In the Democratic Republic of the Congo, Nigeria, South Africa,

[59]Xinshen Diao, Margaret McMillan and Dani Rodrik, 'The Recent Growth Boom in Developing Economies: A Structural Change Perspective', National Bureau of Economic Research Working Paper No. 23132, February 2017.
[60]Deborah Brautigam, Xinshen Diao, Margaret McMillan and Jed Silver, 'Chinese Investment in Africa: How Much do we Know?' *PEDL Synthesis Series*, 2 (October 2017) https://pedl.cepr.org/sites/default/files/PEDL_Synthesis_Papers_Piece_No._2.pdf [Accessed October 2018]

Sudan, Zambia, Tanzania, Kenya and Ethiopia, Chinese investment flows very much remain a driver.

What all these numbers are forcefully telling us is that this is a time of dynamic change in many African countries. However, imbalances remain and it is not clear whether Africa's institutions are strong enough to oversee the regulation of African capitalism as a modern entity requiring high levels of investment in people and technology. Rodrik et al. argue that 'essential change stabilising institutions through the rule of law and the independence of the judiciary as well as large scale investment in health, education, and communities is still in deficit compared to the raw effects of market opening'.[61] It helps to clarify matters by looking at the export-import relationship between China and Tanzania as a case in point.

Tanzania's main exports are very traditional and include: dry seafood, raw leather, logs, copper and wooden handcrafts. It imports pricier items with greater value such as: foodstuffs, vehicles, textiles, light industrial products, chemical products, mechanical equipment, electric appliances and steel. One way to read the trade figures is that this is a conventional commercial relationship, and that China's investments have not yet been as transformative as predicted. By contrast, China's trade relationship with Kenya has been marked by the flow-through effects of OBOR investments.

As a 2014 World Bank report points out, Chinese exporters have targeted more sectors than natural resources in Kenya: the communications sector in Nairobi benefited from $150 million in investments from China, and automotive manufacturing received $68 million.[62] High import rates from China are attributed to increased OBOR infrastructure projects in Kenya, with the ongoing construction of standard gauge railways accounting for a large chunk of imports. According to leading economic indicators by Kenya's

[61]Diao, McMillan and Rodrik, op. cit.
[62]Peter Buxbaum, 'What in the World is China doing in Kenya?' *Global Trade,* 24 May, 2016 http://www.globaltrademag.com/global-trade-daily/commentary/what-in-the-world-is-china-doing-in-kenya [Accessed October 2018]

National Bureau of Statistics, Kenya imported $3.4 billion worth of goods to China in 2017.[63] If this trend persists, imports from China will reach $4 billion for the first time, dethroning India as the biggest net exporter to Kenya.

Ethiopia is another special case highlighting the importance of partnering with China's OBOR. Even before China's global infrastructure initiative was launched, it was already outperforming most other African countries. Its GDP grew at a rate of 10.9 per cent from 2003 to 2013 as compared with 4 per cent from 1993 to 2003. This period of high growth rates in Ethiopia was marked by an intensification of Ethiopia-China economic relations. Bilateral trade between the two countries has expanded rapidly, and China now accounts for over one-fifth of Ethiopia's total imports and is the principal source for manufactured goods, machinery and transport equipment for Ethiopia.[64]

From a developmental perspective, Ethiopia is most convergent towards the Chinese economic model of development through international economic cooperation. It has struck a balance between its own painfully slow growth trajectory of gradual industrialisation and integration into China's global supply chain. Manufactured goods and machinery and transport equipment together account for over 90 per cent of Ethiopian imports from China. Capital goods such as transport vehicles, building structures and parts, mechanical shovels, telecommunications equipment and accessories are the leading import items from China. Indeed, there is a beachhead of investment and China is displacing other competitors in Addis Ababa's leading sectors, including construction, transportation and manufacturing.

[63]Apurva Sanghi and Dylan Johnson, 'Three myths about China in Kenya', Brookings (blog), 16 May, 2016 https://www.brookings.edu/blog/future-development/2016/05/16/three-myths-about-china-in-kenya/ [Accessed October 2018]
[64]Malancha Chakrabarty, 'Ethiopia-China Economic Relations: A Classic Win-Win Situation?' World Review of Political Economy 7(2) (2016), pp. 226–248 https://www.questia.com/library/journal/1P3-4173781401/ethiopia-china-economic-relations-a-classic-win-win [Accessed October 2018]

PROGRESS BUT NO SILVER BULLET

So what is happening here? One tangible effect is that China's investment and export relationship has raised productivity, technology and other norms, but obviously not enough. The current boom is possible only because of China's investment in infrastructure and its reliance on resource exports. How else would such economies support a modern infrastructure, the nervous system of a market economy? Indeed, the industrial base is still small and inadequate. The danger is always growing indebtedness, the volatility of international commodity markets and the constant pressure on public finance to meet its debt obligations. The good news is that China is loaning money at very low rates, which no private multinational can match. Ethiopia is also a special case because it is part of China's core constituency of post-revolutionary countries where non-market relations can play a large role in debt repayment.

There is no simple lesson to be learned because African and Asian countries do not share a common template and state-market relations are organised so differently between and among countries. China seems to have understood the 'varieties of capitalism' argument, which, in effect, sends policymakers the unambiguous message that the timing and sequencing of investments reflect divergent conditions and not a universal imperative of supply and demand signals.

From such a complex public policy perspective, the margins between winners and losers will vary depending on the region and its proximity to mainland China. Does this mean that Asia will do better than Africa in the long run? Countries successful at building institutions that are stable and embedded in the social order are likely to prosper. For those that cannot solve the governance trap, no amount of innovative infrastructural development can be a shortcut.

Beijing will have to work hard to convince its partners and neighbours that its oversized infrastructural initiative has more to offer than the US-led order. The economic benefits of acquiring a modern infrastructure and a financial boost from China are too tempting for many 'poor and forgotten' Southeast Asian and African countries to pass up. Still, countries have yet to eliminate the crippling effects of their developmental gaps linked to poverty, resource dependency, blocked market access, footloose MNCs and precious little new technology.

For some policy experts, it is a kind of chicken and egg situation. Do you first upgrade and modernise a country's transportation system, which, in turn, becomes a trigger point in the development cycle to create an environment for investment in new industries? Or is the timing and sequencing the reverse? The New Silk Road has partially settled this vexatious debate about economic geography and technology by providing the resources to start at both ends of the process.

7

Beijing's Power-drivers: What Could Go Wrong? Or Right?

THE OVERSELLING OF OBOR

There is always a very real and immediate danger of overselling China's One Belt, One Road to the many countries looking for an infrastructural fix. Most of its members are second- and third-tier countries that are economically deprived and struggling with their development. Others are a mixture of middle-income, market-emerging economies and advanced high-income states. Economic powerhouses like Japan and the EU are not formally part of it, and could join at a later date. So, China still has a long way to go to create a viable Eurasian coalition with institutions and a fully developed legal framework. If experts have learned anything, it is that the Chinese policy reflex needs globalisation to ensure the supply of resources it lacks. It is locked into the global economy for its survival. The One Belt, One Road global infrastructural strategy is the best geopolitical insurance for China's robust new identity.

China faces other difficult challenges from the subcontinent, which may reorient its soft power applied calculus. For instance, the escalating rhetoric between India and China is only one example of how dangerously incendiary Asian politics can be. In China's own backyard, Vietnam, Laos, Thailand, Sri Lanka, Pakistan and Cambodia have unprecedented debt levels. China's commercial loans have an octopus quality, taking hold of many different sectors, according to Mahindra Rajapaska, the powerful president for a decade and now a Sri Lankan opposition politician. He is attacking the deal that he negotiated and is quite typical in his scepticism that Sri Lanka is caught in the middle of China's infrastructural plans. Just beneath the surface is a lot of anti-China resentment. Japan and South Korea, other potential members of the anti-China front, have kept a low profile because they are significant trading partners with China.

In the eyes of some experts, the absence of any collective security provision is a design defect in China's global project.[1] But it could also be an asset for others. Certainly, China does not want to be encumbered by a formal commitment to send Chinese soldiers to the rescue of another state faced with a major security threat.[2] It would surprise few experts if China were to continue to expand its use of private security contractors to protect projects in which it has invested hundreds of millions of dollars.[3]

CHINA: A RISING MILITARY POWER

China has increased its military spending dramatically over the past five years to become a powerful regional presence. Yet it still faces a permanent and large military presence of American forces in the region, with both hard and soft power working together. The US military has 28,500 troops stationed in South Korea, 5000 troops stationed on Guam, 50,000 troops stationed in Japan, active military bases in the Philippines, and a carrier strike group permanently based at Yokosuka, Japan.[4] Beijing's 'hard power' build-up is often difficult to separate from its soft power strategy to construct a parallel global system. This could have serious implications for the future of BRI.

---

[1] An important feature of NATO is Article 5, which commits members to a collective security provision in the event of aggression.
[2] Unlike the US-led coalition of NATO, China has only one standing mutual defence pact with North Korea entitled the 'Sino-North Korean Mutual Aid and Cooperation Friendship Treaty'.
[3] Charles Clover, 'Chinese private security companies go global', *Financial Times*, 26 February, 2017.
[4] "The US has a massive military presence in the Asia-Pacific. Here's what you need to know about it', *Agence France-Presse*, 11 August, 2017 https://www.pri.org/stories/2017-08-11/us-has-massive-military-presence-asia-pacific-heres-what-you-need-know-about-it [Accessed October 2018]

Such distinctions have collapsed as China's disputes over islands in the South China Sea continue to escalate. Whether China will step back from soft power diplomacy and replace it with great power bullying remains an open question. So far it has settled its conflicts with its partners such as Pakistan, Kenya and Rwanda, all part of China's investment club, renegotiating the terms and conditions of bilateral agreements that, with hindsight, were seen to be too costly when originally negotiated. On the global stage, it would be a mistake to think that Beijing is all about soft power and, in fact, the modernisation of its army and the upgrading of its national security suggest quite the reverse.

The use of military force by Beijing is a risky flashpoint that could seriously damage China's soft power image-building exercise to promote cooperation and development.[5] It does not take much imagination to see that China's reliance on its growing military presence would be a game-changer. Nonetheless, China has invested heavily in settling contractual or border disputes with Turkey, Pakistan, Kenya, the UK, Russia, Vietnam, Laos and the Philippines, among others. It is significant that some of these commercial disputes with Russia and Pakistan involved hundreds of millions of dollars in agreements and were renegotiated to the astonishment of many, without the help of a Western-backed, private-state-investor, dispute-resolution mechanism.

These messy examples of bilateral relations gone sour are also case studies of state-to-state conflict resolution. The increasing spread of the OBOR projects through the Asia-Pacific region are particularly complicated by the fact that the South China Sea area may hold more than 200 billion barrels of oil, up to 750 trillion cubic feet of natural gas, 12 per cent of the world's remaining fish catch and key routes for the transportation of commodities. Such unresolved tensions around sovereignty and resources show no signs of de-escalating in the near future.[6]

---

[5]For an overview of the South China Sea, see: 'South China Sea', *Eia*, 7 February, 2013 https://www.eia.gov/beta/international/regions-topics.cfm?RegionTopicID=SCS [Accessed October 2018]
[6]Chas Freeman, 'The United States and China: Game Of Superpowers', 8 February, 2018 https://chasfreeman.net/the-united-states-and-china-game-of-superpowers/ [Accessed October 2018]

SMART ECONOMICS AND THE RETURN OF THE LEADING ROLE OF INFRASTRUCTURE

Economists have always been divided about the trade-off between the debt burden of building infrastructure and higher GDP growth from infrastructural stimulus. Despite being by far the largest dynamic economy in the Asia-Pacific region, China has not escaped this fundamental dilemma, nor can it. It was not so long ago that infrastructural spending was the mainstay of modern post-war mainstream developmental economics for industrialising capitalist countries. Spending on infrastructure, except defence, has been pushed to the sidelines, one of the casualties of the rise of neoliberalism, the world's troubled financial framework.

Neoclassical economics have systematically abandoned the older Keynesian public policy narrative. The renowned economists Ragnar Nurkse,[7] Gunnar Myrdal[8] and Joseph Stiglitz[9] all highlighted the vital link between infrastructure and development, and accorded it a central place of honour in post-Second World War global governance discourses. Countries emerging from colonialism or devastated by war understood, instinctively, the important role infrastructure played in winning the war and later, in the postcolonial era, as a leading factor of modernisation, international competitiveness and industrialisation.

According to economic historian Robert Gordon, technology, large-scale infrastructural investment and high rates of capital accumulation were the key to the record-high US productivity growth post-1945.[10] Strong financial regulation after World War II stabilised the business cycle with fewer highs and lows. Crisis

---

[7]Ragnar Nurkse, *Problems of Capital Formation in Underdeveloped Countries* (Oxford University Press, 1967); Albert O. Hirschman, *The Strategy of Economic Development* (Yale University Press, 1958).

[8]Gunnar Myrdal, 'What is Development?', *Journal of Economic Issues* 8 (1974), pp. 729–736.

[9]Joseph Stiglitz, 'More Instruments and Broader Goals: Moving toward the Post-Washington Consensus', in WIDER *Perspectives on Global Development, United Nations University World Institute for Development Economics Research* (from the 1998 WIDER Annual Lecture, January 1998) (Palgrave MacMillan, 2005), pp. 16–48.

[10]Robert Gordon, *The Rise and Fall of American Growth: The US Standard of Living since the Civil War* (Harvard University Press, 2016).

and panics were seen to have been relegated to the past. Public investment reached record levels in both hard and soft infrastructure spending, particularly in the education and health sectors, as well as housing and defence. American governments invested in science and technology, and many of the innovations in the fields of medicine, computing and new information-based technologies contributed to private productivity growth.

Ironically, the policy rationale justifying substantial investments in massive infrastructure projects borrowed from orthodox free market theories narrowly focused on the powers of the self-regulating market. The modern gift of infrastructure made the market appear to operate efficiently in response to supply-and-demand signalling.[11] The post-war welfare state's retreat from 'the commanding heights of the economy' was dramatic and long-lasting, and needs no retelling here.[12] Importantly, there were other surprises waiting in store to challenge the global balance of power.

What took Anglo-American economics by complete surprise were the high-performing tiger economies of Hong Kong, Singapore, South Korea and Taiwan in the 1990s, which rejected the standard model of market fundamentalism. They had, in the words of the World Bank's controversial 1993 report, challenged mainstream economics with their market-driven policies. They 'had achieved unusually low and declining levels of inequality, contrary to historical experience and contemporary evidence in other research'.[13] The

[11]John Galbraith, *The Affluent Society* (Paw Prints, 1958).

[12]The popular phrase, 'the commanding heights of the economy', refers to existing private industry essential to the economy like public utilities, natural resources, heavy industry and transport as well as control over foreign and domestic trade. This phrase emerged from a branch of modern political economy concerned with organising society and can be traced back to Karl Marx's idea on socialism, which stresses commanding heights and advocates for government control of them. When Deng Xiaoping introduced the Chinese economic reforms, he was inspired by this concept. Moreover, the Communist Party of China still advocates that the state needs to control the economy's commanding heights. See Daniel Yergin and Joseph Stanislaw, *The Commanding Heights: The Battle Between Government and the Marketplace That Is Remaking the Modern World* (Free Press, 1998).

[13]*The East Asian Miracle: Economic Growth and Public Policy* (Oxford University Press, published for the World Bank, 1993) http://documents.worldbank.org/curated/en/975081468244550798/pdf/multi-page.pdf [Accessed October 2018]

tigers economies were more risk-driven and committed to the idea that the state's proper role was to design both industrial and financial policy so as to pick sectorial winners.

Like China would replicate 25 years later, the tigers channelled cheap credit to strategic sectors of their choosing and invested in infrastructure as the cornerstone of development, a policy condemned by most mainstream American economists on the grounds that only markets could pick winners. The tiger economies were the success story of the decade until the East Asia crisis of 1997–98 struck. The US treasury and IMF were blamed for advice to cut back on state expenditures, imposing austerity and pushing these economies into recession.[14] These experiences help us better understand how China appropriated and intensified the idea of the 'development state' for its own purposes. And OBOR is a direct legacy effect.

IS CHINESE AID AS EFFECTIVE AS WESTERN AID?

Recently, China's investment in infrastructure has given new legitimacy to the importance of highly engineered, efficient public transportation systems, bridges, automated ocean-going ports, clean water, publicly built housing, oil pipelines and innovative green energy projects, all of which can be thought of as the third phase in developmental economics. This is a branch of economics analysing the economic aspects of the development process in low-income countries.[15] As a result, China has positioned itself as a leading global financier of the 'hardware' of economic development.

China's emphasis on economic and social infrastructure stands in contrast to Western suppliers of development finance, which have scaled back their involvement in the infrastructure

[14]Robert Wade, *Governing the Market: Economic Theory and the Role of Government in East Asian Industrialization* (Princeton University Press, 1990). Also see: Deena Khatkhate, 'East Asian Financial Crisis and the IMF: Chasing Shadows', *Economic and Political Weekly*, Vol. 33, No. 17 (Apr. 25 – May 1, 1998), pp. 963–969.
[15]Colin Crouch, *Political Economy of Modern Capitalism: Mapping Convergence and Diversity* (Sage Publications, 1997).

sector.[16] As infrastructural investments can ease structural barriers to economic growth and spur development, it is plausible that Chinese aid might have stronger impacts than aid from other bilateral and multilateral donors.[17] Moreover, despite claims about Chinese inefficiency and corruption from countless Sinophobics, the 2017 report by AID Data uncovered that Chinese, US and OECD-DAC aid produce similar economic growth impacts. Interestingly, it also found no evidence to support the idea that Western aid is less effective at accelerating economic growth in countries that also have significant access to Chinese aid.[18]

On the other hand, Crouigneau and Hiault argue that Chinese 'aid' can also work to dampen the growth prospects of its recipient and borrower countries.[19] If China finances unproductive, 'white elephant' capital investment projects that deliver weak financial and economic returns, host governments may find it difficult to service their debts and cover their recurrent expenditures.[20] For example, in the case of Tonga, concessional loans from China account for 65 per cent of the nation's debt stock, and as Philippa Brant observes, it will be difficult for Tonga to service these debt obligations.[21]

[16]David Dollar, *Lessons from China for Africa*, World Bank Policy Research Working Paper Series, February 2008 https://ssrn.com/abstract=1098629 [Accessed October 2018]; Robert L. Hicks, Bradley C. Parks, J. Timmons Roberts and Michael J. Tierney, *Greening Aid?: Understanding the Environmental Impact of Development Assistance* (Oxford University Press, 2008); Michael J. Tierney, Daniel L. Nielson, Darren G. Hawkins, J. Timmons Roberts, Michael G. Findley, Ryan M. Powers, Bradley Parks, Sven E. Wilson and Robert L. Hicks, 'More Dollars than Sense: Refining Our Knowledge of Development Finance Using AidData', *World Development* 39(11), (2011), pp. 1891–1906.
[17]Axel Dreher, Andreas Fuchs, Bradley Parks, Austin M. Strange and Michael J. Tierney, 'Aid, China, and Growth: Evidence from a New Global Development Finance Dataset', *AIDDATA: A Research Lab at William & Mary*, working paper 46, October 2017 http://docs.aiddata.org/ad4/pdfs/WPS46_Aid_China_and_Growth.pdf [Accessed October 2018]
[18]Ibid.
[19]Françoise Crouigneau and Richard Hiault, 'World Bank hits at China over lending', *Financial Times*, 23 October, 2006.
[20]Axel Dreher, Andreas Fuchs, Bradley Parks, Austin M. Strange and Michael J. Tierney, op. cit.
[21]Philippa Brant, 'The Geopolitics of Chinese Aid: Mapping Beijing's Funding in the Pacific', *Foreign Affairs*, 4 March, 2015 https://www.foreignaffairs.com/articles/china/2015-03-04/geopolitics-chinese-aid [Accessed October 2018]

Despite high-level overtures to Beijing, former Tongan prime minister Lord Tu'ivakanō was unsuccessful in having these loans converted to grants. Repayment of one loan would have accounted for over 17 per cent of government revenue. China recently agreed to defer repayments for five years, as it also renegotiated the terms and conditions of its loan to Ethiopia. But the original 20-year loan term to Tonga does not change, meaning that annual repayments will be larger when they begin in 2018–19. Other debt-laden partners are also wondering what will happen if they cannot repay Beijing. They could find themselves using more public funding than would otherwise be necessary to keep up with interest payments. The failure to maintain their infrastructure would further deter foreign investors who perceive that it is high risk.

THE SELF-MADE DEBT TRAP

Normatively, Chinese lending practices depart in significant ways from the international standards of development-lending banks, the IMF and the World Bank.[22] China offers some high-risk countries loans at a level beyond their ability to repay and, as a result, a host government that has taken on a high level of Chinese debt might experience foreign exchange shortages, which can lead to import shortages and constrain export growth.[23]

Will there also be domestic fallout with China's middle class turning against the BRI when their taxes increase because these generously funded infrastructural initiatives go over budget and demand still more money? Will Chinese public opinion become disenchanted and ask why Beijing is investing so much money in low-return projects in high-risk countries when China needs to invest in domestic Chinese development? Will China escape this colossal debt trap of its own making? The truthful answer is, with

[22]Moises Naím, 'China Is Not a Rogue Donor', *Foreign Affairs*, 15 October, 2015.
[23]M. Iyoha, 'External Debt and Economic Growth in Sub-Saharan African Countries: An Econometric Study', AERC research paper 90 (Nairobi: African Economic Research Consortium, 1999).

the global economy so volatile, no one can predict the success or failure rate. The only certainty is that the next five years will be critical.

After all, the amount of money that Beijing is spending on the BRI is often misunderstood. In some ways, much of the cost of the initiative will be passed down to the Chinese population, who will have to pay for this 'great leap outward'. As Yuan Li, Professor of East Asian studies at the University of Duisburg-Essen, points out, the benefits of global infrastructural investment on Chinese consumers are usually diffused, but losses on workers in a few sectors are concentrated.[24] Workers from traditional low-wage sectors are especially likely to get hurt. Offshoring may cause job polarisation, which could lead to rising relative demand in well-paid skilled jobs and falling demand in the low-paid, less-skilled 'middling' jobs, and least-skilled jobs. This combination of increasing inequality, the disappearance of the middle class and stagnating wages for low-skill workers is very worrisome.[25]

When coupled with new tariffs from the Trump Administration on $250 billion of Chinese imports, tightening of rules on Chinese investments in the US, screening of supply chains for national security vulnerabilities, and boosting military spending by $82 billion, it is apparent that Beijing faces serious challenges to implementing its vision moving forward.[26] However, many Chinese economists have estimated that the export losses can be amply offset by stimulating domestic demand.[27] China is already one of the world's largest

[24]Li Yuan and Hans-Jörg Schmerer, 'Trade and the New Silk Road: Opportunities, Challenges, and Solution', *Journal of Chinese Economic and Business Studies* 15, no. 3 (2017): 205-213 https://www.tandfonline.com/doi/full/10.1080/14765284.2017.1347473

[25]Maarten Goos and Alan Manning, 'Lousy and Lovely Jobs: The Rising Polarization of Work in Britain'. *Review of Economics and Statistics* 89, no. 1 (2007): pp. 118–133.

[26]'The US is Hunkering Down for a New Cold War with China', *Financial Times*, 12 October, 2018 https://www.ft.com/content/666b0230-cd7b-11e8-8d0b-a6539b949662

[27]Ni Tao, 'How China can Turn the Trade War into a "Strategic Opportunity" to ascend to Global Leadership', *South China Morning Post*, 25 October, 2018 https://www.scmp.com/comment/insight-opinion/united-states/article/2169955/how-china-can-turn-trade-war-strategic

consumer markets, offering a wealth of opportunities to businesses selling merchandise from garments to hi-tech gadgets, from imported foods to travel products. In January of 2018, the *Washington Post* predicted that retail sales in China would reach $5.8 trillion by the end of the year, equalling or surpassing the US.[28]

Zheng Bijian, an influential Chinese intellectual on globalisation, identified the origins of China's resilience as part of market capitalism with Chinese characteristics. It is the fifth pillar after 'sustained productivity growth, strong national defence, unique cultural power and unparalleled social governance'. He also talked up the Belt and Road Initiative, calling it a 'mega world market' that would be China's best shot at breaking free from Trump's chokehold on trade. At the same time, this is by no means a foregone conclusion as mounting personal debt levels are also squeezing Chinese consumers' ability and willingness to buy other big-ticket items. For instance, the country's household debt-to-income ratio reached 107 per cent at the end of 2017, according to a recent research report published by the Shanghai University of Finance and Economics.[29]

Along the BRI, data released by China's National Bureau of Statistics and Ministry of Commerce shows that Chinese trade with countries along the planned routes has reached $5 trillion in five years. Moreover, China has directly invested more than $60 billion in the countries and, according to official statistics, more than 200,000 jobs have been created, likely a guestimation.[30] While a significant number of bad debts are on its books in a handful of countries, some experts argue that OBOR has become 'too big to fail'. The role of China's financial institutions in this complex balancing act continues to confound many Western experts. The Chinese command-control

---

[28]Heather Long, 'The Chinese are now Buying as much Stuff as Americans, a Gamer-Changer for the World Economy', *Washington Post*, 11 January, 2018 https://www.washingtonpost.com/news/wonk/wp/2018/01/11/the-chinese-are-now-buying-as-much-stuff-as-americans-a-game-changer-for-the-world-economy/?noredirect=on&utm_term=.d0d4cb7d0d50

[29]http://www.bjreview.com/Opinion/201808/t20180820_800138574.html

[30]Ni Tao, op. cit.

system is often understood as a simplistic one-way, top-to-bottom dynamic. As explored in Chapter 3, China's deep pockets give those in command sufficient institutional flexibility to address disasters when they occur from overspending to low rates of return on these projects.

A different threat is the question of whether, if the Chinese economy faces a jolting financial setback, hundreds of projects will be cancelled or postponed. Recently, a major study of dozens of domestic bridges built by China in the past decade concluded that a significant number suffer from underuse and poor construction.[31] Issues of a loss in trust and confidence can also be earth-shaking in their consequences. This is why the Chinese authorities' promise of financial reform needs to be monitored closely to determine whether they are keeping their word.

They have the money and the appetite to finance more and bigger projects across the Global South, and particularly in Central Asia. China has already surpassed $2 trillion, the original budget target. A recent report from the Center for Global Development has new data that China is spending as much as $8 trillion across deals in Belt and Road initiatives in more than 80 countries covering Asia, Africa and Europe.[32] The final accounting could easily show a much higher figure. So where does this leave us? Can China look to historical examples to confirm that it is on the right path with its massive infrastructural strategy?

THE NEW DEAL: AN OBOR-LIKE SOCIAL INVESTMENT STRATEGY?

The most successful case of public capital having long-term transformative effects was Roosevelt's New Deal, which helped rescue the American economy from the depths of the Great Depression in the 1930s. Along with other measures, the New Deal injected hundreds of

[31]Bruce Einhorn, 'The Big Problem with China's Bridge and Tunnel Addiction', *Bloomberg*, 2 March, 2017 https://www.bloomberg.com/news/articles/2017-03-02/the-big-problem-with-china-s-bridge-and-tunnel-addiction [Accessed October 2018]
[32]John Hurley, Scott Morris and Gailyn Portelance, 5 March, 2018, op. cit.

millions of dollars into upgrading America's infrastructure. For many economists, its generic focus on thousands of small, community-based local projects combined with national visionary public works was the prototypical ideal.

Even by today's standards, the Public Works Administration (PWA) relying on federal leadership was diverse, often innovative, and far-sighted. It partnered with private money and 'hired over millions of workers and eventually built 78,000 bridges, 650,000 miles of road, and 700 miles of airport runways, 13,000 playgrounds and 125,000 military and civilian buildings including more than 40,000 schools'.[33] It was a defining achievement in planning, coordination, conceptualisation, and execution and the Chinese model, as we have demonstrated, shares many of these same features with its managerial expertise and flexible centralised planning, providing a highly malleable framework with the Party firmly in control. The Chinese experience in conceptualisation and execution has created a unique economic culture and model that has its origins in the Asian century with its own varieties of capitalism models.

Today, no account of the transformative strategic role of public capital would be complete without the mention of South Korea and Japan – both Asian success stories of a state steering the economy after devastating wars in the Pacific. It is worth highlighting that their governments created powerful industrial ministries with special links to Korean and Japanese banks in order to target and invest in strategic sectors of the economy and develop globally competitive industries.

Korea's and Japan's industrial revolutions could not have occurred without massively funded, superior models of efficient public works and high-performance transportation systems that linked rail, road, air and ocean-going freighters to transform leading export industries

[33]James Stewart, 'Trump-Size Idea for a New President: Build Something Inspiring', New York Times, 17 November, 2016.

into powerful engines of growth.[34] We are obliged to ask, is this Asian-centred vision of industrialisation driving China's massive investments in infrastructure globally and regionally? Fundamentally, the answer is yes.

Further, we need to know whether these examples are, in some aspirational way, precursors of the Chinese strategic model of global infrastructure investment. The answer is, again, yes, if you have a top-down, state-directed economy with limited labour rights and a lot of corruption that takes charge of development and has a strategic plan and the resources to pull it off. Certainly, Deng regarded Japan's post-war economic development as important enough to study in detail. He visited Japan to see for himself how technology, strategic targeting and investment in science had catapulted Japan into the front ranks of global power, concluding that the two neighbours should 'set aside disputes and pursue joint development'.[35]

For many in the Global South, the absence of a fully developed efficient infrastructure is now considered a central factor in the wealth disparity gap between the North and the South. As Acemoglu and Robinson point out, for all of the work being done to 'close the gap', 'even the poorest citizens of the United States have incomes and access to health care, education, public services and economic and social opportunities that are far superior to those available to the vast mass of people living in sub-Saharan Africa, South Asia and Central America'.[36]

The gap in access to services between the poor and the vulnerable living in the Global North and South is larger than ever, according to recent reports. Highly industrialised South Korea and Japan, in the area of services, have pulled away from the pack. China's ascendancy

[34]Ha-Joon Chang, op. cit.
[35]'Set aside dispute and pursue joint development', *Ministry of Foreign Affairs of the People's Republic of China* http://www.fmprc.gov.cn/mfa_eng/ziliao_665539/3602_665543/3604_665547/t18023.shtml [Accessed October 2018]
[36]Daron Acemoglu and James Robinson, op. cit., p. 78.

has not put a dent in the sovereignty of these countries, but global value chains are a much more important threat.

In Trump's world, American citizens are no longer certain they will continue to have access to these basic necessities. With its social market, the EU is much closer to China in terms of long-term structural investment in public works. Infrastructural investment and structural adjustment remain major EU priorities. Brussels has many funding instruments offering financial support to projects implementing its marquee trans-European transport network. These include: the Connecting Europe Facility (CEF), the European Fund for Strategic Investment (EFSI), Horizon 2020, the European Structural and Investment Funds (ESIFs), the Cohesion Fund (CF) and the European Regional Development Fund (ERDF). Planning for the long term, Brussels spends billions of dollars annually to build and maintain infrastructure as the nervous system of economic integration.

From a global perspective, Washington is following a model of decentralisation, leaving it to individual American states and the private sector to rebuild America's neglected infrastructure with a minority share of financing provided by Washington. So, where does this leave the BRI conversation?

Certainly, you could conclude that the completion rate of infrastructural winners in China's infrastructural coalition outnumbers the losers by a substantial margin. Yet many projects are only partially completed and do not take into account the impact of infrastructural investment on people's lives. Some projects are troubled in Laos, Vietnam and Malaysia, and will need to be renegotiated. None of China's neighbours are yet quitting the BRI or breaking off relations with China.

But the strategic question to ask is: how are 'successes' to be decided? Should they be measured conventionally, by China's return on investment? By increased GDP growth? By a strong export performance? By the expansion of networks of cultural and economic connectivity between communities, regions and people? A lot of metrics come into play. Without reliable and comprehensive data,

Chinese policy elites may also share worries and anxieties about the future of the OBOR initiative.[37]

One region that is particularly promising is the Balkans. China has a long-standing presence in the former Yugoslavia, particularly building railroads, tunnels, highways and a coal-fired thermal nuclear station. The politics and economics are entangled, but, despite this, China has built a durable, somewhat conflictual, relationship with all the states in the region. Most of the project work is dominated by Chinese engineering firms and Serbians have complained that more work has not been sourced locally. Serbia had a lot of international expertise, but many of Serbia's leading companies never recovered after the Balkan wars. According to Dragana Mitrović, a full-time professor at the University of Belgrade and an expert on China-Balkans relations, 'China's intention is to create a corridor from the Piraeus port towards Central Europe', and when it comes to the most important infrastructures, like the port, it wants to be directly involved in their operation.[38]

At the same time, Serbia and China have a long tradition of close bilateral relations. 'Serbia always supported the "One China" Policy, while China is a very important ally for Belgrade when it comes to backing Serbia's territorial integrity and sovereignty.'[39] At the practical level, 'the Serbian public opinion is not happy with the current state of affairs and would prefer a more visible spill-over in the local economy, especially in terms of new jobs creation'. Similarly, Hungary has had a lot of trouble from the European Commission because of irregularities about not following EU rules in awarding public contracts. These also seem to be worked out for the time being and, in respect to market rules and procedure like in the Greek case, 'Chinese companies may not

---

[37]For an insightful overview of the views of the Chinese elites on the New Silk Road initiative, see the European Council on Foreign Relations, '"One Belt, One Road": the great leap outward', June 2015 http://www.ecfr.eu/publications/summary/one_belt_one_road_chinas_great_leap_outward3055 [Accessed October 2018]

[38]Francesco Martino, op. cit.

[39]Ibid.

win the bidding process'.[40] Serbians expect more contracts to be awarded locally.

BALANCING ON THE NARROW BEAM OF WORLD POLITICS

There is a final question to address. Will the OBOR become collateral damage in the deteriorating US-China relationship? In American elite circles, there is a lot of angry talk that globalisation has now made China a 'monster' and, by implication, tainted its global infrastructural initiative.[41] It appears that Trump is determined to give Beijing 'a kicking, and a licking' as the centrepiece strategy to make 'America great again'. Getting tough on China is now the major talking point in Republican circles. There is a lot of speech-making and sabre-rattling about China being America's enemy and that China needs 'a good jab to the jaw' to bring it to its senses.[42]

The politics of resentment always risk disaster. There used to be a cycle during the Cold War of moves and countermoves, mutual deterrence and nerve-racking showdowns in Cuba and across the globe. Trump has not filled out his vision of how he plans to cut China down to size.[43] He first attempted a charm offensive during Xi's visit to Washington in 2017 in the hopes of convincing China to cooperate on cutting the US trade deficit by $50 billion. When that failed, he reversed course and labelled China a 'predatory threat' to US national security. Invoking article 232 of the 1962 US Trade Expansion Act, Trump has changed the rules of the game. He is piling on punitive tariffs against Chinese imports, starting with $34 billion on 6 July, 2018 on a range of products. He has also threatened

[40]Ibid.
[41]Emile Simpson, 'Globalization Has Created a Chinese Monster', *Foreign Policy Magazine*, 26 February, 2018 https://finance.yahoo.com/news/globalization-created-chinese-monster-201300153.html [Accessed October 2018]
[42]Peter Baker and Ana Swanson, 'Trump Authorizes Tariffs, Defying Allies at Home and Abroad', *New York Times*, 8 March, 2018.
[43]Michael Schuman, 'Who Gains From Trump's Tariffs? China', *Bloomberg*, 2 March, 2018 https://www.bloomberg.com/view/articles/2018-03-02/china-stands-to-gain-from-donald-trump-s-steel-tariffs [Accessed October 2018]

to impose another $200 billion and yet another $200 billion when China retaliates.

No one is exactly sure how much of the world's trade will be affected since the numbers cited do not include EU and NAFTA tariffs from Mexico and Canada. The Trump trade wars could easily surpass $1 trillion in exports in the name of US national security. Tit-for-tat trade retaliation is a highly flammable dynamic. It is very different from the previous trade wars of the George H.W. Bush presidency between the US and Japan over autos, which look more like a skirmish than a full-frontal economic confrontation from today's vantage point.

Normally, trade wars have an escape hatch and a back door so that disputing parties can climb down from their maximum position and negotiate a compromise. What makes this trade war so unique is that Trump is presenting its major trading partners with what amounts to 'terms for surrender'. What this means is that Trump would in effect be dictating domestic policy for China or the EU, Mexico and Canada. It would be occupying another country's policy space. Brazenly, it is challenging China's national sovereignty to make policy in its national interest. The United States has made a fundamental error of judgement in assuming that China will abandon its Made in China 2025 industrial high-tech strategy and accept American terms of surrender without a major, bitter confrontation.

Much the same point needs to be made about Trump's auto wars, which demand the return of highly paid auto jobs from Europe and tens of thousands of jobs from Canada and Mexico. Armed with such a transactional mindset, the heavyweight trade knockout fight will be nasty. No global rival is ready to capitulate to American bullying if there is no room for compromise. So far, Washington has underestimated the effectiveness of Beijing's global strategy of investing in economic corridors, beachheads, high-speed transportation systems and its string-of-pearls ocean ports.

But things could easily change. A sudden bout of American pushing and Chinese shoving could escalate quickly. Big power bumping and jostling, driven by the prospect of winner-take-all outcomes rather than the need for compromise, looks more and more likely. One way to understand the new political landscape is that China's soft power will be tested to its limits. If the American hegemon strikes back with a prolonged trade war of three or four years or a hot war in the South China Sea, China's commitment to deploy its hard power to defend its core interests could well become inevitable.

The United States has clearly stated its intention to remain the dominant presence in the Asia-Pacific region, where the New Silk Road has numerous projects.[44] This is not a small point for China, but a major challenge to its power and rapid ascendancy in the world economy. In the words of the former president of the China Institute of Contemporary International Relations, 'It is not normal for China to be under US dominance forever. You can't justify dominance forever.'[45] So, if the United States' political and military role has to be 'readjusted', what does 'readjusted' mean, practically and politically, for the Bretton Woods institutions?

Would multilateralism, as a system of rules and practices, survive Trump's attack on the constitutional order? What core American interests in the Asia-Pacific region will be defended? Which are to be sacrificed? At the moment, the White House's unambiguous answer would be none.

The US government has various policy weapons in its war chest, in addition to the far-reaching US trade legislation, to levy collateral damage against China's global initiative. One of the most important is the powerful intergovernmental Committee on Foreign Investment in the United States (Cifius), which has the discretionary power to block multibillion dollar international takeovers and acquisitions of American companies by Chinese investors.

[44]Joshua Kurlantzick, 'Growing U.S. Role in South China Sea', *Council on Foreign Relations*, 7 October, 2011 https://www.cfr.org/expert-brief/growing-us-role-south-china-sea [Accessed October 2018]
[45]Jane Perlez, 'Xiu Jingpiung Extends Power, and China Braces for New Cold War', *New York Times*, 27 February, 2018.

In doing so, the US is using national security doctrine to circumvent the WTO's rules about treating foreign companies on the same footing as they would domestic ones. The test for national security is very broad, and, as many trade experts argue, rather arbitrary.[46] After all, all countries reserve the right to step in and prevent a foreign takeover when it is deemed to be in their national interest. What is dramatically different is that this rarely invoked practice has become the new protectionist normal for the Trump Administration, incensing many trade experts.[47]

WEAPONISING TRADE IN THE NAME OF NATIONAL SECURITY: A DANGEROUS PRECEDENT

The committee was created to review, screen and reject inbound foreign investment for potential national security threats. It could directly impact Beijing's commitment to open markets and investment flows. Negative decisions to prevent legitimate Chinese investment in American companies could be perceived as having an implicit anti-China bias. The reason that the committee is so powerful is that these threats can be interpreted very broadly, and it is the ideal instrument to knock China down a peg or two. Its recent security doctrine report, tabled in December 2017, has given the president the power to label China a 'strategic competitor' to what the National Security Report sees as the threat China presents should it become the leader in artificial intelligence, self-driving vehicles and other new industries.[48]

Even though most Chinese foreign direct investment is in real estate, hospitality and transportation, it is evident that China

[46]Chad Bown, 'For Trump, it was a summer of tariffs and more tariffs. Here's where things stand', *Washington Post*, 13 September, 2018 https://www.washingtonpost.com/news/monkey-cage/wp/2018/09/13/for-donald-trump-it-was-a-summer-of-tariffs-and-more-tariffs-heres-where-things-stand/?noredirect=on&utm_term=.5c517c2ee270=
[47]Chad Bown and Melina Kolb, 'Trump's Trade War Timeline: An Up-to-Date Guide', *Peterson Institute of Economics*, 1 December, 2018 https://piie.com/blogs/trade-investment-policy-watch/trump-trade-war-china-date-guide
[48]*National Security Strategy of the United States of America* (The White House, December 2017), https://www.whitehouse.gov/wp-content/uploads/2017/12/NSS-Final-12-18-2017-0905.pdf [Accessed October 2018]

also wants to be a global leader in the high-tech world of artificial intelligence and intellectual property innovation. So, the committee has created an administrative backstop to prevent Chinese companies from acquiring US high-tech firms. Given its broad mandate, the committee would be within its authority to reject the takeovers that would challenge American dominance in the transition to 5-G networks, the leading edge in new information technology. This restriction is designed to prevent corporations like Huawei Technologies from competing with US interests in other markets in the global telecom business.

This labelling of China as an 'enemy' is a game-changer in China's public policy lexicon. Controversially, the committee decision to veto Jack Ma's bid to buy MoneyGram was more about politics than it was about privacy. Of course, it can be argued that a Chinese parent company should not have access to the personal data of Americans for reasons of national security. But what of American companies like Facebook, who continue to emerge relatively unscathed from data breach after data breach? Where are the meaningful regulatory mechanisms through which other corporate invasions of personal privacy will be adequately scrutinised? Putting China in its place now appears to be the principal focus of the Cifius' mandate.[49] In this regard, Washington's priority is to contain China's infrastructural ambitions.

In October 2018, the US Senate approved a $60 billion foreign development bill to go head to head against the OBOR initiative. With this challenge in mind: where do the trade and investment wars leave OBOR as a soft power initiative? Will China be forced to wear the 'black hat' of a global disruptor? Or is its long-term goal to create a parallel universe beyond liberal internationalism? Western countries need to respond, and they have a possible option in the AIIB.

---

[49]BBC Business, 'US pushes back on foreign takeover deals', available at: https://www.bbc.com/news/business-45177254

AIIB: A SMART BET

For many countries the safe policy alternative is to join the AIIB. More than 27 countries initially joined the Board and many are from Latin America, including Argentina, Chile, Ecuador, Bolivia, Peru and Venezuela. In 2018 China's Developmental Bank had some 84 countries with more coming on board, including a lot of Washington's friends such as the UK, Australia, South Korea, Germany and Canada. Importantly, joining the AIIB requires a contribution to the infrastructural fund. As for American membership of the AIIB, the United States, along with Japan, have isolated themselves and not joined, even though they have an open invitation from Beijing. Presently the United States and Japan are a minority of two holdouts among major economies. They are banking on the fact that private infrastructure investment with government guarantees is the next frontier for global capital.[50]

Beijing has been careful to organise the Development Bank and the BRICS Bank with enough transparency safeguards and accountability provisions to satisfy international norms. For this reason, many global development banks are cooperating with the AIIB on investment projects, such as the Islamic Development Bank, the largest of its kind in the Islamic world. AIIB has co-financed a group of projects with the Asian Development Bank. The IMF's Managing Director, Christine Lagarde, has recently invited China to work more closely with them on development aid and China, for the time being, is on board. In this sense, China has received an international vote of confidence in its global governance banks, as many countries are applying to join.

Certainly, at the regional level the AIIB has found a niche for itself, and is supporting loans to high-risk countries such as Myanmar and Tajikistan. It has made itself into a very flexible institution, financing projects that are connected to the BRI and those that were not part of China's infrastructural initiative. The AIIB is increasing the amount

[50]Martin Arnold, op. cit.

of money it has for loans to $2.7 billion from $1.6 billion in 2016. According to its spokesperson, the bank will loan between $3 billion and $3.5 billion in infrastructure spending. He added, 'The AIIB is having no problem developing a pipeline for its projects.'[51]

According to the Asian Development Bank Report 2016, the globe will require $32 trillion over the next two decades for infrastructural investment including for roads, hydroelectricity, high-speed trains, dams, and water and sanitation systems, as well as social infrastructure such as hospitals, schools and communication systems.[52] Beijing has the political will and the deep pockets to make a substantive commitment to address the long-term developmental crisis under China's leadership umbrella.[53] It can't solve the issue on its own. For the moment there is no slowing down of the initiative, and underestimating China's interest and staying power to defend its core interests in the new world order would be a big mistake.

FOR SURE SOME THINGS ARE ON TRACK

For the moment, the trade in goods and services between China and various countries making up BRI is turning in a record performance. A lot of things are going right. The Chinese are feeling very bullish, announcing that in the first four months of 2018 they signed deals worth $189.1 billion, according to the Ministry of Commerce. If anything, they seem to be accelerating the acquisition of new projects, some of which are major undertakings financially. They have built 75 economic and trade cooperation zones along the Belt and Road countries, with a total investment of $25 billion. If the figures are to be believed, almost 4000 companies have joined the cooperation

[51]James Kynge, 'AIIB set to extend reach to Latin America and Africa', *Financial Times*, 7 May, 2018.

[52]*Meeting Asia's Infrastructure Needs* (Tokyo: Asian Development Bank Institute, February 2017) https://www.adb.org/sites/default/files/publication/227496/special-report-infrastructure.pdf [Accessed October 2018]

[53]Daniel Drache, 'Post Brexit and the Crisis of Trade Multilateralism: Heartbreak or Mess? Ought We Be Worried?' *TLI Think!* Paper 84/2017 https://papers.ssrn.com/sol3/papers.cfm?abstract_id=3046810

zones, with factories creating 220,000 jobs.[54] Trade also increased by 26 per cent in the first quarter of 2017 to $240 billion, according to the Chinese Ministry of Commerce. It is reported that Chinese exports to the China club of investment beneficiaries grew by 28 per cent.

At this point, there is a trade imbalance in China's favour and authorities are confident that commercial transactions with ASEAN nations will continue to surge as its bilateral partners become important suppliers to China's global value chain.[55] China has come a long way as a global power. In 2006, the United States was the largest trading partner of 127 countries compared to China's 70 countries. A scarce five years later the situation was reversed. Beijing is now the top trading partner of 126 countries while Washington is the primary trading partner of only 76 countries.[56] Palpably, the Asian century is quickly coming of age and a shift in global power structures has already happened.

Despite all its promises, Wall Street has shown little interest in loaning money on a grand scale to poor, high-risk countries without government guarantees. The International Finance Corporation, the World Bank's private sector arm, has been pushing for public-private partnerships to fund infrastructure in the developing world. They are involved in refinancing a $900 million hydroelectric power plant in Uganda, partly owned by the Blackstone group. There has been a lot of controversy about the spiralling cost of the dam, cost overruns, and dangers to the environment and worker safety.[57]

Even if many legal obligations have not been met, private global capital groups like Blackstone are eager, in principle, to take a larger share of infrastructure business away from China in the future with the active support of the World Bank. The big banks have held many

[54]'China Signs More Trade Deals with Belt and Road Countries', *Xinhua*, 31 May, 2018.
[55]Silk Road Briefing, China-OBOR trade increases 26%, 2 May, 2017.
[56]Quoted in Lei Zou, op. cit.; Lu Zheng, 'Treating "Export No.1" with Calm', *China Securities Journal*, 11 February, 2010, p. A02.
[57]David Pilling, 'World Bank set for Uganda dam refinancing talks despite criticism', *Financial Times*, 8 March, 2018 https://www.ft.com/content/9218ca3e-214b-11e8-a895-1ba1f72c2c11 [Accessed October 2018]

conferences about their role in China's initiative. Some believe it is a 'generational opportunity to expand the scale and reach of their business'.[58] Behind the world of business-talk, many in the private sector still have numerous doubts about working with local high-risk governments for financing and joint partnerships.

CHINA AND LIBERAL INTERNATIONALISM'S GOVERNANCE ORDER

No one should have any doubts that China would like to imagine its future as a world hegemon. In the space of five years, China has begun to build networks of connectivity globally. Deeper regional trade is both a driver and an investment frontier with many opportunities for all kinds of connectivity between China and its South Asian neighbours. Beijing is only at the beginning of the process and it has a long route ahead of it. By comparison, intraregional trade accounts for more than 50 per cent of total trade in East Asia and the Pacific and 22 per cent in sub-Saharan Africa. The critical figure is that for South Asia as a regional entity, intraregional trade forms only 5 per cent and so the mutual gains from regional cooperation and shared economic development have significant potential according to the World Bank.[59]

It is evident that China is betting its future on its geopolitical repositioning to ramp up investments in communities and transnationally. China's multi-nation infrastructure initiative has excelled in providing new railway services from China to Europe. It connects approximately 35 Chinese cities with 34 European cities, according to a recent report.[60] Rail services are much cheaper than air and faster than sea. China is investing hundreds of billions of

---

[58]Ibid.

[59]"South Asia Should Remove Trade Barriers for Mutual Economic Gains: New World Bank Report', *The World Bank,* 24 September, 2018 https://www.worldbank.org/en/news/press-release/2018/09/24/south-asia-remove-trade-barriers-mutual-economic-gains-report [Accessed October 2018]

[60]Jonathan Hillman, 'The Rise of China-Europe Railways', *Center for Strategic & International Studies,* 6 March, 2018 https://www.csis.org/analysis/rise-china-europe-railways [Accessed October 2018]

dollars in this third connectivity option. The report emphasises that 'rail's share of cargo by value is already growing, increasing 144 per cent during the first half of 2017, as compared to the same period in 2016'. A study commissioned by the International Union of Railways estimates that 'China-Europe rail services could double their share of trade by volume over the next decade'.[61]

China has accomplished much in the first five years of its grand coalition of common interest. Its imposing design can be understood by looking at five main projects, which are drawn from the extensive BRI coverage by the *South China Morning Post*.[62] The first completed project is the direct railway link from London to China, including freight and passenger services that can cover the 12,000-km (7450-mile) journey in just 18 days. The China-Pakistan Economic Corridor is the second project. It is the biggest and most ambitious project of the five. This multi-decade undertaking now boasts overland links from China's Xinjiang province to Pakistan's Gwadar Port, a gateway to the seagoing links of Western China and Central Asia. The third is less well known in the Western press, a new China-Iran railway network that China has completed. The Chinese promote its achievement as 'building peace and security through regional integration in the Middle East'.

Fourth on the list is the Central Asia-China Gas Pipeline in Turkmenistan, comprising four lines, the construction of which is still underway. When completed, the four lines will supply China with 70 billion cubic metres of natural gas. Coming in at a cost of $8 billion, the pipelines are part of China's green strategy to replace coal-fired hydro plants with cleaner energy. Finally, the Khorgos Gateway connects Kazakhstan to China by rail and will soon enter the record books as the world's biggest dry port. The new

[61]Ibid.
[62]"The five main projects of the Belt and Road Initiative: A visual explainer', *South China Morning Post*, http://multimedia.scmp.com/news/china/article/One-Belt-One-Road/index. html [Accessed October 2018]; not surprisingly, the coverage from the Hong Kong newspaper is focused entirely on the Asian region, overlooking the important role of the BRI's infrastructural investments in Africa, Latin America, the Middle East and the Antarctica region.

development area joins the borders between China and Kazakhstan. It is projected that the railway border crossing will initially handle up to 15 million tonnes of freight a year. Volume is expected to eventually increase to 30 million tonnes per year, opening up the second Europe-China rail link.

With all this activity, it stands to follow that diplomatically China has also been pumping billions of renminbi into support for these infrastructural initiatives. Expenditures on foreign diplomacy have almost doubled since the One Belt, One Road initiative was first announced in 2013. It is hard to believe that 'China's growth rate in foreign affairs spending is roughly double that of defence spending which is on course to increase by 8.1 per cent to Rmb 1.1 trillion in 2018'.[63] The dramatic increase in foreign diplomacy spending sends the unmistakable message that China is mobilising its resources for a major role as a global power. It is an entirely different question whether China will win its long battle against liberal internationalism's multilateral governance order and bring the United States down a notch or two.

At this point, China is the engineer driving the 21st-century railway transportation revolution forward at high speed. What a contrast to when China turned inward over 400 years ago. In the 19th century, China functioned much like a giant clam. Its borders were closed to outsiders until the 'century of humiliation' of Western occupation, civil war and Japanese military invasion formally ended in the victory of the Communist Revolution. Under Mao and until Deng there was a long period when China turned in on itself. That option is permanently off the table now that China has become the world's workshop, number one global exporter and the planet's leading infrastructural developer. So what is next for China's club of nations?

AT CIVILISATION'S CROSSROADS ONCE AGAIN
The Chinese are highly pragmatic and Beijing is intent on building, brick by brick, multi-tiered economic, scientific and cultural networks

[63]Charles Clover and Sherry Fei Ju, 'China's diplomacy budget doubles under Xi Jinping', *Financial Times,* 6 March, 2018.

with Europe as its master economic corridor and beachhead. Some would consider this the ultimate prize of high-impact diplomacy and soft power politics. The influential historian Peter Frankopan has added much to our understanding of the importance of China's historic Silk Road because, as he demonstrates in his path-breaking history, there were many silk roads knitting together Asia as a region in world history. Over the centuries, they formed many civilisational meeting points in Persia, Syria, India, Afghanistan and beyond.[64]

Seen in this way, the 'community of common destiny' is less of an elusive anchor point of China's grand plan for the global economy. It is a view of the world that is deeply embedded in China's modern psyche – what occurs on one continent inevitably impacts another. The aftershocks of what transpires in Kazakhstan, Italy and Saudi Arabia can be felt immediately in New York, Nairobi and Copenhagen.

The challenge for the Western world is that at the present time, China is the only superpower 'with a truly global, geo-strategic idea', and the West can only blame itself, in Sigmar Gabriel's formulation, former German Minister of Foreign Affairs, '[for] not having a strategy to find a new balance.'[65] Many Western elites resent China's rise as a world power. In Martin Wolf's prescient words: 'After the financial crisis and the rise of populism, the ability of the West to run its economic and political systems well has come into doubt. For those who believe in democracy and the market economy as expressions of individual freedom, these failures are distressing. They can only be dealt with by reforms. Unfortunately, what the West is getting instead is unproductive rage.'[66]

It is worth recalling that for China's many critics, the OBOR is pigeonholed as a classic example of a potentially disastrous policy

---

[64]Peter Frankopan, *The Silk Roads: A New History of the World* (Bloomsbury, 2015).

[65]Nick Miller, 'China undermining us "with sticks and carrots": Outgoing German Minister', *The Age*, 19 February, 2018 https://www.theage.com.au/world/europe/china-undermining-us-with-sticks-and-carrots-outgoing-german-minister-20180219-p4z0s6.html [Accessed October 2018]

[66]Martin Wolf, 'How the West should judge a rising China', *Financial Times*, 15 May, 2018.

of sino-colonialism; for others, it is seen primarily as a challenge to the status quo that needs to be contained, not accommodated; still, for others, it is a colossal developmental programme that could fulfil crucial infrastructural demands for the least developed countries, which only China is prepared to finance.

In the business press there are many assessments of its failures and shortcomings with hyperbolic titles such as 'Soviet Collapse Echoes In China's Belt And Road'.[67] The unstated assumption is that the private sector would do a better job. There is no evidence for making this leap of faith because global finance would not invest in most of the projects. The story so far is that in such a massive undertaking, investment expectations will not always be met. China will always be wedged between the narrow market criteria of global efficency and the complex needs of infrastructural development. To believe otherwise would be naïve. Of the hundreds of projects, some will be underutilised and others will not generate the revenue and traffic hoped for in the planning stages. For others still, corruption and theft of public funds will create an environment of debt distress.

SMART STRATEGY TO MEND FENCES

What is now apparent is that OBOR has the momentum and support to grow even larger, with countries facing a mountain of debt. This is a constant worry for African countries and many Asian governments as well. The new Malaysian Prime Minister Mahathir Mohamad recently cancelled a China-backed railway project. What's more, the new leadership in Pakistan is publicly outspoken about the unsustainability of its infrastructural debt burden. China has not been silent in responding to events like these.

At a China-Africa summit in 2018, Beijing said, for the first time publicly, that it would work 'to ensure that its projects on the continent met real needs'. The Vice Minister of Commerce added that 'as a next step, we will discuss with African countries about how to

[67]David Fickling, op. cit.

promote a sustainable model for debt'.[68] Few details are available, but it marks a shift in the BRI official narrative. After all, many of China's bilateral partners are equally concerned about their low-performing infrastructural projects and debt burden. They are worried that unpaid loans will not be forgiven by Chinese leaders unless they make concessions about ownership and protection of their core interests.

Xi's speech demonstrates that China is not tone deaf to the dangers of debt trap diplomacy. We need to wait and see if Beijing is willing to abandon its old rhetoric in order to address the challenge of sustainable debt. At this stage, after five years of start-ups, a definitive assessment of China's premium foreign policy initiative can only be partial; it is too early in the process to be fully reliable.

For the time being, BRI remains an international anomaly outside the rules and norms of liberal internationalism because it is largely freestanding and, as some critics posit, comprises a rapidly expanding group of countries without a recognisable institutional form. China's elites have raised their variant of Keynesianism to a new level and, in Adam Tooze's well-chosen words, 'Xi's "Chinese dream" is the most spectacular Keynesian promise ever made'.[69] Still, there are no signs that it is becoming a 'coalition of the willing', nor is it an economic bloc with a fixed goal. Rather, it could be summed up as membership in an open-door investment club where China's deep pockets pay the membership fees and China guards the keys. At this point in time, it is on the verge of a lot of success from its first five years of accomplishments, but still there are many things that could go wrong – and will.

CHINA'S LONG GAME

The Belt and Road infrastructural initiative occupies centre stage in China's long game, with its competing priorities operating on many fronts and levels. The first priority is to achieve energy security by

[68]Catherine Wong, 'China aims for "sustainable" debt with Africa as Belt and Road Initiative comes under fire From West', *South China Morning Post*, 28 August, 2018 https://www.scmp.com/news/china/diplomacy-defence/article/2161737/china-aims-sustainable-debt-africa-belt-and-road [Accessed October 2018]
[69]Adam Tooze, op. cit., pp. 19–21.

building dozens of gas and oil pipelines across the world. A second is to acquire new markets for its industries with their excess capacity, particularly in Africa and Asia where more than three-quarters of the world's population live and consume on a scale unimaginable a decade ago. To recall Dean Acheson's memorable words spoken at a time of American ascendancy in the 1940s, Beijing intends to be present 'at creation' of one of the world's largest consumer markets.

Finally, China's elites have even greater ambition for the Middle Kingdom. Their commercial beachheads and economic corridors are part of China's long-term goal of making Eurasia its geopolitical partner in the Asian century and they are the pivot to rebalance power between Washington and Beijing. As the global economy becomes more fractured and unpredictable with the Learian White House, great power rivalries and American-driven trade wars are a logical outcome of an international order dominated by inter-capitalist conflict: the EU in fierce competition against Washington, India going head-to-head against China, the White House battling Canada and Mexico, Turkey and Germany, and Brussels squaring off against the UK over Brexit. It is unlikely that the multilateral system in its current configuration will survive as liberal internationalism looks for an institutional fix to accommodate the fallout from long-term structural change. China will have an even larger leadership role if it chooses, provided that, domestically, it continues to prosper and its leadership remains united.

As a recent report from the Carnegie Endowment points out, imports, investments, loans and aid from China along the OBOR can make recipient countries more economically linked, but such dependency can also produce political resentment instead of strategic trust.[70] Beijing's soft power diplomacy is an attempt to break the curse of hot economics and unpredictable politics, where established rules no longer seem to matter.

[70]Xie Tao, 'Chinese Foreign Policy With Xi Jinping Characteristics', *Carnegie Endowment for International Peace*, 20 November, 2017 http://carnegieendowment.org/2017/11/20/chinese-foreign-policy-with-xi-jinping-characteristics-pub-74765 [Accessed October 2018]

The principal takeaway of *One Road, Many Dreams* is that, in the final analysis, China's global infrastructural initiative is like a giant puzzle with 10,000 pieces that Beijing is patiently assembling, piece by piece, while the West is caught flat-footed. Will the puzzle ever be completed? While long-term outcomes remain uncertain, many countries are already reconsidering their strategic options by seeking pathways between the US and the development of closer relationships with China.[71]

WHO IS ON FIRST?

So, what happens next? Will OBOR get bigger and better? Will Beijing back off and downsize its global initiative if American hegemony strikes back? What misgivings and second thoughts do global publics have? For the Chinese leadership, the geopolitical end game is to provide an alternative to a crisis-prone, market-driven fundamentalism under the American flag. Beijing does not offer 'pure' socialism as an alternative model; instead, it is adapting, redefining and redirecting its state-driven market capitalism with the BRI, its collectively driven global project. That is the political strategic wager China has made; the stakes are high and the returns unclear in Africa and parts of Asia. The Chinese dream may end well or badly if Xi's structural reforms are derailed and an undiluted privatisation takes command – as it did in the former Soviet Union in the mid-to-late 1990s.

The removing of constitutional term limits on Xi's presidency, so that he can stand for a third term, introduces a fundamental change to China's state party system. The concentration of so much power in the hands in Xi will have far-reaching consequences. After all, he is the architect and champion of BRI and his presidency is dependent on its success. Pragmatic as 'the China dream' may be in their use of soft power, the Chinese authorities have hunkered down to build a different economic infrastructure-centred future

[71]Dunford and Liu, 2018, p. 29.

for themselves, with multiple economic corridors and beachheads and with Europe as the strategic goal.

Whatever its many shortcomings, Beijing's global ascendancy is irreversible and, unlike German, British, French, Japanese and American hegemony, China's rise has been peaceful so far.[72] For many countries, partnership with China along the OBOR comes with substantive cultural and political baggage, but importantly, this baggage is not a repeat of war-torn Vietnam, Afghanistan, Iraq, or the countless other states whose sovereignty has previously been interfered with by an imperial hegemon. China's renewed sense of international destiny has required it to proceed always cautiously with intense determination.

[72]Eric X. Li, op. cit.

AFTERWORD

AFTERWORD

Towards 2049

GROWTH PAINS AND MISSTEPS

So, inside China, what is next for its premier global initiative? For now, China's global project is busy recruiting new members from the Caribbean, the Russian Federation, Latin America, central Asia, the EU and Africa. It would like to recruit important holdouts such as Mexico, Argentina and Brazil, which have not signed up as yet, as well as more states in the EU such as Italy, the first of the G7 countries formally to join in 2019. Without them, China's investment club of nations will increasingly look like a parallel UN assembly, where China can conceivably broker global public policy on issues such as climate change, regional security and poverty eradication. For the moment, all this is in the future, but China is already busy establishing its own free trade zone and organisation in conjunction with 16 Asia-Pacific and Southeast Asian countries.

Chinese elites have also pulled off some high-powered diplomatic triumphs. Its ability to attract new members remains impressive by any standard. The number of 'One Roaders' has more than doubled from the original 30 odd countries to more than 80. In another five years, China is expected to have a hundred or more countries, with over three-quarters of the world's population, under its investment umbrella.

No country has quit its ranks despite much public criticism by researchers and journalists about debt distress, corruption and contracts heavily weighted in China's favour.[1] Publicly, China has

---

[1]Minxin Pei, 'Will China let Belt and Road die quietly?', *Nikkei Asian Review*, 15 February, 2019, https://asia.nikkei.com/Opinion/Will-China-let-Belt-and-Road-die-quietly

faced a growing chorus of criticism from Pakistan, Malaysia, Kenya, Sri Lanka, the Maldives and Myanmar to renegotiate their debts after receiving BRI loans

In Israel, controversially China's state-owned enterprises are building the port of Haifa as well as investing heavily in Iran, one of Israel's sworn enemies. India and Pakistan are on a war footing with each other, but are also large-scale recipients of China's investment dollars for massive infrastructure projects. China makes these investments through the Asian Investment Infrastructural Bank, a Chinese creation that now funds projects in more than 90 countries. China and Russia are 'frenemies' but have found common ground to cooperate through One Belt, One Road. At any moment, however, their core interests could abruptly end for political or other reasons.

In addition, there are many complex spin-offs which receive very little coverage in the American or British press. You would have no idea London has won the race to be the world's biggest renminbi trading hub outside China. The UK did not want to miss the opportunity to dominate offshore markets potentially worth billions of pounds in tax revenues.

FINANCIAL OUTREACH AND DEBT DISTRESS

Certainly, global capital wants to do business with China even though different actors are increasingly vocal in their criticism of China's one-party political system and the forced removal of Uighur Muslims into 'education centres'. All this public disapproval has not prevented the Islamic Development Bank, the largest bank of its kind in the Islamic world, from joining forces with China's AIIB. They are injecting new funding into joint projects to address a yawning infrastructure gap in African and other developing regions.

The plan is to co-lend to projects in the Islamic world to boost the international footprint of the China-led development bank, launched in spite of US opposition in 2015. 'We will partner with the AIIB,' Bandar Hajjar, IDB president, said in an interview with the *Financial Times*. 'We will co-finance many projects [with AIIB] in the future in Africa. Africa needs about $150 billion USD a year to finance infrastructure and there are about 650 million people in Africa without access to electricity.'[2]

One of the attention-grabbing partnerships China has entered into is China's Development Bank's (CDB) partnership with the UK's Standard Chartered Bank. Standard has inked a $1.6 billion deal to fund trade and investment projects linked to the Beijing-backed Belt and Road Initiative. According to press reports, the two banks signed a memorandum of understanding during British Prime Minister Theresa May's visit to Beijing. The agreement will see a total of $12.8 billion worth of business deals covering construction, finance, agriculture and technology.[3]

Yet Malaysia's 93-year-old Prime Minister Mahathir Mohamed perhaps spoke for many of China's investment club members when he publicly criticised Beijing's lending practices as 'neocolonial'. The newly elected government suspended Chinese projects worth close to $25 billion, and several months later cancelled three Chinese-financed oil and gas pipelines. Theoretically, you might expect Malaysia, a rational state actor, to quit the One Belt, One Road, angered by the high costs of corruption, but so far there is no indication of any desire to exit. Instead, there is a consistent pattern in this part of Asia of renegotiating more balanced agreements with Beijing. High-level talks are already in progress to reduce Malaysia's inflated investment contracts.

In the case of the Maldives, Chinese diplomats saddled the country with a huge debt due in part to local corruption and lack of transparency. All of China's loans are protected by sovereign guarantees. The finance minister of the new government is asking China to forgive part of the loan, reduce the interest rates and adjust the repayment schedule.

For the time being, China remains an important partner for the government, but any future deals will obviously have to be negotiated with far greater care. The Maldives are going to lobby Beijing for

[2]James Kynge, 'Islamic Development Bank to join forces with China-led AIIB', *Financial Times*, 20 February, 2018.
[3]Pan Che, 'China Development Bank, Standard Chartered Sign $1.6 Billion "Belt and Road" Deal', *Caixin*, 2 February, 2018 https://www.caixinglobal.com/2018-02-02/china-development-bank-standard-chartered-sign-16-billion-belt-and-road-deal-101206810.html [Accessed February 2019]

debt forgiveness and are asking China for a $1 billion emergency loan.[4] In Myanmar, many of the same issues around public tender transparency have cast a long shadow over its diplomatic partner and talks are underway to renegotiate these one-sided contracts.

BEIJING'S PURSUIT OF ITS CORE INTERESTS

There is little that is altruistic about Beijing's investment blitzkrieg and much that could be called transactional, hardball investment tactics to get the best deal possible. But it is more complicated than that. The closest China comes to socialist messaging is when President Xi invokes the fuzzy ideal of a 'community of destiny' and the virtues of the 'Chinese dream' as the visionary pillars. However, the consensus among China experts is that these are very small conceptual handles for such an ambitious globalist undertaking. The net result is that ideology is not the central message of China's investment drive; instead, 'dollar diplomacy' is by far and away the royal jelly of its spin doctors. So far, Beijing's biggest accomplishment has been its ability to successfully internationalise the Belt and Road Initiative in the first five years by building complex networks of regional commercial corridors and beachheads, interlinked on land and sea. Inside China, the BRI has also grown in importance, funding many large-scale public works projects in regions hardest hit by rising unemployment in export-oriented sectors.

Beijing has scored a lot of points as an outspoken defender of the rules-based multilateral order attacked by Trump and Republicans intent on dismantling much of its architecture.[5] At Davos, Xi made headlines saying, 'The economic and social well-being of countries in the world is increasingly interconnected. The need for reform of the global governance system is picking up speed.'[6]

---

[4]Simon Mundy and Kathrin Hille, 'The Maldives counts the cost of its debts to China', *Financial Times*, 10 February, 2019.
[5]China has publicly positioned itself as a defender of the WTO's embattled legal order. So far, the Trump administration has refused to appoint an American judge to the Appellate Body and without this appointment the WTO's legal arm will cease to function without a quorum to hear cases, make findings and issue rulings. Effectively, if no appointment is made, Washington will be quitting the WTO.
[6]Evelyn Cheng and Everett Rosenfeld, 'China's Xi again talks up commitment to "free trade"', *CNBC*, 4 November, 2018 https://www.cnbc.com/2018/11/05/china-president-xi-jinping-again-talks-up-commitment-to-free-trade.html [Accessed February 2019]

COUNTING THE BILLIONS

It is still an open question how China is going to cope with these 'turbulent headwinds' of protectionism and unilateralism that are likely to outlive the Trump presidency. Democrats also share many of the same convictions that China is using subsidies to promote its heavily favoured state-owned giants. If China continues to favour local companies over American multinationals, will China's rulers have any incentive to support 'a new round of high-standard opening up ...[of] its market access to the rest of the world'? Will China scale down its infrastructural initiative and adopt a different model of state capitalism, less reliant on forced technology transfers? In the long run, will it be more compliant with WTO subsidy codes?

In the next five years in the race to become the world leader in core technologies, there are going to be many systemic changes at all levels of Chinese government. Some experts believe the Belt and Road's deep pockets are likely to be smaller and less generous. For the moment, it is impossible to get accurate, comprehensive information on its infrastructural spending binge. The low estimate is $2 trillion and the high guesstimate as much as $9 trillion by 2049, the official end date that coincides with a century of Chinese Communist rule. The final figure could easily surpass $9 trillion, depending on how Chinese authorities intend to pay for the next wave of state infrastructure development projects, which now include many new investments located in China's provinces to address rising unemployment and other structural problems.

China's rulers are doubling down on infrastructure projects to rescue the economy from the looming downturn. The share of bank lending to state firms at the heart of the BRI project has doubled since 2013. This fast growth of investment is intended to boost China's flagging growth rate and deliver a stimulus punch big enough to offset the slowdown in exports. This kind of policy rebalancing is expected to have supply and demand, medium-term effects. In early 2019, the government announced 16 new infrastructural projects costing over

$163 billion.[7] By comparison, Beijing had announced a much smaller package a year earlier, approving just seven projects worth a total of $16 billion.

Some are impressive, such as the expansion of the Shanghai urban rail transit system, with a price tag of $45 billion, which will better integrate the financial hub's two airports and two major railway stations. One can see that the government is speeding up project approvals, easing the rules of finance and lowering the reserve requirement for banks, making it easier for businesses to borrow money. China is worried that it has to do much more to safeguard its economy from an escalating trade war with Washington and the slowing down of growth.

The pressures from the downturn have already forced the government to take new measures in these tougher times. It is reported that 17 of China's 31 provinces missed their economic growth targets in 2018. The worst performer, according to the *South China Morning Post*'s special report, was Chongqing, the fastest growing information and manufacturing powerhouse. Guangdong, the wealthiest province in China, also missed its growth target and, as one of the anchors of China's export-led growth, suffered a significant slowdown.[8] Beijing is speeding up efforts to support the private sector and counter the mounting job losses by returning to Keynesian-style fundamentals at the highest levels. Modernising the infrastructure in key industrial provinces is now front and centre of the Chinese economic policy for a soft landing.

BRI: TOO BIG TO FAIL?
Keeping its foot on the accelerator by doubling down on infrastructure spending as growth slows is China's best bet for the moment. The economy still has to address the twin dangers of out-of-reach inflated housing prices and the bad debts of the SOEs. While lower growth rates

[7]Cissy Zhou, 'China's top 10 infrastructure projects to rescue its slowing economy', *South China Morning Post*, 5 February, 2019 https://www.scmp.com/economy/china-economy/article/2184999/chinas-top-10-infrastructure-projects-rescue-its-slowing [Accessed February 2019]
[8]Orange Wang, 'China's wealth gap widens as more than half of its provinces missed growth targets last year', *South China Morning Post*, 12 February, 2019 https://www.scmp.com/economy/china-economy/article/2185738/chinas-wealth-gap-widens-more-half-its-provinces-missed-growth [Accessed February 2019]

have cut deeply into China's foreign exchange reserves and its exports to the US have fallen sharply, China's stocks have staged a remarkable comeback in 2019 in a sharp reversal of last year's sharp downturn as the worst equity market in the world. The 2019 markets index has roared back, putting China in the top ranks of the world's best performers, jumping more than 10 per cent in the year to date. Now Chinese equity valuations are much cheaper, looking like a bargain relative to the US.[9]

Despite predictions of gloom and doom by many forecasters, China's money machine seems to be working overtime once again. Investors poured a record of $9 billion into Chinese equities in January 2019, the single largest inflow month on record.[10] The *Financial Times* reported that 'The global index provider is increasing the volume of Chinese stocks on its flagship emerging markets benchmark'. China is expecting a record amount of foreign inflows. Evidence mounts that key drivers of the Chinese economy still have plenty of bounce and policy capacity to stay the course.

On the trade front, expect a mix of modest and substantial reform measures from the high beam trade confrontation between the world's superpowers. If and when some kind of face-saving deal is reached, investor rights, subsidies and intellectual property rights are likely to be made more WTO-compliant.[11] It is a reasonable hypothesis that will surely be tested. Chinese exports to its 80-odd infrastructural partners are already providing a badly needed growth dividend for many Chinese industries. We should not underestimate how many levers the Chinese state has to steer a slowing economy out of its worst troubles.

Turning on the taps to fund a third wave of BRI projects is good news for job creation and a boost for its struggling exporters in the face of volatile global headwinds. After five years, China's global infrastructural project is now 'too big to fail', but whether Beijing's transformative vision for the world order succeeds is a different

---

[9]Emma Dunkley, 'China stocks roar back after grim 2018', *Financial Times*, 15 February, 2019 https://www.ft.com/content/99dfb798-30ca-11e9-8744-e7016697f225 [Accessed February 2019]
[10]Ibid.
[11]Gregory C. Shaffer and Henry S T Gao, *A New Chinese Economic Law Order?* (April 11, 2019). UC Irvine School of Law Research Paper No. 2019-21. Available at SSRN: https://ssrn.com/abstract=3370452

matter entirely. Inter-capitalist rivalry has intensified across the global economy, pitting market economy against market economy for control of regional markets. It should be evident by now that globalism has entered a new and dangerous, unpredictable phase as liberal internationalism unravels and American protectionism upends an already precarious multilateral trading order.

The politics of fear and anger of anxious publics of a systemic meltdown has worked to Beijing's advantage with many countries. China has accomplished much in the first five years and the road ahead is long and unpredictable. Still, it would be an enormous mistake to underestimate China's deft use of soft power to develop an alternative to liberal internationalism's post-war global consensus.

For the moment, Beijing does not have a detailed roadmap of its global vision for public consumption. Elements of where it is headed are, however, already apparent in providing an unprecedented investment bonanza in public goods for an expected 100 countries. The BRI is only a down payment along with its global infrastructure investment bank (AIIB), RCEP, its mega-sized free trade bloc and other security arrangements.

Driving its ambition is the fierce inter-capitalist rivalry between the US, an aging, powerful hegemon, and a self-confident, assertive challenger pushing hard to be number one producing 19 per cent of the world's output in 2018, more than double the 7 per cent recorded in 2000. Finally, it is hard to say how all the pushing and shoving of the current trade war will resolve their systemic enmity, whatever deal is struck in the short term. In the near future, this many-sided rivalry promises more confrontation till it finds its new equilibrium point. The possibility for a grand bargain to accommodate rather than constrain the newly emergent Asian structures of power of China, India, Indonesia and Thailand, home to half the world's middle classes, cannot be ruled out.[12] Let time be the final arbiter as the Asian century continues its irreversible, jarring ascent. For our now badly polarised world order, there is no turning back.

[12] Valentina Romei and John Reed, 'The Asian century is set to begin, Financial Times', March 25, 2019. https://www.ft.com/content/520cb6f6-2958-11e9-a5ab-ff8ef2b976c7

APPENDIX I

THE 21 PROJECTS THAT HAVE PROVIDED INFORMATION OF THEIR FUNDING SOURCES

Project	Estimated Investment Amount (in billions of USD)	Destination Country
Jakarta-Bandung High Speed Railway	5.135 (60 per cent of which is invested by Indonesia, 40 per cent by China)	Indonesia
Kendari Ferro-nickel Smelting Industrial Park	929 million (all investment from China, for phase 1 of the project only)	Indonesia
First Pacific Nickel Industrial Park	2 (all investment from China)	Indonesia
KIBING Glass Malaysia Production Line	0.19 (all investment from China)	Malaysia
Steel Industry Cluster of Kuantan Industrial Park	1.4 (all investment from China)	Malaysia
Bandar Malaysia Project	2.0 (all investment from China)	Malaysia
Massive Forest City Project	38.5 (all investment from China)	Malaysia
China Railway Group Limited Asia-Pacific Regional Centre	2 (all investment from China)	Malaysia
China-Laos Railway Project	6.8 (70 per cent of which is invested by China, 30 per cent by Laos)	Laos

Project	Estimated Investment Amount (in billions of USD)	Destination Country
Hai Doung Thermal Power Plant	1.8 (70 per cent of which is financed by China)	Vietnam
Karot Hydropower Project	1.6 (93 per cent of which is invested by the constructor, the Three Gorges Group of China)	Pakistan
Qasim Coal-fired Power Plant Project	2.5 (75 per cent of which is financed by the China EXIM Bank)	Pakistan
Thar Coalfield Coal-pit and Power Station	2.0 (40 per cent of which is financed by China)	Pakistan
Punjab 900 MW Solar Farm	1.5 (all investment from China)	Pakistan
Dawood Windpower Project	0.115 (all investment from China)	Pakistan
China-Pakistan International Science and Technology Trade Logistics Industrial Park	1.5 (all investment from China)	Pakistan
Tehran-Mashhad Railway Electrification Project	2.1 (85 per cent of which will be financed by loans from China)	Iran
Golbahar-Mashhad Railway Electrification Project	0.35 (85 per cent of which will be financed by China)	Iran
Hungary-Serbia Railway Project	2.89 (80 per cent of which is financed by China)	Hungary, Serbia

Project	Estimated Investment Amount (in billions of USD)	Destination Country
China-Belarus Industrial Park	1.41 (60 per cent of which is financed by China, for phase 1 of the project only)	Belarus
Mombasa-Nairobi Railway	3.8 (90 per cent of which is financed by CHEXIM Bank)	Kenya

Source: China Pivot Working Group, Robarts Centre for Canadian Studies, York University 2017.

APPENDIX II

THE INVESTMENT DESTINATIONS OF PROPOSED NEW PROJECTS

Area	Destination Country	Number of Projects	Total Investment (in billions of USD)
Southeast Asia	Indonesia	10	11.273
	Malaysia	6	44.1565
Southern Asia (Including Indian Oceanian Countries)	Laos	2	7.2
	Vietnam	5	3.6235
	Cambodia	1	–
	Burma	3	0.7
	Thailand	1	1.55
	Pakistan	8	11.915
	Nepal	1	1.6
	India	1	10
Middle Asia	Kazakhstan	4	3.26
	Kyrgyzstan	3	0.121
	Uzbekistan	1	–
Western Asia and Middle East	Iran	3	2.45
	The United Arab Emirates	1	1.8
	Turkey	1	1.6

Area	Destination Country	Number of Projects	Total Investment (in billions of USD)
Europe	Hungary and Serbia	1	2.89
	Belarus	1	1.41
Others	Russia	3	30.368
	Mongolia	2	1.098
	Kenya	1	3.8

Source: China Pivot Working Group, Robarts Centre for Canadian Studies, York University, 2017.

SELECT BIBLIOGRAPHY

Aglietta, Michel and Bai, Guo, 'China's 13th Five-Year Plan. In Pursuit of a "Moderately Prosperous Society"', *CEPII Policy Brief*, 12 September, 2016. Available online: http://www.cepii.fr/PDF_PUB/pb/2016/pb2016-12.pdf [Accessed October 2018]

Albert, Eleanor, 'China's Big Bet on Soft Power', *Council on Foreign Relations*, 9 February, 2018. Available online: https://www.cfr.org/backgrounder/chinas-big-bet-so -power [Accessed October 2018]

Alkire, Sabina and Robles, Gisela, 'Global Multidimensional Poverty Index 2017', *OPHI Briefing* 47 (2017). Available online: http://www.ophi.org.uk/wp-content/uploads/B47_Global_MPI_2017.pdf [Accessed October 2018]

Andersen, Lars Erslev, Ehteshami, Anoush, Sunuodula, Mamtimyn and Jiang, Yang, '"One Belt, One Road" and China's Westward Pivot: Past, Present and Future', *Danish Institute for International Studies*, 2017. Available online: http://pure.diis.dk/ws/les/1258174/Durham_OBOR_Conference_ Report.pdf [Accessed October 2018]

Anderson, B, *Imagined Communities: Reflections on the Origin and Spread of Nationalism* (Verso Books, 1983).

Armstrong, Philip, Glyn, Andrew, and Harrison, John, *Capitalism Since World War II: The Making and Breakup of the Great Boom* (Fontana Press, 1984).

Anheier, Helmut K. 'The Decline of the West, Again', Project Syndicate, 2018. Available online: https://www. project-syndicate.org/onpoint/the-decline-of-the-west-again-by-helmut-k--anheier-2018-10? [Accessed November 2018]

Ansar, Atif, Flyvbjerg, Bent, Budzier, Alexander and Lunn, Daniel, 'Does Infrastructure Investment Lead to Economic Growth or Economic Fragility? Evidence from China', *Oxford Review of Economic Policy* 32, (2016).

'Arbitration System of China', China International Trade Lawyers, 17 January, 2012. Available online: http://www.cn-linked.com/en/view.php?id=237 [Accessed October 2016]

Asian Development Bank Institute, *Meeting Asia's Infrastructure Needs* (Asian Development Bank Institute, February 2017). Available online: https://www.adb.org/sites/default/files/publication/227496/special-report-infrastructure.pdf [Accessed October 2018]

Bayoumi, Tamim, *Changing Patterns of Global Trade* (International Monetary Fund, Strategy, Policy and Review Department, 2011) https://www.imf.org/external/np/pp/eng/2011/061511.pdf [Accessed October 2018]

Bermingham, Finbarr, 'AIIB Extends Clean Energy Push in Pakistan', *Global Trade Review*, January 23, 2017. Available online: https://www.gtreview.com/news/asia/aiib-extends-clean-energy-push-in-pakistan/ [Accessed October 2018]

Bernanke, Ben and Olsen, Peter, 'China's transparency challenges', Brookings Institute, 8 March, 2016. Available online: https://www.brookings.edu/blog/ben-bernanke/2016/03/08/chinas-transparency-challenges [Accessed October 2018]

Blyth, Mark, *Austerity: The History of a Dangerous Idea* (Oxford University Press, 2015).

Brautigam, Deborah, *The Dragon's Gift: The Real Story of China in Africa* (Oxford University Press, 2009).

Brautigam, Deborah, *Will Africa Feed China?* (Oxford University Press, 2015).

Bourguignon, François and Pleskovic, Boris, *Rethinking Infrastructure for Development* (International Bank for Development and Reconstruction, 2008).

Bown, Chad and Kolb, Melina, 'Trump's Trade War Timeline: An Up-to-Date Guide', Peterson Institute of Economics, 1 December, 2018. Available online: https://piie.com/blogs/trade-investment- policy-watch/trump-trade-war-china-date-guide [Accessed October 2018]

Boyer, Robert and Drache, Daniel (eds), *States Against Markets* (Routledge, 1996).

Bradsher, Keith and Yuan, Li, 'China's Economy Became No. 2 by Defying No. 1,' *New York Times*, 25 November, 2018. Available online: https://www.nytimes.com/interactive/2018/11/25/world/asia/china- economy-strategy.html [Accessed October 2018]

Braudel, Ferdinand, *The Mediterranean and the Mediterranean World in the Age of Philip II* (University of California Press, 1995).

Buckley, Chris and Bradsher, Keith, 'Xi Jinping's Marathon Speech: Five Takeaways', *New York Times*, 18 October, 2017.

Buckley, Chris and Bradsher, Keith, 'China Moves to Let Xi Stay in Power by Abolishing Term Limit', *New York Times*, 25 February, 2018.

Buxbaum, Peter, 'What in the World is China doing in Kenya?' *Global Trade*, 24 May, 2016. Available online: http://www.globaltrademag.com/global-trade-daily/commentary/what-in-the-world-is-china-doing-in-kenya [Accessed October 2018]

Chan, Lai-Ha and Power, Pak K. Lee, 'Ideas and Institutions: China's Emergent Footprints in Global Governance of Development Aid', Working Paper, 281/17, University of Warwick, 2017.

Chanda, Nayan, *Bound Together: How Traders, Preachers, Adventurers, and Warriors Shaped Globalization* (Yale University, 2007).

Chang, Ha-Joon, *Kicking Away the Ladder: Development Strategy in Historical Perspective* (Anthem Press, 2002).

Chin, Greg T., 'Asian Infrastructure Investment Bank: Governance Innovation and Prospects', *Global Governance* 22 (2016), pp. 11–25. Available online: http://journals.rienner.com/doi/pdf/10.5555/1075-2846-22.1.11?code=lrpi-site [Accessed October 2018]

Collier, Paul, *The Bottom Billion: Why the Poorest Countries are Failing and What can be Done About It* (Oxford University Press, 2007).

Committee on Infrastructure Innovation, National Research Council, *Infrastructure for the 21st Century: Framework for a Research Agenda* (Academy Press, 1987).

Crouch, Colin, *Political Economy of Modern Capitalism: Mapping Convergence and Diversity* (Sage Publications, 1997).

Cripps, Francis, 'Narrowing the Development Gap Africa, Europe, ASEAN in the World to 2040: Macro Perspectives' (seminar, 'Narrowing the Development Gap, Ismeri-Europa, Poggio Mirteto, 18–20 June, 2018).

Dambisa, Moyo, *Dead Aid: Why Aid is Not Working and How There is a Better Way for Africa* (Penguin, 2009).

Diao, Xinshen, McMillan, Margaret and Rodrik, Dani, 'The Recent Growth Boom in Developing Economies: A Structural Change Perspective', NBER Working Paper No. 23132 (National Bureau of Economic Research, 2017).

Djankov, Simeon and Miner, Sean (eds), *China's Belt and Road Initiative: Motives, Scope, and Challenges* (Peterson Institute for International Economics, 2016).

Dollar, David, 'Lessons from China for Africa', World Bank Policy Research Working Paper Series, February 2008. Available online: https://ssrn.com/abstract=1098629 [Accessed October 2018]

Dinkel, Jürgen, *The Non-Aligned Movement. Genesis, Organization and Politics 1927–1992* (Brill, 2019).

Drache, Daniel and Jacobs, Lesley (eds), *Linking Global Trade and Human Rights New Policy Space in Hard Economic Times* (Cambridge University Press, 2014).

Drache, Daniel, 'Post Brexit and the Crisis of Trade Multilateralism: Heartbreak or Mess? Ought We Be Worried?' (conference draft, TLI Think! Paper 84, 10 December, 2017). Available online: https://papers.ssrn.com/sol3/papers.cfm?abstract_id=3046810 [Accessed October 2018]

Drache, Daniel and Jacobs, Lesley (eds), *Grey Zones of Governance: Linking Trade and Human Rights* (UBC Press, 2018).

Dunford, Michael and Liu, Weidong, 'Xi Jinping Thought and Chinese Perspectives on China's Belt and Road Initiative' (Institute of Geographical and Natural Resources Research, Chinese Academy of Sciences, 2018).

Economist, 'The great fall of China?' 13 May, 2004.

Economist, 'Hard landing looms in China', 14 October, 2016.

Eder, Thomas S., 'Mapping the Belt and Road Initiative: Where We Stand', Mercator Institute for Chinese Studies, 7 June, 2018. Available online: https://www.merics.org/index.php/en/bri-tracker/ mapping-the-belt-and-road-initiative [Accessed October 2018]

Eikenberry, John and Lim, Darren J., *China's Emerging Institutional Statecraft Asian Infrastructure Investment Bank and the Prospects for Counter Hegemony* (Brookings Institute, April 2017).

Fenby, Jonathan, *Tiger Head, Snake Tails: China Today, How it got here and Why it has to Change* (Simon & Schuster, 2012).

French, Howard W., *China's Second Continent: How a Million Migrants are Building a New Empire in Africa* (Alfred A. Knopf, 2014).

French, Paul, *City of Devils: The Two Men Who Rule The Underworld Of Old Shanghai* (Picador, 2018).

Frankopan, Peter, *The Silk Roads, A New History of the World* (Bloomsbury, 2015).

Gallagher, Kevin, 'China Global Energy Finance: A New Interactive Database', GEGI policy brief 002, March 2017. Available online: https://

www.bu.edu/pardeeschool/files/2017/03/China-Global-Energy.-Gallagher.Finaldraft.pdf [Accessed October 2018]

Gallagher, Kevin P., Kamal, Jin Rohini, Chen Junda and Xinyue Ma, 'Energizing Development Finance? The Benefits and Risks of China's Development Finance in the Global Energy Sector', *Energy Policy* 122 (2018).

Gittings, John, *The Changing Face of China: From Mao to Market* (Oxford University Press, 2005).

Grossman, Gene and Helpman, Elhanan, 'Endogenous Innovation in the Theory of Growth', *Journal of Economic Perspectives* 8 (1994).

Hansen, Valerie, *The Silk Road: A New History* (Oxford University Press, 2012).

Hicks, Robert L., Parks, Bradley C., Roberts, J. Timmons, and Tierney, Michael J., *Greening Aid? Understanding the Environmental Impact of Development Assistance* (Oxford University Press, 2008).

Jacques, Martin, *When China Rules the World: The Rise of the Middle Kingdom and the End of the Western World* (Penguin Books, 2012).

James, Harold, 'Deglobalization as a Global Challenge', CIGI Papers, 135 (June 2017).

Johns Hopkins School of Advanced International Studies, 'China-Africa Trade, China-Africa Research Initiative', December 2017. Available online: http://www.sais-cari.org/data-china-africa-trade/ [Accessed October 2018]

Jinping, Xi, *Important Speeches at the Belt and Road Forum for International Cooperation* (Foreign Languages Press, 2017).

Krugman, Paul, *Geography and Trade* (MIT Press, 1993).

Lui, Xinru, *The Silk Road in World History* (Oxford University Press, 2010).

Mattern, Janice Bially, 'Why "Soft Power" isn't so Soft: Representational Force and the Sociolinguistic Construction of Attraction in World Politics', *Millennium: Journal of International Studies* 33 (2005).

Mahbubani, Kishore, *Has the West Lost It? A Provocation* (Penguin, 2018).

Monson, Jamie, *Africa's Freedom Railway: How a Chinese Development Project Changed Lives and Livelihoods in Tanzania* (Indiana University Press, 2009).

Nye, Joseph S., *Soft Power: The Means to Success in World Politics* (Public Affairs, 2004).

Pei, Minxin, *China's Crony Capitalism: The Dynamics of Regime Decay* (Harvard University Press, 2016).

Piketty, Thomas, *Capital in the Twenty-first Century* (Harvard University Press, 2014).

Rezakhani, Khodadad, 'The Road that Never Was: The Silk Road and Trans-Eurasian Exchange', *Comparative Studies of South Asia, Africa and the Middle East* 30 (2010).

Rolland, Nadège, *China's Eurasian Century? Political and Strategic Implications of the Belt and Road Initiative* (National Bureau of Asian Research, 2017). Available online: http://www.nbr.org/publications/issue.aspx?id=346 [Accessed October 2018]

Streeck, Wolfgang. *How Will Capitalism End?* (Verso, 2016).

Sturzenegger, Federico and Zettelmeyer, Jeromin, *Debt Defaults and Lessons from a Decade of Crises* (MIT Press, 2006).

Tao, Xie, 'Chinese Foreign Policy With Xi Jinping Characteristics', *Carnegie Endowment for International Peace*, 20 November, 2017. Available online: http://carnegieendowment.org/2017/11/20/chinese- foreign-policy-with-xi-jinping-characteristics-pub-74765 [Accessed October 2018]

Tooze, Adam, *Crashed: How a Decade of Financial Crisis Changed The World* (Allen Lane, 2018).

Tracy, Elena F., Shvarts, Evgeny, Simonov, Eugene and Babenk, Mikhail, 'China's New Eurasian Ambitions: The Environmental Risks of the Silk Road Economic Belt', *Eurasian Geography and Economics* 58 (2017).

Wang, Dong, *China's Unequal Treaties: Narrating National History* (Lexington Books, 2005).

Watkins, Derek, Lai, K.K. Rebecca, and Bradsher, Keith, ,The World Built by China', *New York Times*, 18 November, 2018. Available online: https://www.nytimes.com/interactive/2018/11/18/world/asia/world-built-by-china.html [Accessed October 2018]

Wolf, Martin, 'How the West should judge a rising China', *Financial Times*, 15 May, 2018.

Wolf, Martin, 'Too Big, Too Leninist – A China Crisis is a Matter of Time', *Financial Times*, 13 December, 2016.

Woods, Ngaire, 'Whose Aid? Whose Influence? China, Emerging Donors and the Silent Revolution in Development Assistance', *International Affairs* 84(6) (2008).

World Bank, *The East Asian Miracle: Economic Growth and Public Policy* (Oxford University Press, 1993). Available online: http://documents. worldbank.org/curated/en/975081468244550798/ pdf/multi-page.pdf [Accessed October 2018]

Yamada, Go and Palma, Stefania, 'Is China's Belt and Road working? A progress report from eight countries', *Nikkei Asian Review*, 28 March, 2018.

Ye, Zicheng, *Inside China's Grand Strategy: The Perspective from the People's Republic* (University Press of Kentucky, 2011).

Yuan, Li and Schmerer, Hans-Jörg, 'Trade and the New Silk Road: Opportunities, Challenges, and Solution,' *Journal of Chinese Economic and Business Studies* 15, no. 3 (2017).

Zou, Lei, *The Political Economy of China's Belt and Road Initiative* (World Scientific Publishing, 2018).

ACKNOWLEDGEMENTS

We have been fortunate to be able to draw on the expertise and knowledge of Professor B. Michael Frolic, York University, Toronto, a leading Canadian scholar who has been going back and forth to, as well as living in, China for different periods since the 1960s. Many thanks to him for his valuable insights, our many discussions and the vast amounts of information that he enthusiastically shared with the authors. We are indebted for his critical support, many reads of the manuscript, and timely advice. He has been a steadfast supporter of the project throughout. Professor Ed Dosman has had a major impact on refocusing the final manuscript and made many valuable suggestions. Special thanks to Professors Greg Chin, Roger Keil and Harry J. Glasbeek, York University, and to Stephen Minas, Peking Transnational Law School, who made some very useful suggestions early on. Arthur Donner and Selwyn Kletz provided critical feedback throughout. Robert Fothergill gave excellent editorial oversight in the later stages. Guy Standing gave a critical push at the right time. Simon Archer, Peer Zumbansen, Priya Das Gupta, Bob Kellermann, Irene Frolic and Scott Guan assisted with extra maintenance. Marilyn Lambert-Drache, Charlotte Drache-Lambert and Lina Nasr El Hag Ali were steadfast, enthusiastic and early supporters of the project. Special thanks to Lynn Tougas for body work.

We have also been fortunate to receive backing and encouragement from Chinese researchers. In particular, special thanks to Professor Qiyan Chen and Professor Feng Zhongren, Wuhan University of Technology, for their many kindnesses during my visits to Wuhan and for introducing me to parts of China I wouldn't have seen without them. We are grateful to the Mercator Institute for Chinese Studies (Merics), Berlin, for special permission to reproduce their 2018 map of BRI. In October 2017, I was invited to give a TEDx Talk in Beijing, available at: http://v.youku.com/v_show/id_ XMzEwOTgzMDg4NA==.html.

During the latter part of the visit, I gave a group of seminars at Fudan University's law school, the Faculty of Law at Wuhan University, and Shanghai University of Finance and Economics. Special thanks to Professors Bohua Gong, Jianqiang Nie, and Allen Ding, respectively, as well as to Professor Haifeng Wang, Shanghai Academy of Social Sciences. In December 2017 at the 4th Global China Dialogue: The Belt and Road: Trans-Cultural Cooperation for Shared Goals, at the London University of Westminster, I was an invited speaker. On a visit to Hong Kong, I was fortunate to spend a morning visiting the Hong Kong History Museum, which had a marvellous exhibition on the historic Silk Road, entitled *Miles Upon Miles: World Heritage Along The Silk Road*. On another visit I spoke at HKUST thanks to Professor David Zweig. Thank you as well to Professor Qian Jiwei who arranged a seminar at the National University of Singapore. Many thanks are also due to the Canadian Embassy in Tokyo, which arranged at short notice my briefing to the embassy staff on the significance of the One Belt, One Road Initiative in December 2017.

In April 2018, I was invited to Addis Ababa, Ethiopia, by the United Nations to be part of their Inter-Agency Expert Group Meeting on Poverty Eradication. Poverty eradication is, sadly, no longer a primary goal of most Western nations.[1] There are still hundreds of millions of people barely surviving on two dollars a day, despite the success of China's anti-poverty policies, which have lifted millions of Chinese people out of poverty. In India, we can see a parallel story of achievement, where India's high growth rate has significantly reduced the number of people living in poverty according to the UN Human Development Index. Millions more are in danger of being left behind and abandoned by the world system. The expert panel brought together some of the best researchers from across the UN system. Special thanks to the participants for sharing their data.

Girum Worku of Escape Tours excellently organised my Ethiopian visit and I was able to see first-hand the impact of Chinese investment

[1]The background papers and agenda are available at https://www.un.org/development/desa/dspd/2018-expert-group-meetings-and-panel-discussions/world-without-poverty.html [Accessed October 2018]

on Addis' urban culture. They also made possible my visits to the textile factory, the African Union and the Addis-Djibouti railway, as well as a ride on its brand-new Metro. The accumulated experience of visiting, even for a week, a Chinese beachhead is not easily forgotten. A special thank you to Harry and Penny Arthurs for connecting me with this talented young man.

Another individual who especially helped towards the end of this project is Enrico Wolleb, president, Ismeri, Rome, who invited me to participate in the international seminar on 'Narrowing the Development Gap', which took place on 18–20 June, 2018 in Poggio Mirteto, Italy. I am specially indebted to Francis Cripps, Pascal Petit, Robert McDowell, Michael Dunford and Alice Sindzingre for sharing their research, which helped me better understand China's global initiative in a European and African context.

Finally, Professor Sarah Biddulph, a distinguished China scholar from the University of Melbourne, read the manuscript in draft form early on. We have relied on Professor Duan Qi, Beihang University, for his detailed knowledge of China and his tenacity in digging behind the headlines of China's print media and official publications. Professor Michèle Rioux, L'Université du Québec à Montréal, and Directrice of the Centre d'entreprises et d'innovation de Montréal, supported us with funds from our collaborative SSHRC grant, making possible A.T. Kingsmith's employment and research on all aspects of our book. He is a doctoral candidate in the Department of Politics, York University.

Matt Lowing, our editor at Bloomsbury, was an early, enthusiastic supporter of our project from beginning to end. His critical input throughout has made the final manuscript stronger, tighter and accessible. Special thanks are due. Lastly, we have also been very fortunate to have the manuscript professionally copy-edited by Amy Verhaeghe, Toronto. We are in her debt for her editorial thoroughness and the time and energy that she invested in the final assembly under a pressing deadline. Errors and omissions are our own making.

Daniel Drache, Toronto, 2019.

ABOUT THE AUTHORS

Daniel Drache is professor emeritus of political science and a senior research fellow, Robarts Centre for Canadian Studies, York University, Toronto. His work and interests focus on understanding the changing character of the globalisation narrative in its economic, social and cultural dimensions. He has published widely on globalisation, the public domain, trade governance and citizen activism. Among his books are *Defiant Publics: The Unprecedented Reach of the Global Citizen* (Polity, 2008), *Linking Global Trade and Human Rights: New Policy Space in Hard Economic Times* (Cambridge University Press, 2014), edited with Lesley A. Jacobs. *The Daunting Enterprise of the Law: Essays in Honour of Harry Arthurs* (McGill Queen's University Press, 2017), edited with Simon Archer and Peer Zumbansen, and *Grey Zones in International Economic Law and Global Governance Crises* (UBC University Press, 2018), edited with Lesley A. Jacobs. Homepage: www.danieldrache.com.

drache@yorku.ca

A.T. Kingsmith is a doctoral candidate in the Department of Politics at York University, Toronto. His research examines the effects of labour, media, and infrastructure on social and economic conceptions of anxiety in Canada and the Asia-Pacific region. His most recent book is *The Radical Left and Social Transformation: Augmentation and Reorganization* (Routledge, 2019), co-edited with Julian von Bargen, Karen Bridget Murray and Robert Latham.

akingsmith@protonmail.ch

Duan Qi received a doctorate in economics from Peking University and is currently an assistant professor at Baihang University, Beijing, where he teaches a range of courses. In 2015–2016, he was a visiting researcher in the Department of Economics, York University, Toronto.

duanqi@buaa.edu.cn

INDEX

Note: page numbers in *italic* indicate figures; page numbers followed by 'n' indicate footnotes.

250